EMBEDDED SYSTEMS

AUTHOR

Santanu Chattopadhyay
Professor,
Electronics and Electrical Communication Engineering
Indian Institute of Technology, Kharagpur

REVIEWER

Srinivasulu Tadisetty
Professor,
Kakatiya University, Warangal,
Vidyaranyapuri, Hanamkonda,
Warangal, Telagana

KHANNA BOOK PUBLISHING CO. (P) Ltd.
4C/4344, Ansari Road, Darya Ganj,
New Delhi, India

All India Council for Technical Education
Nelson Mandela Marg, Vasant Kunj,
New Delhi, India

Dear Readers,

To prevent the piracy, this book is secured with HIGH SECURITY HOLOGRAM on the front title cover. In case you don't find the hologram on the front cover title, please write us to at contact@khannabooks.com or whatsapp us at +91-99109 09320 and avail special gift voucher for yourself.

Specimen of Hologram on front Cover title:

Moreover, there is a SPECIAL DISCOUNT COUPON for you with EVERY HOLOGRAM.

How to avail this SPECIAL DISCOUNT:

Step 1: Scratch the hologram

Step 2: Under the scratch area, your "coupon code" is available

Step 3: Logon to www.khannabooks.com

Step 4: Use your "coupon code" in the shopping cart and get your copy at a special discount

Step 5: Enjoy your reading!

ISBN: 978-93-5538-871-1

Book Code: UG486EN

Embedded Systems

by Santanu Chattopadhyay

First Edition: 2026

Originally Published by:
All India Council for Technical Education, Ministry of Education, GOI

Exclusively Published & Distributed by:
Khanna Book Publishing Co. (P) Ltd.
4C/4344, Ansari Road, Daryaganj,
New Delhi (INDIA)

Visit us at: **www.khannabooks.com**
Write us at: **contact@khannabooks.com**

To view complete list of books, Please scan the QR Code: KPH

Printed in Bharat.

अखिल भारतीय तकनीकी शिक्षा परिषद्
(भारत सरकार का एक सांविधिक निकाय)
(शिक्षा मंत्रालय, भारत सरकार)
नेल्सन मंडेला मार्ग, वसंत कुंज, नई दिल्ली–110070
दूरभाष : 011–26131498
ई–मेल : chairman@aicte-india.org

प्रो. टी. जी. सीताराम
अध्यक्ष
Prof. T. G. Sitharam
Chairman

सत्यमेव जयते

आज़ादी का अमृत महोत्सव

ALL INDIA COUNCIL FOR TECHNICAL EDUCATION
(A STATUTORY BODY OF THE GOVT. OF INDIA)
(Ministry of Education, Govt. of India)
Nelson Mandela Marg, Vasant Kunj, New Delhi-110070
Phone : 011-26131498
E-mail : chairman@aicte-india.org

FOREWORD

Engineers are the backbone of any modern society. They are the ones responsible for the marvels as well as the improved quality of life across the world. Engineers have driven humanity towards greater heights in a more evolved and unprecedented manner.

The All India Council for Technical Education (AICTE), have spared no efforts towards the strengthening of the technical education in the country. AICTE is always committed towards promoting quality Technical Education to make India a modern developed nation emphasizing on the overall welfare of mankind.

An array of initiatives has been taken by AICTE in last decade which have been accelerated now by the National Education Policy (NEP) 2020. The implementation of NEP under the visionary leadership of Hon'ble Prime Minister of India envisages the provision for education in regional languages to all, thereby ensuring that every graduate becomes competent enough and is in a position to contribute towards the national growth and development through innovation & entrepreneurship.

One of the spheres where AICTE had been relentlessly working since past couple of years is providing high quality original technical contents at Under Graduate & Diploma level prepared and translated by eminent educators in various Indian languages to its aspirants. For students pursuing 2nd year of their Engineering education, AICTE has identified 87 books, which shall be translated into 12 Indian languages - Hindi, Tamil, Gujarati, Odia, Bengali, Kannada, Urdu, Punjabi, Telugu, Marathi, Assamese & Malayalam. In addition to the English medium, books in different Indian Languages are going to support the students to understand the concepts in their respective mother tongue.

On behalf of AICTE, I express sincere gratitude to all distinguished authors, reviewers and translators from the renowned institutions of high repute for their admirable contribution in a record span of time.

AICTE is confident that these outcomes based original contents shall help aspirants to master the subject with comprehension and greater ease.

T. G. Sitharam

(Prof. T. G. Sitharam)

ACKNOWLEDGEMENT

The author is grateful to the authorities of AICTE, particularly Prof. T.G. Sitharam, Chairman; Dr. Abhay Jere, Vice-Chairman; Prof. Rajive Kumar, Member Secretary; Dr. Sunil Luthra, Director, and Reena Sharma, Hindi Officer Training and Learning, for their planning to publish the book on *Embedded Systems* and other subjects. I sincerely acknowledge the valuable contributions of the reviewer of the book *Dr. Srinivasulu Tadisetty*, Professor, Kakatiya University, Warangal for going through the entire manuscript line-by-line and providing valuable suggestions for content improvements. My sincere thanks to my wife *Santana* for being the constant source of inspiration to write this, as well as, several other books in the past. I would also like to mention about our son *Sayantan*, who always pushes me to newer challenges to put my knowledge into black and white – leading to this book as well.

This book is an outcome of various suggestions of AICTE members, experts and authors who *shared their opinion and thought to further develop the engineering education in our country*. Acknowledgements are due to the contributors and different workers in this field whose published books, review articles, papers, photographs, footnotes, references and other valuable information enriched me at the time of writing the book.

Santanu Chattopadhyay

PREFACE

Embedded Systems are computing systems present in electronic/electrical devices and appliances, controlling their overall operation and often going unnoticed by the user. Unlike general computing systems, an embedded computing system has a limited set of activities based upon the intended system functionality. The design is highly constrained in terms of resources like size, speed, power consumption, and stringent time-to-market. Designer must have knowledge of contemporary developments in hardware, software, networking, sensors and communication, as decision is needed regarding the suitable target architecture for the system.

This book attempts to provide a good understanding of various angles involved in the process. Features of embedded systems, the design metrics and the design flow for a complete system has been discussed. Embedded processors differ from general ones in terms of features like I/O handling, timers/counters, data converters etc. Microcontrollers are typically used in embedded systems. One of the most popular microcontrollers, ARM has been covered. Digital Signal Processors (DSPs) have been discussed as the natural choice for signal processing applications. To address performance criticality, the hardware platforms like FPGA and ASIC have been enumerated. Embedded hardware often contains nonconventional interfaces. Some such interfaces are Serial Peripheral Interface (SPI), Inter Integrated Circuits (I^2C), Infrared communication (IrDA), Controller Area Network (CAN), Bluetooth etc. Traditional interfaces like RS-232, Universal Serial Bus (USB) are also used.

Relatively large embedded applications like network switch, aviation equipment, missile etc. contain a number of interacting processes that work at real-time. In order to ensure the satisfaction of their requirements, a Real-Time Operating System (RTOS) is needed. Designing a process is also challenging, as the code will have both computation and hardware interactions. This comes under the broad paradigm of embedded programming.

For an embedded application, all its modules may not be equally critical in meeting the area, performance and power constraints. To keep the overall system cost low, the target platform may contain both hardware and software modules interacting with each other. Hardware-Software Codesign and Cosimultaion paradigm has come up to address this partitioning.

The book is an outcome of the author's experience of handling the theory and laboratory courses on subjects like Microprocessors, Microcontrollers, and Embedded Systems for more than two decades. It is expected that the book will be highly useful to the students and the subject teachers.

It may also be useful to anybody starting a career as an embedded system designer. Any constructive suggestion to improve the quality of the book in its future editions is most welcome.

Santanu Chattopadhyay

OUTCOME BASED EDUCATION

For the implementation of an outcome based education the first requirement is to develop an outcome based curriculum and incorporate an outcome based assessment in the education system. By going through outcome based assessments evaluators will be able to evaluate whether the students have achieved the outlined standard, specific and measurable outcomes. With the proper incorporation of outcome based education there will be a definite commitment to achieve a minimum standard for all learners without giving up at any level. At the end of the programme running with the aid of outcome based education, a student will be able to arrive at the following outcomes:

PO1. Engineering knowledge: Apply the knowledge of mathematics, science, engineering fundamentals, and an engineering specialization to the solution of complex engineering problems.

PO2. Problem analysis: Identify, formulate, review research literature, and analyze complex engineering problems reaching substantiated conclusions using first principles of mathematics, natural sciences, and engineering sciences.

PO3. Design/development of solutions: Design solutions for complex engineering problems and design system components or processes that meet the specified needs with appropriate consideration for the public health and safety, and the cultural, societal, and environmental considerations.

PO4. Conduct investigations of complex problems: Use research-based knowledge and research methods including design of experiments, analysis and interpretation of data, and synthesis of the information to provide valid conclusions.

PO5. Modern tool usage: Create, select, and apply appropriate techniques, resources, and modern engineering and IT tools including prediction and modeling to complex engineering activities with an understanding of the limitations.

PO6. The engineer and society: Apply reasoning informed by the contextual knowledge to assess societal, health, safety, legal and cultural issues and the consequent responsibilities relevant to the professional engineering practice.

PO7. Environment and sustainability: Understand the impact of the professional engineering solutions in societal and environmental contexts, and demonstrate the knowledge of, and need for sustainable development.

PO8. Ethics: Apply ethical principles and commit to professional ethics and responsibilities and norms of the engineering practice.

PO9. Individual and team work: Function effectively as an individual, and as a member or leader in diverse teams, and in multidisciplinary settings.

PO10. Communication: Communicate effectively on complex engineering activities with the engineering community and with society at large, such as, being able to comprehend and write effective reports and design documentation, make effective presentations, and give and receive clear instructions.

PO11. Project management and finance: Demonstrate knowledge and understanding of the engineering and management principles and apply these to one's own work, as a member and leader in a team, to manage projects and in multidisciplinary environments.

PO12. Life-long learning: Recognize the need for, and have the preparation and ability to engage in independent and life-long learning context of technological change.

COURSE OUTCOMES

After completion of the course, the students will be able to:

1. Understand advanced concepts of embedded system architecture
2. Design systems for various embedded applications
3. Design software systems such as RTOS using embedded controllers
4. Analyze hardware software co-design trade-offs

Course Outcomes	Expected Mapping with Programme Outcomes *(1-Weak Correlation; 2- Medium Correlation; 3- Strong Correlation)*											
	PO-1	**PO-2**	**PO-3**	**PO-4**	**PO-5**	**PO-6**	**PO-7**	**PO-8**	**PO-9**	**PO-10**	**PO-11**	**PO-12**
CO-1	3	3	3	3	2	2	1	1	1	1	1	2
CO-2	3	3	3	1	2	1	1	1	1	1	1	2
CO-3	3	3	3	3	3	1	1	1	1	1	1	2
CO-4	3	3	3	2	3	1	1	1	1	1	1	2

GUIDELINES FOR TEACHERS

To implement Outcome Based Education (OBE) knowledge level and skill set of the students should be enhanced. Teachers should take a major responsibility for the proper implementation of OBE. Some of the responsibilities (not limited to) for the teachers in OBE system may be as follows:

- Within reasonable constraint, they should manipulate time to the best advantage of all students.
- They should assess the students only upon certain defined criterion without considering any other potential ineligibility to discriminate them.
- They should try to grow the learning abilities of the students to a certain level before they leave the institute.
- They should try to ensure that all the students are equipped with the quality knowledge as well as competence after they finish their education.
- They should always encourage the students to develop their ultimate performance capabilities.
- They should facilitate and encourage group work and team work to consolidate newer approach.
- They should follow Blooms taxonomy in every part of the assessment.

Bloom's Taxonomy

Level	Teacher should Check	Student should be able to	Possible Mode of Assessment
Creating	Students ability to create	Design or Create	Mini project
Evaluating	Students ability to Justify	Argue or Defend	Assignment
Analysing	Students ability to distinguish	Differentiate or Distinguish	Project/Lab Methodology
Applying	Students ability to use information	Operate or Demonstrate	Technical Presentation/ Demonstration
Understanding	Students ability to explain the ideas	Explain or Classify	Presentation/Seminar
Remembering	Students ability to recall (or remember)	Define or Recall	Quiz

GUIDELINES FOR STUDENTS

Students should take equal responsibility for implementing the OBE. Some of the responsibilities (not limited to) for the students in OBE system are as follows:

- Students should be well aware of each UO before the start of a unit in each and every course.
- Students should be well aware of each CO before the start of the course.
- Students should be well aware of each PO before the start of the programme.
- Students should think critically and reasonably with proper reflection and action.
- Learning of the students should be connected and integrated with practical and real life consequences.
- Students should be well aware of their competency at every level of OBE.

LIST OF ABBREVIATIONS

ABS	Anti-lock Braking System
ADC	Analog-to-Digital Converter
AGU	Address Generation Unit
AHB	Advanced High-performance Bus
ALAP	As Late As Possible
AMBA	Advanced Microcontroller Bus Architecture
APB	Advanced Peripheral Bus
API	Application Programming Interface
ASAP	As Soon As Possible
ASB	Advanced System Bus
ASIC	Application Specific Integrated Circuit
BER	Bit Error Rate
CAD	Card Acceptor Device
CAN	Controller Area Network
CCD	Charge Coupled Device
CISC	Complex Instruction Set Computer
CLB	Configurable Logic Block
CPSR	Current Program Status Register
CSC	Current System Ceiling
CTS	Clear To Send
DAC	Digital-to-Analog Converter
DCE	Data Communication Equipment
DCT	Discrete Cosine Transform
DDR	Double Data Rate
DFT	Design For Test
GA	Genetic Algorithm
GDS II	Graphical Data Stream Information Interchange
GPIO	General Purpose Input Output
GUI	Graphical User Interface
HDD	Hard Disk Drive
HLP	Highest Locker Protocol
ICE	In-Circuit Emulator
IDE	Integrated Development Environment
IIC/I2C	Inter Integrated Circuit
ILP	Integer Linear Programming
IPC	Interprocess Communication
IrDA	Infrared Data Association
IRQ	Normal Interrupt Processing
ISO	International Standards Organization
ISR	Interrupt Service Routine
LCM	Least Common Multiple
LUT	Look-Up Table
MAC	Message Authentication Code
MAC	Multiply Accumulate
MISO	Master In Slave Out
MOSI	Master Out Slave In
MRAM	Magneto-resistive Random Access Memory
NRE	Nonrecurring Engineering
NVRAM	Non-Volatile Random Access Memory
PAL	Programmable Array Logic

DMA	Direct Memory Access
DMA	Deadline Monotonic Algorithm
DP	Instruction Dispatch
DPC	Deferred Procedure Call
DRAM	Dynamic Random Access Memory
DSP	Digital Signal Processor
DSR	Data Set Ready
DTE	Data Terminal Equipment
DTR	Data Terminal Ready
ECC	Error Correcting Code
ECU	Electronic Control Unit
EDF	Earliest Deadline First
EOC	End-of-Conversion
FeRAM	Ferroelectric Random Access Memory
FIQ	Fast Interrupt Processing
FPGA	Field Programmable Gate Array
RTL	Register Transfer Level
RTOS	Real-Time Operating System
RTS	Request To Send
RZ	Return-to-Zero
SAR	Successive Approximation Register
SCL	Serial Clock
SCLK	Serial Clock
SDA	Serial Data
SIMD	Single Instruction Multiple Data
SOC	System-On-a-Chip
PCIe	Peripheral Component Interconnect Express
PCP	Priority Ceiling Protocol
PG	Program Address Generate
PIP	Priority Inheritance Protocol
PLA	Programmable Logic Array
PLD	Programmable Logic Device
PPM	Pulse Position Modulation
PR	Program Fetch Packet Receive
PS	Program Address Send
PSO	Particle Swarm Optimization
PW	Program Access Ready Wait
RISC	Reduced Instruction Set Computer
RMA	Rate Monotonic Analysis
RMS	Rate Monotonic Scheduling
ROM	Read Only Memory
SPI	Serial Peripheral Interface
SPSR	Saved Program Status Register
SRAM	Static Random Access Memory
SS	Slave Select
SSD	Solid State Drive
TWI	Two-Wire Interface
UI	User Interface
UML	Universal Modelling Language
USB	Universal Serial Bus
UX	User Experience
VLIW	Very Large Instruction Word

LIST OF FIGURES

Unit 1

Unit 2

Unit 3

Unit 4

Unit 5

Unit 6

CONTENTS

1 Embedded System Basics

UNIT SPECIFICS

Through this unit we have discussed the following aspects:

- *Defining an embedded system and its difference from other general electronic systems;*
- *Features of an embedded system;*
- *The metrics that an embedded system designer attempts to optimize;*
- *The step-by-step design process of an embedded system;*
- *Role of various synthesis and simulation tools that aid in the design process;*
- *Predesigned libraries to reduce the time to market for embedded systems;*
- *Three typical examples of embedded systems – smart card, digital camera and automobiles have been elaborated.*

The overall discussion in the unit is to give an overview of embedded systems, starting with its definition and illustrating its features. It has been assumed that the reader has a good understanding of System Design with hardware and software design processes. A basic understanding of tools and libraries will be helpful. A good number of examples have been included to explain the concepts, wherever needed.

A large number of multiple choice questions have been provided with their answers. Apart from that, subjective questions of short and long answer type have been included. A list of references and suggested readings have been given, so that, one can go through them for more details. The section "Know More" has been carefully designed so that the supplementary information provided in this part becomes beneficial for the users of the book. This section mainly highlights the initial activity, history of the development of embedded systems, recent developments and application areas.

RATIONALE

This unit on embedded system basics helps the reader to understand the definition of an embedded system, its features and design process. Starting with the conceptual view of an embedded system, it goes into the details of important features that distinguishes an embedded system from general electronic systems. The designers target a specific set of goals to optimize while designing such systems. The unit details all those aspects. The design process for any system goes through a set of interdependent hierarchical steps. The unit explains the process of refining a system specification, passing through several stages into a set of processes implemented either in hardware or in software. The synthesis process passes the system specification (or its refinement) through several tools. Some of these tools help in the synthesis process, whereas some others are used for verification and testing. Predesigned libraries play a major role in reducing the turn-around time. The unit takes the reader through an overview of all these steps to give complete picture of the embedded system design paradigm. To explain the functionality of embedded systems, three examples have been taken up. The dedicated nature of these examples makes the reader acquainted further with embedded systems. Thus, this unit gives a bird's-eye-view of embedded systems and their design process.

PRE-REQUISITES

System Design

UNIT OUTCOMES

List of outcomes of this unit is as follows:

U1-O1: Define an embedded system

U1-O2: Differentiate embedded systems from general electronic systems

U1-O3: List features of embedded systems

U1-O4: Enumerate the metrics of embedded system design

U1-O5: Illustrate the design flow of embedded systems

UI-O6: List examples of embedded systems

Unit-1 Outcomes	*EXPECTED MAPPING WITH COURSE OUTCOMES (1- Weak Correlation; 2- Medium correlation; 3- Strong Correlation)*			
	CO-1	*CO-2*	*CO-3*	*CO-4*
U1-O1	3	2	-	-
U1-O2	3	2	-	-
U1-O3	3	1	-	-
U1-O4	3	-	-	-
U1-O5	3	2	-	-
U1-O6	3	2	-	-

1.1 Introduction

Information Technology has made information processing the heart of modern electronic systems. Over the decades, there have been significant changes in the devices employed for such processing. Traditional systems possess separate computational and physical systems (such as, mechanical, chemical etc.). For example, an algorithm running on a computer may decide upon the concentration of various chemicals, temperature requirements etc. to synthesize an end product in a chemical process. However, the actual chemical process is carried out separately. The two systems here are distinct from each other and are easily differentiable by an outside observer. On the other hand, a new class of instruments/equipments have emerged in which the computational and physical systems have got integrated into a single one. Looking from outside, as a user of the system, it is not possible to demarcate between its computational part and physical part. A typical example of such a system is an automobile which has got a number of computational processors integrated with its mechanical components. New electronic gadgets are being developed in all fronts of life that put computation inside the gadget itself. The effort of embedding computational elements inside the bigger devices, which is often unnoticed by the system user, has given rise to the new class of devices, called *embedded systems*. Conceptual representation of an embedded system has been shown in Fig 1.1.

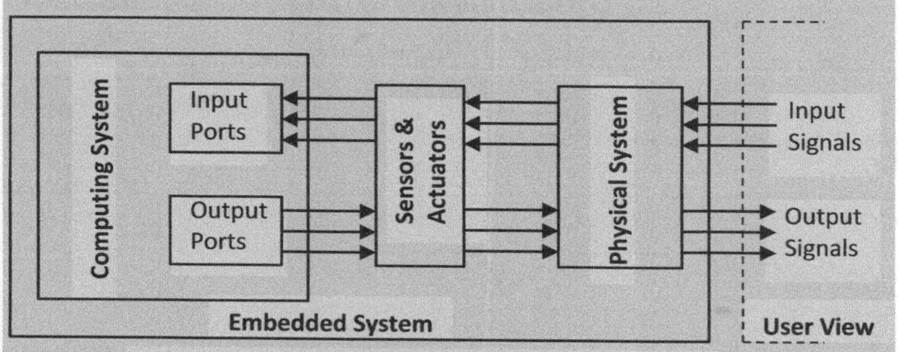

Fig 1.1: Conceptual view of Embedded System

The design goals of embedded systems differ significantly from the general computational systems. Embedded systems contain a very strict performance requirement, while meeting many other design constraints. Hence, an embedded system may be defined as a computing device contained within a larger electronic device, performing a single task, or a specific set of tasks repeatedly, often going unnoticed by the user. Though this given definition is not very precise, giving a complete definition of embedded system is quite difficult. In a wider sense, an embedded system can be thought to be computing systems excepting desktops and other higher configuration computers. Gadgets designed around embedded processors are available in plenty around us. It can be predicted that each and every electrical device will have some computational component in it, if not already integrated. The following are a few example domains for the embedded systems.

- Automobiles (components like anti-lock brake, fuel-injection system etc.)
- Home appliances (like refrigerator, washing machine, microwave oven etc.)
- Consumer electronics (with devices like cell-phone, pager, video camera etc.)
- Office automation devices (like fax, printer, EPBX etc.)
- Guided missiles
- Aviation equipments

The list is ever increasing as newer domains are ventured for electronic automation. The systems are highly heterogeneous in nature. Thus, bringing them under the common umbrella of embedded systems is a daunting task. The operating principle of the devices vary significantly. However, the devices coming under embedded systems share certain common features as depicted in the next section.

1.2 Features of Embedded Systems

The commonly seen features of embedded systems have been noted in the following. It may be mentioned that all such features may not be exhibited by all embedded systems.

1. *Single functioned*: Most embedded systems execute a single function. For example, a washing machine contains an embedded controller optimized to carry out the washing job efficiently. It takes the user inputs in terms of some knob settings and executes the control algorithm to carry out the desired washing task. A cell-phone has the primary responsibility of communicating between two users. Its operation is optimized for such communication. However, a cell-phone has got some additional capabilities also, such as, sending/receiving SMSs, taking photograph/video using add on camera, tuning to radio stations, playing music, browse internet etc. However, the computational capabilities of cell-phone processors are not comparable to desktops – it cannot be programmed that way to carry out complex scientific computations. Similar to cell-phone, many embedded systems are multifunctional in nature, however, the set of functionalities are limited in nature.
2. *Interactive*: Embedded systems are mostly interactive in nature. The systems interact with the environment by means of sensors and actuators. While the sensors are used to read-in the values of some physical quantities, the actuators are used to control the physical system parameters. For example, a room temperature control system may have multiple temperature sensors installed at various places in a room. The system gets the temperature inputs and may actuate the heating/cooling systems installed at different places in the room to maintain the set temperature profile.
3. *User Interface*: Instead of familiar user interfaces (like keyboard, mouse, screen etc.), an embedded system may contain special interfaces, such as, push buttons, LED displays, steering wheels and so on. Presence of such peripherals give the users the impression of absence of any computing element in it. It also hides the information processing that goes on in the system.
4. *Dependability*: Many of the embedded systems work in safety-critical application domains, such as, medical implants, nuclear plants etc. Thus, high dependability is an essential requirement of such systems. Systems working in autonomous mode interact with the environment and cause impact upon the plant directly. This enhances the dependability requirement further. A dependable system must also ensure high maintainability, good availability and high degree of safety to its environment. The information processing task carried out by the embedded processor must also be secured from external security threats.

5. *Tight Constraints*: The constraints put on an embedded system design are often much more stringent than the general purpose systems. Typically, it should be a low-cost solution to meet the computational needs, so that, the overall system is cheap. Often, the non-engineering constraints are given more importance in choosing the technology alternative to be adopted for the system design. For example, to keep the system size small, power budget must be low for an autonomous system, so that a small battery may suffice for the requirement. Unlike high-performance general-purpose systems, separate cooling arrangement may not be possible. Finally, to reduce the design time, predesigned hardware and software modules may be utilized which may not be optimized for the present application.
6. *Real-Time*: A real-time system responds to a request within a finite and fixed time. As embedded systems are interactive in nature, most of them face the requirement of responding in a time-bound manner. Failure to meet the time-line may or may not mean failure of the system as a whole. Some systems, named as *hard real-time* systems, must respond within the time limit, after an event has occurred. For example, the fire extinguishers must be actuated within a fixed time after a fire detector detects a fire. On the other hand, in a live video streaming application, if a few frames arrive late, the video may become jittery, but not considered as a system failure. In contrast, for a general-purpose system, it is only expected that the system works fast enough after getting the user inputs. Systems with a relaxed timing requirement are termed as *soft real-time* ones.
7. *Hybrid Structure*: Most embedded systems contain both analog and digital components. This is primarily because of the fact that in the environment, most of the physical parameters are analog in nature, while the processing is on digital data in a computing platform. Analog-to-Digital and Digital-to-Analog Converters (ADCs and DACs) are used for interfacing. General computing systems take inputs in digital format and produce outputs in digital format, as well.
8. *Reactive*: A reactive system interacts with the environment. Such a system possesses internal states and transits between the states on occurrence of events in the environment. Embedded systems are reactive in nature as they respond automatically with changes in the environmental parameters. On the other hand, a *proactive* system is not interactive in nature. Once initiated, a proactive system continues along the pre-decided execution sequence to produce outputs. General-purpose systems without interrupt facilities are proactive in nature.

1.3 Embedded System Design Metrics

Embedded system designers attempt to optimize certain design goals known as *design metrics*. Some such important metrics are as follows.

1. *System Cost*: This is the most important metric deciding the acceptability of the embedded system product. The system cost has two components – the *nonrecurring engineering* (*NRE*) cost and the per unit *recurring* cost. The one-time NRE cost is incurred in the design stage of the system. Once the design has been completed, additional units can be developed at a much lower cost. Typical example of such scenario occurs in the VLSI chip manufacturing process. The NRE cost in this case is pretty high as it may take several man-months to finalize the chip design and prepare the masks. However, once the mask has been prepared, it can be replicated over a large silicon die to produce large number of chips in a single-go, making unit cost low.
2. *Size*: Size of the design is very important as it will affect the overall size of the product. An embedded system often consists of a hardware part and a software part. The hardware part area is decided by the silicon area usage. The software part corresponds to the code size, determining the memory space requirement.
3. *Performance*: There are certain performance requirements that any embedded system needs to meet. In the system requirement itself, the desired speed of the system is specified. This becomes an important factor in deciding the target platform for implementation. For example, if the speed requirement is not very stringent, the computation may be implemented in software. On the other hand, a high speed computation necessitates hardware implementation. Within the hardware implementation also, there are several alternatives, such as, Field Programmable Gate Array (*FPGA*), Application Specific Integrated Circuit (*ASIC*) etc. To make a design trade-off, the speed-critical part of the embedded system may be put into hardware, whereas, the non-critical portions may be implemented in software.
4. *Power Consumption*: This is one of the most important design metrics, particularly for battery-operated portable embedded systems. Such systems are expected to be light-weight with long battery-life. This may necessitate plastic packaging and devoid of cooling arrangements. Hence, the size and weight of the battery pack should be kept at the minimum, affecting the allowed power consumption limit for the system. Excessive power consumption also leads to good amount of heat generation affecting circuit reliability, particularly in the absence of cooling arrangements.

5. *Design Flexibility*: Requirement and specification of a system may change over the time, after a system has been put into operation. The design should be flexible enough to accommodate such change requests. A software implementation of the system is generally much more flexible compared to a hardware based one. Among the hardware implementations also, FPGA based realizations can be modified with much less effort, compared to an ASIC realization.
6. *Design Turnaround Time*: This is defined as the time taken from starting the design specification to taking the product into market. Many of the consumer electronics products (such as, mobile phones, camera, smart watch) have very high rate of obsolescence. Hence, it is imperative to keep the turnaround time small. To meet a stringent turnaround time, the designer may have to go for off-the-shelf and predesigned components, foregoing the possibility of designing optimized subcomponents targeted towards the application in hand. *Design reuse* becomes the key to achieve this turnaround time reduction.
7. *Maintainability*: It corresponds to the ease of maintaining and monitoring the system, after it has been put into operation. Proper design documentation is necessary so that the design can be easily understandable by those intending to augment the system functionality, fix bugs etc., even if they are not part of the initial design team.

1.4 Embedded System Design Flow

Similar to any other system, design of an embedded system goes through certain stages as enumerated in Fig 1.2. In the process, several automated tools and libraries of predesigned components play important roles in converting a system specification into a final implementation. The design flow consists of the following stages.

1. *System Specification*: Based on the analysis of system requirements, the initial specification is prepared which may be refined to finalize the same. Specification may be informal or formal in nature. A simple English language description of the system functionality is an example of an informal specification. On the other end, a set of mathematical equations depicting the system behavior is a formal way of giving specification. Many other specification techniques have been reported in the literature and are also available as tools. Detailed description of the same is beyond the scope. Suitable references have been added at the end of the chapter. Some such widely used techniques include *PetriNet*, *StateChart*, *UML Chart* etc. Ideally, a specification should be executable, so that the desirable behavior of the system could be checked to ensure that those are

captured completely in the specification. This is easy for a formal specification, compared to an informal one. For example, if the specification is written in some programming language like C/C++, it may be executed to confirm the input-output behavior of the system to be designed. The *system synthesis tools* transform a formal specification into a set of interactive sequential processes. The individual processes can then be realized by the later synthesis steps. Individual processes may be implemented in software on a general-purpose processor or in hardware, such as, FPGA and ASIC. The decision to put a process in hardware or software is often determined by the availability of pre-designed modules, which may significantly reduce the time-to-market for the product. These modules form the *system-level library* consisting of complete solutions to some previous problems. Verification of system specification is carried out by tools commonly called *model simulators/checkers*. Such tools model the entire specification using some mathematical logic. The desired behavior of the system is also captured into a few logic formula. The tools verify whether the logic formula are valid on the model or not. In case some formula turns out to be false on the model, the tool generates a counter-example for the situation. This counter example can help the designer to refine the specification rectifying the error.

2. *Behavioral Specification*: The system synthesis tool generates behavioral specification for the constituent processes. Each process is marked to be implemented either in software or in hardware. While the software parts are to be implemented in general-purpose processors, the hardware parts are to be realized by dedicated hardware modules. Verification at behavioral specification level is carried out by *hardware-software co-simulation*. It may be noted that standalone hardware simulator can work only on the hardware part, while software simulator can work only on the software processes. Thus, to check the correctness of the combined system, a co-simulation of hardware and software parts is essential.
3. *Register Transfer (RT) Specification*: The behavioral specification is refined into register transfer level specification by the behavioral synthesis tools. For the software processes to be executed by general-purpose processors, the code is compiled/assembled into machine language instructions. Since these instructions operate on machine registers only, the machine language program itself is the register transfer specification for software processes. On the other hand, for the processes to be realized in hardware, synthesis tools, commonly known as *high level synthesis* tools, are used which convert the behavioral specification into a netlist of library components. The library typically contains components, such as, registers, counters, ALUs etc. While the RT specification of the

software processes are directly executable, the RT specification of the hardware parts are simulated by hardware simulators, normally used for hardware description languages like VHDL and Verilog.

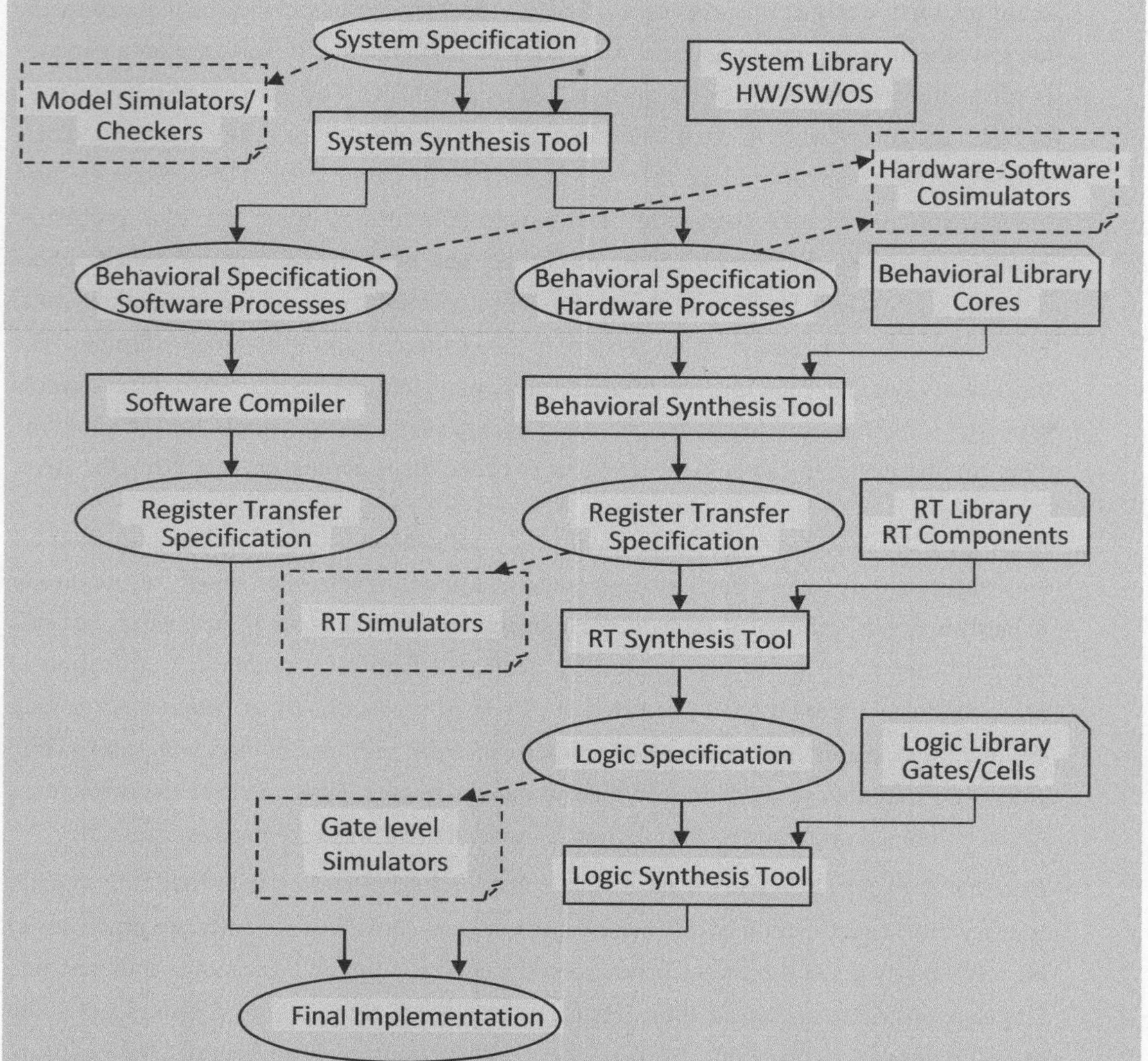

Fig 1.2: Embedded System Design Methodology

4. *Logic Specification*: Register transfer synthesis tool converts the hardware RT specification into corresponding logic specification. The logic specification consists of a set of Boolean equations. These equations can then be converted into realizations in terms of modules in some target technology. It results into a gate-level realization of the hardware part. A gate-level simulator can simulate the behavior of logic specification. It may be noted that for the software part, no further refinement is needed at this stage.

1.5 Embedded System Examples

In this section, we shall look into the structure of a few embedded systems used in our day-to-day life. The first example considers a smart card system. The second one is a digital camera, while the third example is the operation of automobiles.

1.5.1 Smart Card

A traditional digital card contains a magnetic strip with information embedded into it. In contrary to that, a smart card, apart from providing memory information, also has computational capabilities. As a result, the smart cards do not require any external hardware/software for data protection. Application of smart cards include debit/credit cards, medical cards, identification cards, entertainment cards, voting cards, mass transit cards and access cards.

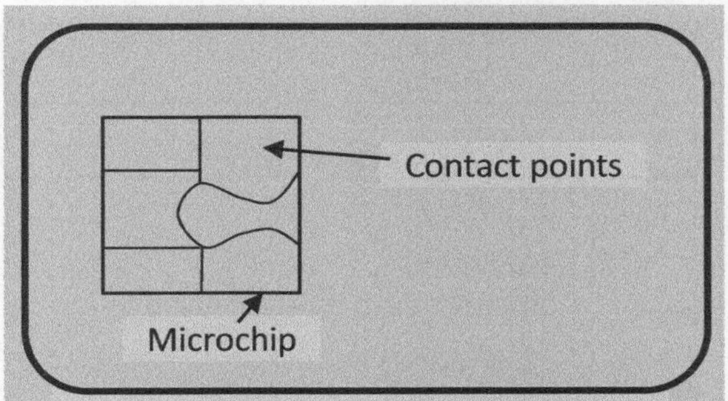

Fig 1.3: Smart Card Physical Structure

The specification of a smart card is standardized by the International Standards Organization (ISO). As per that specification, a smart card has three key physical elements – a plastic card, a printed circuit and an integrated circuit chip, as shown in Fig 1.3. The plastic card has a dimension of 85.60 mm × 53.98 mm × 0.80 mm. By specification, the card has to be able to bend upto certain degree, without damage. The printed circuit is a gold plate that acts as communication interface with external components, and also for power. The most important part of a smart card is a microchip. The microchip consists of microprocessor, read-only memory

(ROM), non-static random access memory (RAM) and an electrically erasable programmable read-only memory (EEPROM). As silicon may break easily, the chip must be within a few millimetres in size.

A smart card works in conjunction with an external *Card Acceptor Device* (*CAD*) for power and input/output information. To enhance the security of operation, the following standards are adopted.

1. Data exchange rate between the chip and CAD is limited to 9600 bps while the data exchange is controlled by the microchip processor. Also, the data transfer is half-duplex, reducing the possibility of massive data attacks.
2. A strict authentication protocol has to be followed between the card and the CAD, as shown in Fig 1.4. First, the card generates a random number r_s and sends to the CAD. The CAD, on receiving the number, encrypts it with a symmetric key K_{sc} and transmits back to the card. The card also encrypts r_s and compares the result with the encrypted value just received from CAD. The whole process is then repeated with the roles of card and CAD reversed.

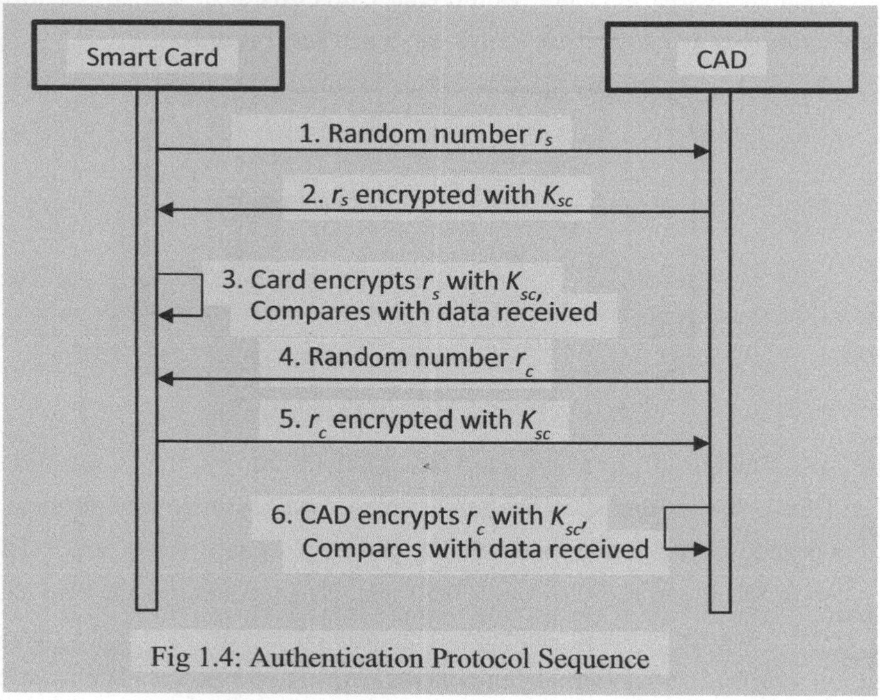

Fig 1.4: Authentication Protocol Sequence

3. After this initial authentication, message transfer between the card and the CAD can proceed. However, each message transmitted is verified by *Message Authentication Code* (*MAC*).
4. Standard encryption algorithms, such as, DES, 3DES and RSA can be used. These algorithms, though breakable, considering the limited computing power of smart card processors, is an acceptable trade-off.

1.5.2 Digital Camera

This is another example of a commonly used embedded system. The general requirements of the device are as follows.

- Capture images of the surroundings.
- Store the captured image in digital format. Unlike analog camera, there is no film in it. Sufficient storage should be available to store a good number of images, the number being determined by the resolution and the format used.
- There should be facility to download images to a computer connected via some communication mechanism.

Some other advanced requirements include high-capacity flash memory, zoom-in/zoom-out, image deletion etc. The block-diagram level representation of a digital camera chip has been shown in Fig 1.5. The overall system qualifies as an embedded system as it is single functioned (works as digital camera only). It is tightly constrained in terms of cost, power consumption, size, weight and required speed of operation. The camera system is reactive and real-time to a limited extent.

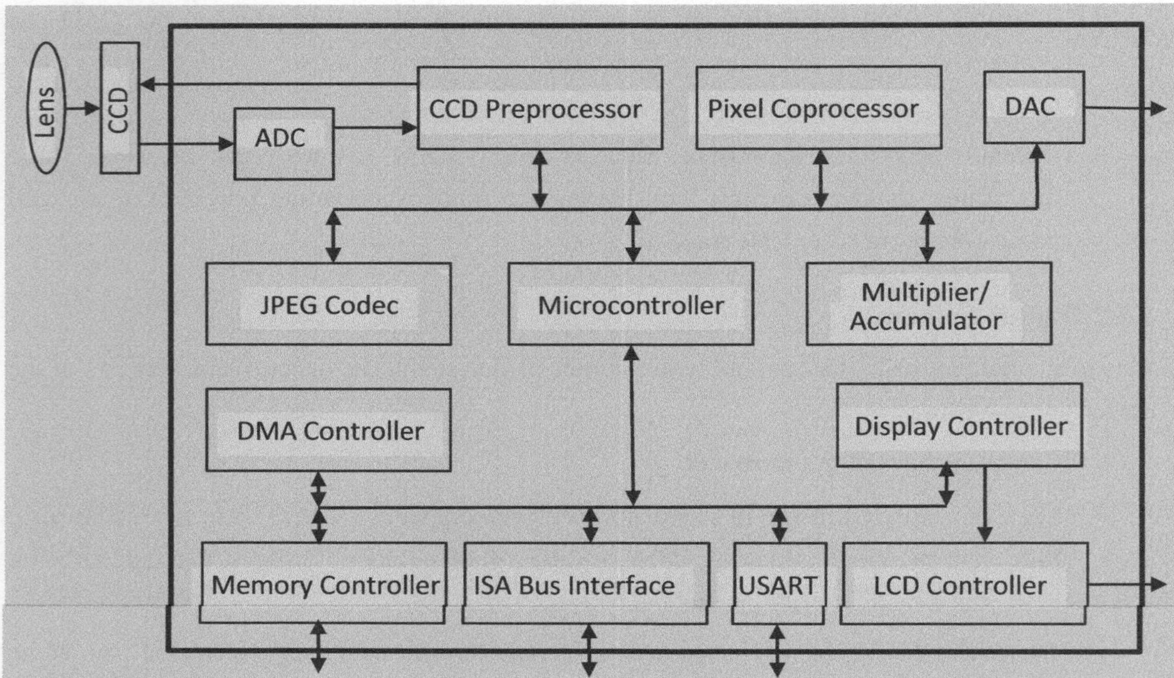

Fig 1.5: Block Diagram of Digital Camera Chip

From the designer's perspective, there are two tasks to be accomplished by the digital camera.

1. *Processing of images and storing in memory*. The process is initiated with the pressing of the mechanical shutter. When the shutter is pressed, the image gets captured. The captured image is then converted to digital form by the *charge-coupled device* (*CCD*) and ADC. The image data is next compressed and archived in the memory.
2. *Uploading of images to computer*. For this, the camera is connected to a computer (via interfaces). The images are transmitted from camera to computer under software control.

The flowchart corresponding to the first task has been shown in Fig 1.6. The charge-coupled device is an image sensor containing a two-dimensional array of light-sensitive silicon solid-state devices, also called cells. To capture an image, the electronic circuitry associated with CCD, discharges the cells, activates the shutter and then reads the digital charge value of each cell. Due to manufacturing errors, the value captured by the cells may be slightly above or below the actual light intensity. The zero-bias adjustment rectifies such errors. The next step, Discrete Cosine Transform (DCT), transforms original 8×8 pixel block into cosine frequency domain. In the transformed representation, the upper-left corner values represent more of the image information, whereas the lower right corner values represent finer details. Thus, the lower right corner values can be stored with lower precision, while retaining reasonable image quality. This is commonly done by reducing the bit precision of the encoded data. The result often passes through a Huffman encoding (which is loss-less in nature) to assign variable length codes to the pixel values. The resulting bit-stream corresponding to the 8×8 block is stored in memory and further such blocks are processed.

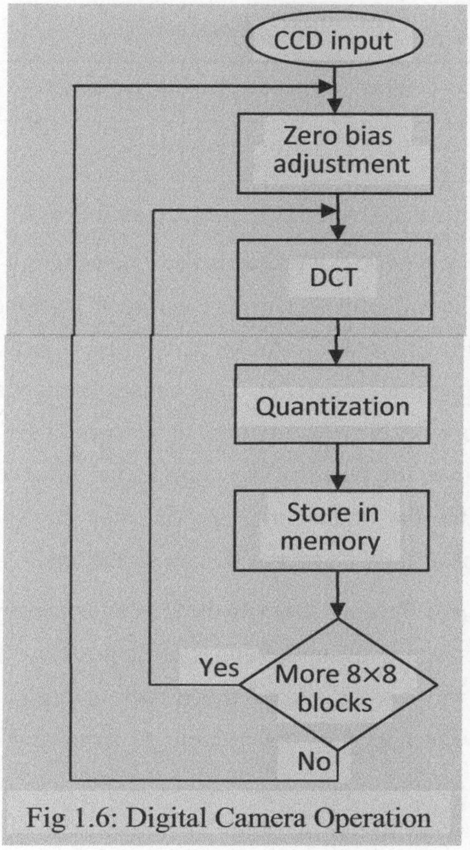

Fig 1.6: Digital Camera Operation

1.5.3 Automobiles

Over the time, cars have become safer, easier to control and more comfortable for the driver as well as the passengers. Embedded systems have played a crucial role in the evolution of automobiles. *Electronic Control Units* (*ECUs*) have become the part-and-parcel to support most of the car features. These ECUs can be various microprocessors, microcontrollers, digital signal processors, FPGAs etc. A high-end vehicle may have more than 100 such ECUs communicating by means of around 5000 signals. Any typical vehicle contains 25-35 such ECUs. Embedded systems are being used in different units of an automobile, some of which are noted next.

Airbags	Anti-lock braking system (ABS)	Black box
Adaptive cruise control	Drive through wire	Satellite radio
Telematics	Emission control	Traction control
Automatic parking	Entertainment system	Night vision
Heads up display	Blind-spot monitoring system	Navigational systems
Climate control	Tyre pressure monitor	Rain sensing system

Some typical embedded systems used in today's cars are as follows.

1. *Anti-Lock Braking System* (*ABS*): It prevents the wheels being locked up during the braking process and is particularly useful on slippery surfaces. In standard braking (without ABS), when the brake pedal is pressed, the brake pads press tightly against the wheel's discs to instantaneously stop the wheel rotation. This causes the wheels to lock up, regardless the vehicle speed. As the wheels stop rotating, these cannot be steered as well, causing the driver to lose control over the wheels. The vehicle now skids due to its momentum and can cause fatal accident. On the other hand, an ABS has the following components – speed sensors, valves, pumps and ECU, to avoid such situations.
2. *Adaptive Cruise Control System*: It controls the car speed by adjusting throttle position. Sensors are used to determine the speed and throttle position. The system enables safe drive on road. If the road is clear, it allows the driver to cruise at a set speed. The system continually monitors the speed of the vehicle in front and adapts the set speed of this vehicle.
3. *Drive Through Wire*: Traditional mechanical control systems in cars utilize hydraulics or cables with electronic control systems. *Drive Through Wire* replaces this technology by using sensors and actuators to control. It covers three control systems noted next.
    - *Steer Through Wire*: There is no physical connection between the steering wheel and tyres.
    - *Electronic Throttle Control*: Physical connection between accelerator pedal and throttle is absent.

- *Brake Through Wire*: Compared to the electromechanical version, this technology does not have any hydraulic part. Instead of that, sensors determine how much force is used.

Steer Through Wire and *Brake Through Wire* technologies are not yet widely used. However, the Electronic Throttle Control has been used widely in cars for decades.

4. *Airbag Control Unit*: It protects the passengers (particularly, the front passengers) from head collision in the case of an accident. Crash sensors installed for the purpose detect speed and rotational speed. Depending upon the severity of the accident, the sensors send information to the ECU to release the airbags. The control unit also stores the crash data that may be beneficial during investigation, to determine the cause of the accident.
5. *Rain Sensing System*: The purpose of this system is to determine automatically the required speed of windshield wipers in case of rain. For this, the optical sensor placed on the front windshield glass emits infrared light. Depending upon the rain severity, certain amount of light is reflected back and is captured by the optical sensor to decide the wiper speed.

UNIT SUMMARY

Embedded systems are computing systems often hidden within a large mechanical, electrical or electronic system. However, their design goals differ significantly from a general-purpose computing system as these systems are highly constrained in terms of size, allowable power consumption, stringent time-to-market etc. The systems are optimized towards a single- or a small set of predefines functionalities only. Most of the embedded systems are reactive in nature and interact a lot with the environment, often through quite nonconventional interfaces. The systems must respond to the events in a time-bound manner, missing deadlines may mean system failures. Like any general system, the design process of an embedded system also starts with its specification. The specification gets refined through a number of intermediary stages to result into the final implementation. Keeping the cost and the performance metrics in view, part of the embedded system is realized in software. However, the speed critical design modules may be required to be implemented in some hardware platform, such as FPGA and ASIC. A number of synthesis and simulation tools take part in this transformation of specification into final implementation. Many predesigned library modules are utilized by the synthesis tools to reduce the turnaround time for the cycle from specification to final implementation. The example embedded systems presented in this unit have brought out the limited features of such systems.

EXERCISES

Multiple Choice Questions

MQ1. Number of functions carried out by an embedded system is

(A) One (B) Two
(C) Fixed (D) No limit

MQ2. Interfaces to an embedded system are

(A) Conventional (B) Non-conventional
(C) Both conventional and non-conventional (D) None of the other options

MQ3. A dependable system should be

(A) Reliable (B) Maintainable (C) Safe (D) All of the other options

MQ4. Constraint(s) on an embedded system is/are

(A) Size (B) Cost (C) Power (D) All of the other options

MQ5. A hybrid system can have modules that are

(A) Analog (B) Digital (C) Reliable (D) Analog or Digial

MQ6. Reactive system

(A) Interacts with environment (B) Performs chemical reactions
(C) Gives measured reaction (D) None of the other options

MQ7. System cost is

(A) Recurring (B) NRE (C) Unit cost (D) None of the other options

MQ8. Size of embedded software is determined by the size of

(A) Code (B) Processor (C) Inputs (D) Outputs

MQ9. Most flexible design of embedded system is via

(A) Software (B) FPGA (C) ASIC (D) None of the other options

MQ10. Design turnaround time is defined as the time needed

(A) From specification to market (B) From design to market
(C) From specification to design (D) None of the other options

MQ11. Verification is carried out on

(A) Design (B) Unit (C) Both design and unit (D) None of the other options

MQ12. Testing is carried out on

(A) Design (B) Unit (C) Both design and unit (D) None of the other options

MQ13. System design starts with

(A) Design (B) Specification (C) Verification (D) Testing

MQ14. Model simulators work with

(A) Specification (B) Design (C) Hardware (D) Software

MQ15. Hardware-Software co-simulators work at

(A) Behavioral level (B) Gate level (C) Specification level (D) All other options

MQ16. RT specification for hardware is generated via

(A) Compiler (B) Cores (C) High-level synthesis (D) None of the other options

MQ17. System level library may include

(A) Hardware (B) Software (C) OS (D) All of the other options

MQ18. RTL simulators are meant for

(A) Hardware (B) Software

(C) Both hardware and software (D) None of the other options

MQ19. RT specification for software is generated by

(A) Compiler (B) Simulator (C) High level synthesis (D) None of the other options

MQ20. Behavioral library may contain

(A) OS (B) Core (C) Gate (D) All of the other options

MQ21. Data exchange rate between smart card and CAD is limited to

(A) 2400 bps (B) 4800 bps (C) 9600 bps (D) None of the other options

MQ22. Data transfer between smart card and CAD is

(A) Simplex (B) Half duplex (C) Full duplex (D) Any of the other options

MQ23. In digital camera image is captured by

(A) Charge coupled device (B) LCD screen (C) ADC (D) DAC

MQ24. The first step in image capturing by digital camera is

(A) Close shutter (B) Activate screen

(C) Discharge CCD (C) None of the other options

MQ25. Number of embedded processors in an automobile is

(A) One (B) Two (C) Many (D) None of the other options

Answers of Multiple Choice Questions

1:C, 2:C, 3:D, 4:D, 5:D, 6:A, 7:B, 8:A, 9:A, 10:A, 11:A, 12:B, 13:B, 14:A, 15:A, 16:C, 17:D, 18:A, 19:A, 20:B, 21:C, 22:B, 23: A, 24: C, 25: C

Short Answer Type Questions

SQ1. Define embedded system.

SQ2. Differentiate between single- and multi-functioned embedded systems with examples.

SQ3. Explain dependability in the context of embedded systems.

SQ4. Explain the requirement of embedded systems being tightly constrained.

SQ5. Distinguish between proactive and reactive systems with examples.

SQ6. Why is power consumption an important issue in embedded system design?

SQ7. Define design turnaround time in the context of embedded system design.

SQ8. How does the RTL of software part differ from the RTL of hardware part in embedded system?

SQ9. What is meant by hardware-software cosimulation and why is it needed?

SQ10. How does anti-lock braking system help in driving an automobile?

Long Answer Type Questions

LQ1. Explain the major features of an embedded system.

LQ2. Enumerate the design metrics that an embedded system designer may try to optimize.

LQ3. Explain the embedded system design flow.

LQ4. Explain briefly the secure mode of operation of a smart card embedded system.

LQ5. Enumerate the major embedded systems that can be found in an automobile.

KNOW MORE

Looking back into the history of embedded systems, the first such system was developed in 1960, used in *Apollo Guidance System*. It was developed by Charles Stark Draper at MIT. In 1965, *Autonetics* developed *D-17B*, an embedded computer used in *Minuteman* missile guidance system. The first embedded system in vehicle was utilized in *Volkswagen 1600*, in the year 1968. The vehicle used a microprocessor to control its electronic fuel injection system. Embedded systems (particularly, in small and medium sized applications) became popular with the progress in microcontrollers. In 1971, *Texas Instruments* developed the first microcontroller *TMS1000*, which was immediately followed by *Intel 4004*. Relatively larger embedded systems are based upon processors hosting embedded operating systems. The first embedded OS, *VxWorks* was released by *Wind River* in 1987. *VxWorks* was eventually used as the operating system for the *Mars Pathfinder Space Mission* in 1997. Versions of embedded Linux systems started appearing by late 1990s. Mobile phones constitute another major category of embedded systems. The first all-in-one embedded mobile device is the original *iPhone* introduced in 2007. The first Android phone was introduced by *T-Mobile* (*T-Mobile G1*) in the year 2008. The embedded market is projected to grow at a very rapid rate and is predicted to be more than 40 billion USD, by the year 2030.

REFERENCES AND SUGGESTED READINGS

[1] S. Chattopadhyay, "Embedded System Design", PHI Learning, 2023.

[2] P. Marwedel, "Embedded System Design", Springer, 2006.

[3] S. Heath, "Embedded Systems Design", Elsevier, 2003.

[4] F. Vahid, T. Givargis, "Embedded System Design A Unified Hardware/Software Introduction", Wiley, 2006.

Dynamic QR Code for Further Reading

1. S. Chattopadhyay, "Embedded System Design", PHI Learning, 2023.
2. Global Embedded Systems Market – Industry Trends and Forecast to 2030.

2 Embedded Processors

UNIT SPECIFICS

Through this unit we have discussed the following aspects:

- *Generic structure and features of an embedded processor;*
- *Guideline for choosing an embedded processor from different processing alternatives and available microcontrollers;*
- *ARM microcontroller basics for embedded applications;*
- *Features of Digital Signal Processors for embedded processing;*
- *Usage of Field Programmable Gate Array as embedded hardware platform;*
- *Application Specific Integrated Circuit chips for high-speed customized embedded system realization;*
- *Memory alternatives available to an embedded system designer.*

The overall discussion in the unit is to give an overview of embedded processor and memory alternatives available to a system designer. It is assumed that the reader has a basic understanding of CPU architecture, memories and digital design.

A large number of multiple choice questions have been provided with their answers. Apart from that, subjective questions of short and long answer type have been included. A list of references and suggested readings have been given, one can go through them for more details. The section "Know More" has been carefully designed, supplementary information provided in this part will be beneficial for the users of the book. It highlights the history of the development of embedded processors along with recent developments in this domain.

RATIONALE

This unit on embedded processors helps the readers to understand the generic and customizable platforms that are available to carry out the computations in an embedded system.

Starting with the generic architecture of an embedded processor and its distinguishing features (compared to general-purpose processors), the unit takes up discussions on microcontrollers for small embedded system design. One of the most widely used microcontrollers, ARM has been explained. Though ARM processors can be used, for signal processing applications, Digital Signal Processors turn out to be an efficient, cost-effective alternative. They possess some typical architectural features, markedly different from other processor classes that make them highly suitable for signal processing. Beyond a certain speed of operation, software-based solutions to an embedded application problem may not work, necessitating exploration of hardware alternatives. Among the hardware platforms, FPGAs are often considered as capable to provide a good trade-off between the Non-Recurring Engineering (NRE) cost of the system and the required performance goal. Due to the programmability of logic blocks and interconnects, it is difficult to achieve a very high speed with reasonably low power consumption in FPGAs. For such applications, fully customized Application Specific Integrated Circuits (ASICs) are to be designed to realize the embedded systems. Different technological alternatives are also available to be used for embedded memories. This unit takes the reader through all these processor and memory alternatives to equip them with the capability to choose the appropriate platform for the application in hand. Once a decision has been made to follow a particular platform, experts from that domain may be consulted to come up with the best possible system implementation.

PRE-REQUISITES

Digital Design, Computer Architecture

UNIT OUTCOMES

List of outcomes of this unit is as follows:

U2-O1: Enumerate generic features of an embedded processor

U2-O2: Choose the embedded platform for realizing an embedded application

U2-O3: State the instruction set architecture of ARM processor

U2-O4: List the architectural features of Digital Signal Processors

U2-O5: Enumerate the design alternatives available with FPGAs

U2-O6: List the basic steps in ASIC design process

U2-O7: Enumerate the memory storage alternatives for embedded systems

Unit-2 Outcomes	***EXPECTED MAPPING WITH COURSE OUTCOMES*** (1- Weak Correlation; 2- Medium correlation; 3- Strong Correlation)			
	CO-1	***CO-2***	***CO-3***	***CO-4***
U2-O1	3	2	-	-
U2-O2	3	2	-	2
U2-O3	3	1	1	-
U2-O4	3	2	-	-
U2-O5	3	2	-	-
U2-O6	3	2	-	2
U2-O7	3	2	-	1

2.1 Introduction

Processor is the heart of any electronic system. Peripheral devices attached to a system either collect data from the environment or modify some parameters of the environment. However, the action to be undertaken, corresponding to some event, is decided by the processor. Naturally, the processor needs to be fast enough to respond to the occurrences of events. The speed of operation of embedded processor is decided by the speed requirement of the application. The requirement may be a relaxed one, in which the processor gets enough time to process events. For such systems, a readily available general-purpose processor may be the ideal choice. However, for more stringent, time-critical embedded applications, dedicated processors may be necessary. For a highly time-critical application, it may be required that the customized processor is implemented directly as semiconductor chips (like FPGA, ASIC).

Compared to general processors, embedded processors require less power, as these are targeted to only a small number of functions. Another significant departure from general processors, while designing an embedded processor, is to have the peripherals on the main processor chip itself. This eliminates the requirements of off-chip communication significantly, thus reducing the delay, power consumption and heat generation in the system. An ordinary processor will need to have separate memory and other peripheral chips (timers, I/O controllers etc.) to build the full system.

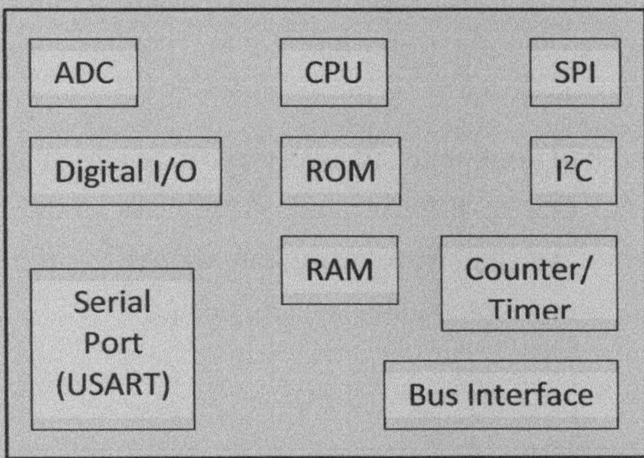

Fig 2.1: Generic Embedded Processor

This increases the size of the printed circuit board for the system. Moreover, off-chip communication also increases both delay and power consumption. Fig 2.1 shows the typical architecture of a generic embedded processor. As can be noted from the figure, apart from the CPU, the processor chip contains memory blocks (ROM and RAM) to hold the program code and data. There are digital I/O pins to drive digital inputs and outputs. Serial interface, in the form of USART is also in-built. To interact with the environment which is mostly analog in nature, *Analog-to-Digital Converters* (*ADC*s) are implemented on-chip. Some special interfacing standards, such as, *Serial Peripheral Interface* (*SPI*), *Inter Integrated Circuit* (*IIC*/I^2C) are often made available on-chip to cater to a large number of special devices having these interfaces. Parallel bus interface is also available which may be utilized to connect to additional memory and peripherals, over and above the available on-chip resources. On-chip timers are often included to help in real-time processing.

Typical examples of such embedded processors are the microcontrollers. These are single-chip computers with relatively simple CPU equipped with timers, serial/parallel, digital/analog input/output lines. On-chip program memory (ROM) of sufficient size is kept that can store the code for small-to-medium complexity embedded systems. To help in storing temporary program variables, small read-write memory block is kept on-chip. External bus interface may extend the memory capacity beyond the on-chip limits. Some example microcontrollers are Intel 8051, ARM, 68HC11, ATmega, PIC, MSP-430 etc. Though targeted towards small applications, there are many high-speed microcontrollers, along with dedicated features like security, wireless communication and signal processing modules. It may be noted that for signal processing applications, there is a dedicated class of embedded processors, called *Digital Signal Processors* (*DSP*s). At architectural level, such processors include hardware for easy implementation of filtering algorithms, parallel computation to reduce overall execution time, and so on. *C6000* series of DSP from *Texas Instruments* is an example of the same.

In the following, we shall look into an overview of each of the embedded processor categories – microcontrollers, DSPs, FPGAs and ASIC. As there are large number of microcontrollers, in this category, we shall be focusing into the ARM processors – one of the most widely used processor series in today's embedded system designs.

2.2 Choice of Microcontroller

With the availability of a large number of microcontrollers, it is often a non-trivial decision to choose the correct one for realizing an embedded application. Hence, before indulging into understanding the architecture of ARM, it is advisable to look into the features that a designer should look for in the target device. In the following, some such features have been noted.

- The highest available speed with the microcontroller should be sufficient for the application.
- Size of the chip should be small to reduce its foot-print on the board. The pin layout (40 pin DIP, QFP) plays a role in determining the board size and routing of signal lines on the board.
- On-chip ROM is expected to be sufficient to hold the program code. Similarly, the RAM should have enough space to cater to the read/write variables.
- Cost of a single microcontroller chip may become a determining factor in fixing the overall system cost.
- It is not possible for a designer to learn the assembly languages of all microcontrollers and develop highly efficient assembly language programs for them. Hence, development platform should be available, such that, the program can be written in some high-level language and subsequently compiled and optimized by the tools provided in the development environment. It should be very easy to download the machine code onto the ROM.
- Facility for on-chip debugging allows a user to single-step through the program and to access the microcontroller memory and registers from the host system. Such a facility can be utilized to carry out the debugging with ease. A microcontroller with this debug facility may be the choice of the designer, particularly for complex program logic.
- Availability of the microcontroller chip in the market is also important to ensure that large number of units can be manufactured for the application system.

2.3 ARM Microcontroller

ARM constitutes one of the most popular microcontroller family used extensively in high-speed embedded applications with tight power budget (such as cell phones). It follows the *RISC* (*Reduced Instruction Set Computers*) architectural philosophy developed into a 32-bit processor. ARM was originally known as *Acron RISC Machine* which later on evolved to *Advanced RISC Machine*. The first microcontroller in the series, *ARM version 1* was introduced by the *Acron* as 26-bit *Acron RISC Machine*, in the year 1985. *ARM version 2* was introduced in 1987. In order to promote the usage of ARM in various applications, the architecture has been licensed to potential manufacturers who can design ARM based CPUs and *System-on-a-Chip* (*SoC*) products. The following are some of the unique features of ARM that has made it a highly efficient embedded architecture today.

1. Compared to the contemporary general-purpose processors, the ARM cores are simple. As a result, an ARM CPU needs much lesser number of transistors. This in turn, leaves lot of space on the silicon floor to house additional circuitry to complete the custom design for an application.

2. As explained later, the ARM CPU design is highly pipelined. The instruction set architecture is designed to minimize energy consumption – a primary requirement for mobile electronic devices. The architecture supports two instruction sets – 32-bit ARM and another 16-bit instruction set known as THUMB. Availability of 16-bit instruction set can lead to better code density and reduced power consumption, while the 32-bit ARM instruction set provides higher CPU efficiency. The instruction set to be used at any point of time can be controlled by the programmer.

3. The ARM architecture is highly modular in nature. The core of the ARM processor is its integer pipeline. While this is the mandatory component of the architecture, the designer has the option to choose one or more of the optional modules, such as, Cache memory, Memory management unit, Floating-point co-processor etc. The provision of this module selection flexibility can save lot of space and power with a module being included in the design only if it is required. The decision can be taken by the system designer.

4. The ARM core possesses built-in JTAG debug port and on-chip embedded ICE (In-Circuit Emulator). The facility allows the designer to access individual system registers and memory locations for debugging in the initial phases of development.

2.3.1 Structure of ARM7 Microcontroller

A block diagram representing the ARM7 microcontroller architecture has been shown in Fig 2.2. The major components of the processor are as follows.

1. *Instruction Pipeline and Read Data Register*: This register receives the 32-bit content of the memory location addressed by the address bus lines *A*[31:0]. Data reaches this register from memory via the external databus lines *DATA*[31:0].

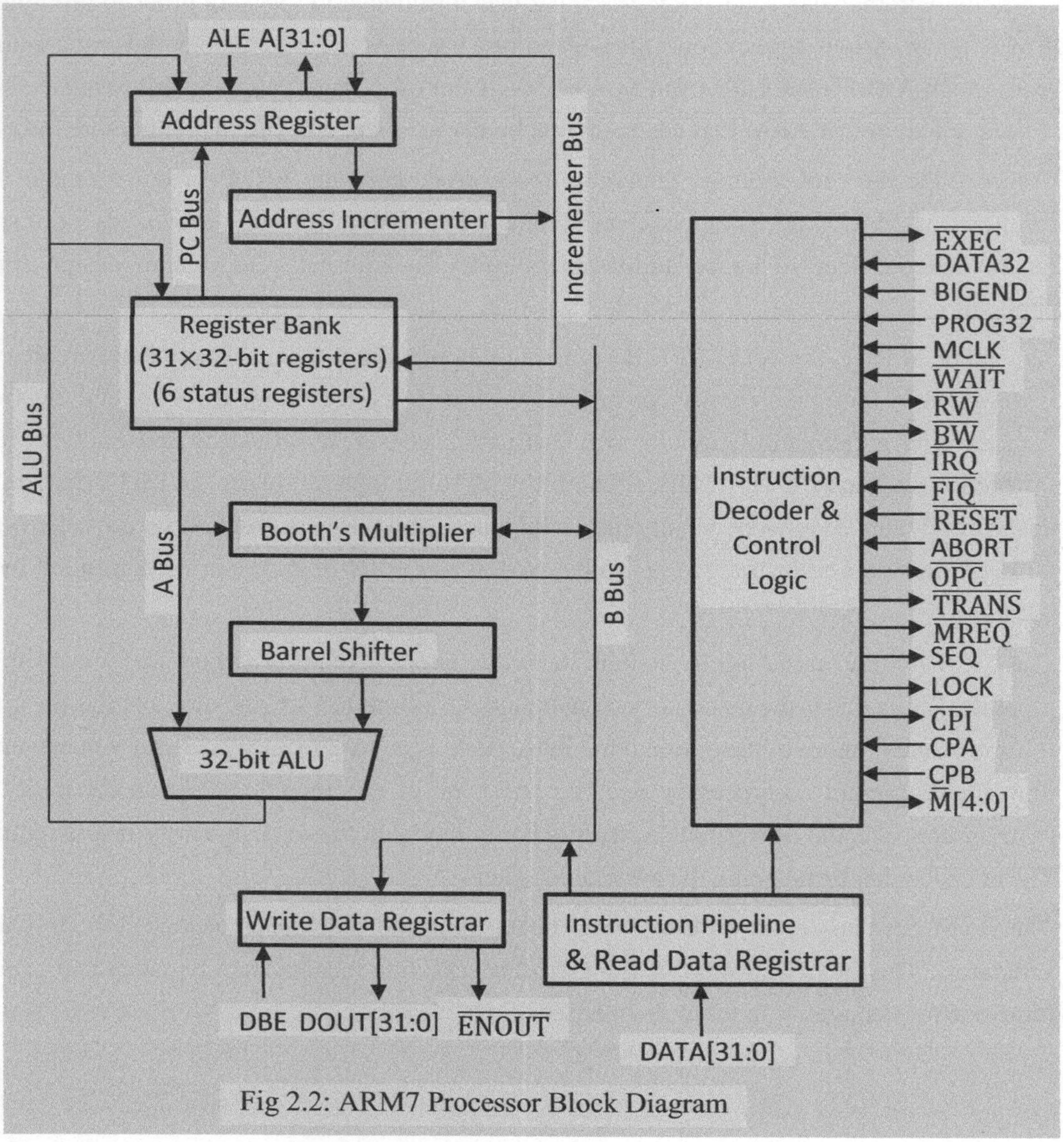

Fig 2.2: ARM7 Processor Block Diagram

2. *Instruction Decoder and Control Logic*: This module controls the overall operation of the ARM7 processor. Several internal and external control and status signals are generated from this module. The external control signals are useful for interfacing the ARM7 processor with memory and peripherals. The signals have been discussed later.

3. *Address Register*: The address register holds the address of the next memory location to be accessed by the processor. It may accessing an instruction or data. The address bus *A*[31:0] is the output of this register. The content of the register is made available on the address bus, as long as the ALE signal is held low by the external memory/device. The role the ALE signal is a marked difference in ARM, compared to the Intel family of processors. In the Intel family, ALE is an output signal used by the external interface to separate out the address bus from the data bus. Whereas, in ARM, the external device controls the availability of address on the bus by instructing the processor accordingly.

4. *Address Incrementer*: This module is responsible to increment the content of Address Register by a proper amount, so that, it points to the next instruction/data, as per requirement.

5. *Register Bank*: ARM contains a large number of registers, some of them are general-purpose, while others are status registers. There are 31, 32-bit registers accessible in different modes of operation. Number of status registers are six. The details of these registers has been elaborated later.

6. *Booth's Multiplier*: ARM7 uses the multiplication module developed around the Booth's algorithm. It has been elaborated while discussing on multiplication instruction.

7. *Barrel Shifter*: The module can be used to shift the operand reaching the ALU for arithmetic/logic operations. The operand can be shifted by a few bits by this module.

8. *ALU*: ARM7 uses a 32-bit Arithmetic Logic Unit (ALU) to carry out the arithmetic/logic operations corresponding to different instructions.

9. *Write Data Register*: The register is used to hold the data to be written onto the memory. This is a 32-bit register, feeding the signal lines *DOUT*[31:0]. The other two signals, DBE and $\overline{\text{ENOUT}}$ have been illustrated later.

The control and status signals of ARM processor can be grouped into some categories. Fig 2.3 shows the functional block diagram of the ARM processor in which the signals have been grouped as per their functionalities.

Processor mode signals $\overline{M}$[4:0]

These are the status lines identifying the current mode of operation of the processor. The internal status bits are inverted to output the $\overline{M}$ lines. The processor modes have been illustrated later.

Clock signals MCLK, $\overline{\text{WAIT}}$

MCLK is the master clock for ARM processor. It has two phases – phase 1 (clock signal is low), phase 2 (clock signal is high). Either phase of the clock can be stretched for slower devices by adjusting the ALE input. If the $\overline{\text{WAIT}}$ signal is low, the ARM processor is made to wait for an integer number of MCLK cycles. These two signals are internally ANDed, $\overline{\text{WAIT}}$ must change only when MCLK is low.

Memory interface signals A[31:0], DATA[31:0], DOUT[31:0], $\overline{\text{ENOUT}}$, $\overline{\text{MREQ}}$, SEQ, $\overline{\text{RW}}$, $\overline{\text{BW}}$, LOCK

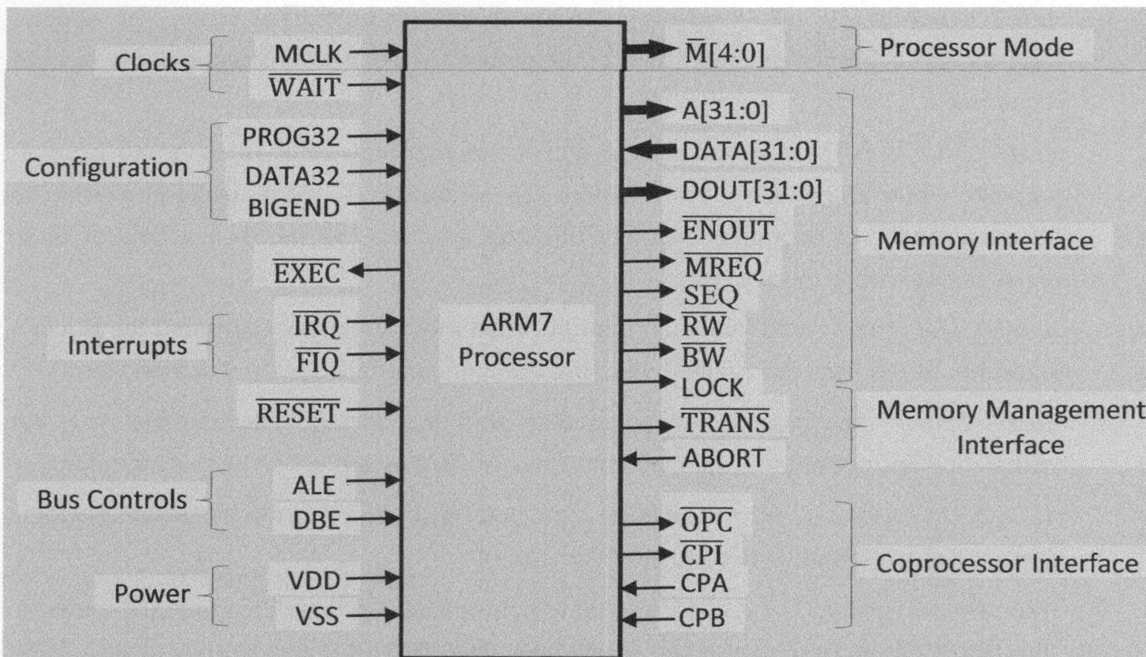

Fig 2.3: ARM7 Functional Diagram

These signals are used for interfacing memory devices with the ARM processor. The lines A[31:0] constitute the 32-bit address bus. The address becomes valid from the phase 2 of the previous clock cycle, while the address is used in phase 1 of the reference clock cycle. DATA[31:0] is the input 32-bit data bus used for read operation. DOUT[31:0] is the output data bus for a memory write operation. Read-write operation is identified by the $\overline{\text{RW}}$ control (0 for read, 1 for write). When the output data is valid on the DOUT lines, the $\overline{\text{ENOUT}}$ signal is made low. Thus, the signal $\overline{\text{ENOUT}}$ can be used to create a bidirectional data bus by joining the signal lines DATA and DOUT. The status signal $\overline{\text{MREQ}}$ indicates the requirement of memory access during the next cycle. The signal becomes low (active) in phase 1 of previous clock and remains low during phase 2, as well. The signal SEQ indicates sequential operation. If the signal is activated (high), the memory accessed in the next cycle is either same as the last memory address, or is four higher. This signal, in conjunction with $\overline{\text{MREQ}}$ indicates *burst mode* memory activity, in which a sequence of memory locations are accessed successively. The signal $\overline{\text{BW}}$ indicates a byte or word transfer. The line is low for a byte transfer and high for a word transfer. The control signal LOCK is used particularly in multiprocessor environment, in which, a memory controller caters to the memory access requests from multiple masters. Upon getting a valid LOCK signal, the memory controller should ensure that no other master is allowed to access memory till LOCK becomes low. It is required to ensure memory data integrity in such environment.

Memory management interface signals $\overline{\text{TRANS}}$, ABORT

The signal $\overline{\text{TRANS}}$ controls the address translation mechanism of the memory controller. If the signal is low, it indicates that the processor is working on user mode and that the memory controller must perform address translation. On the other hand, the signal ABORT is input to the processor. Through this signal, the memory controller can inform ARM that the requested address is not allowed. The processor may decide to abort the current instruction.

Configuration signals PROG32, DATA32, BIGEND

The line PROG32 corresponds to program instruction fetch operation. The signal being high instructs the processor to fetch from 32-bit address space. The signal being low indicates a 26-bit address space. DATA32 is similar to PROG32 but controls the address space size for data memory. The input BIGEND being high tells the processor to assume a *big-endian* data format. The input being low indicates *little-endian* data format. The concept has been illustrated later in conjunction with data transfer instructions.

Interrupt signals $\overline{\text{FIQ}}$, $\overline{\text{IRQ}}$

These two lines are used to interrupt the processor operation. $\overline{\text{FIQ}}$ is asynchronous, low-level sensitive and is of higher priority. It is also responded faster than the $\overline{\text{IRQ}}$. The signals will be discussed in more detail while dealing with interrupts.

Bus control signals ALE, DBE

The input signal ALE is used to extend the stable address on the address bus. The *data bus enable* signal DBE is used for sharing the bus in a *Direct Memory Access* (DMA) mode of operation.

Special signals $\overline{\text{EXEC}}$ and $\overline{\text{RESET}}$

The output signal $\overline{\text{EXEC}}$ is activated (turned low) when the processor has got an instruction for execution, but is not being executed (for example, conditional instruction execution). The input signal $\overline{\text{RESET}}$ is a low-level reset signal for the ARM processor.

The ARM processor architecture is a highly pipelined one. The basic ARM7 processor has a three-stage pipeline – the classical *fetch-decode-execute* cycle. In the first stage, an instruction is read from the memory. The instruction address register is updated. In the next stage, the instruction is decoded to determine the control signals necessary to execute the instruction. The third stage carries out the actual execution. It reads the operands from the register file, performs the ALU operations and writes the result onto the register file, for data processing instructions. For the LOAD/STORE type of instructions, the address computed by the ALU is put onto the address bus and the memory is accessed to carry out the execution phase. The later variants of ARM have more number of pipelined stages. For example, ARM9 has 5-stage pipeline, ARM10 6-stage, while ARM11 has 8-stage pipeline.

2.3.2 ARM7 Instruction Set Architecture

By design, the ARM processors follow the philosophy of *Reduced Instruction Set Computer* (*RISC*) architecture. However, it has also mixed with it several good features from *CISC* (*Complex Instruction Set Computer*) to enhance the performance further. The RISC features present in ARM are as follows.

1. ARM contains a large register file with 16 general-purpose registers.
2. It follows a load/store architecture. Data processing instructions use only on the CPU registers as operands. A load instruction is needed to load an operand into a register. Similarly, to store the result of an operation, an explicit store instruction is needed to transfer data from a register to a memory location.
3. The addressing modes are made simple saving the decoding time.
4. Instruction fields are uniform and of fixed length. The ARM instructions are 32-bit wide with a regular three-operand encoding.

The RISC features, supported by ARM, enhance performance via balanced pipelining. To enhance the performance further, the following CISC features have been included in the instruction set.

1. Each instruction has the capability to utilize both shifter and ALU. This makes the instructions more powerful as two operations could be clubbed in one instruction.
2. Auto-increment and auto-decrement addressing modes have been included in ARM. This allows the index registers to be incremented/decremented automatically after accessing a location. It is particularly useful in array references. The index can be updated while a load or store operation is in progress.
3. Multi-byte load/store operations are permitted. Upto 16 registers may be updated by one instruction. That is, 16-registers may be loaded from memory or stored into the memory via a single instruction. Though it violates the RISC principle of executing one instruction per cycle, the availability of this feature is very much helpful for efficient implementation of procedure invocation, bulk data transfer and creating compact code.
4. Conditional execution is possible for each instruction. The machine code of any *instruction* has the first four bits identifying the desirable values of some of the status flags. The instruction will be executed only if the specified values match with the corresponding bits of the status register. If the code does not match, the operation intended by the instruction is not carried out and can be treated to be equivalent to a 'No operation'. However, the feature has the potential to eliminate small branches in the program code, eliminating pipeline stalls.

ARM7 Registers

There are sixteen general-purpose registers R0-R15 that can be used during the user-mode operation in ARM processor. Out of these 16 registers, the register R15 acts as the program counter. Unlike other processors, the program counter register R15 can also be manipulated as a general-purpose one. The registers R13 and R14 also have some special roles, apart from being used as general-purpose registers. The register R13 is conventionally used as the stack pointer. In fact, in ARM, there is no dedicated stack defined in the architecture. However, programmers may implement a stack using available instructions, it is generally the R13 register that acts as the stack pointer. In the absence of explicit stack, implementing the subprogram calls and returns become an issue. For this, the register R14 is utilized to keep a copy of the return address during a procedure call. For return, the programmer simply needs to copy R14 into R15. The register R14 is aptly named as *link register*. However, this simple arrangement fails to implement nested procedure calls. To support nested calls, the programmer needs to implement a stack separately using R13 as stack pointer.

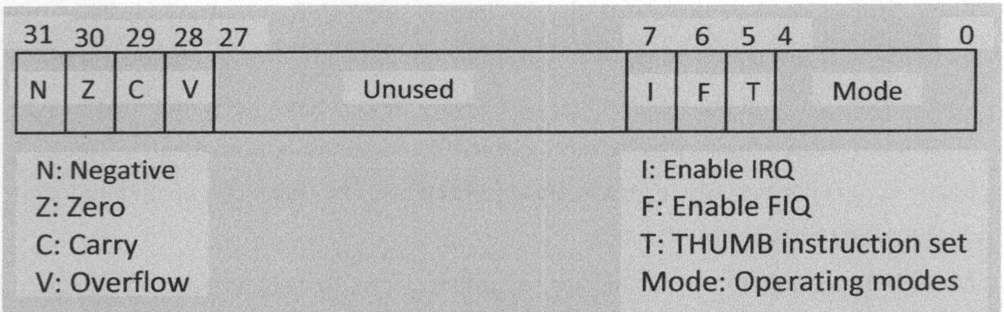

Fig 2.4: CPSR register structure

The processor stores its current status in another 32-bit register, called *current program status register* (CPSR). It has four one-bit status flags, spanning over bits 31 to 28, namely *negative* (*N*), *zero* (*Z*), *carry* (*C*) and *overflow* (*V*). These four bits identify the status of last instruction executed by the processor. The execution of the current instruction may be conditionally dependent on these four bits. The structure of the CPSR register has been shown in Fig 2.4. The bits 27 to 8 are left unused. Bits 7 and 6 are for interrupt enable, bit 7 enables the IRQ interrupt whereas bit 8 enables the FIQ interrupt. Bit 5, called T-bit is used to switch between the instruction sets used by ARM – ARM-to-THUMB or THUMB-to-ARM. Bits 4 to 0 are dedicated to select one of the six execution modes, noted next.

1. *User mode.* This is the mode in which the application code can be executed. The CPSR register cannot be updated in this mode. To change mode, an exception has to be generated.
2. *Fast Interrupt Processing* (*FIQ*) *mode.* The mode is entered on getting the FIQ interrupt. It is a high speed interrupt handler, typically used for a single critical interrupt to the system.
3. *Normal Interrupt Processing* (*IRQ*) *mode.* This is the low speed interrupt processing mode. The mode is entered on getting interrupt on the IRQ line.
4. *Supervisor mode.* The mode is entered on executing a software interrupt instruction. On reset, the processor enters into this mode. The mode is typically used to implement operating system services.
5. *Undefined Instruction mode.* This mode is entered if the opcode of fetched instruction does not match with any of the ARM or coprocessor instructions.

6. *Abort mode.* This mode is entered on occurrence of a memory fault. Typical example is an instruction or data fetch from invalid memory region.

User	FIQ	Supervisor	Abort	IRQ	Undefined
R0	R0	R0	R0	R0	R0
R1	R1	R1	R1	R1	R1
R2	R2	R2	R2	R2	R2
R3	R3	R3	R3	R3	R3
R4	R4	R4	R4	R4	R4
R5	R5	R5	R5	R5	R5
R6	R6	R6	R6	R6	R6
R7	R7	R7	R7	R7	R7
R8	R8_fiq	R8	R8	R8	R8
R9	R9_fiq	R9	R9	R9	R9
R10	R10_fiq	R10	R10	R10	R10
R11	R11_fiq	R11	R11	R11	R11
R12	R12_fiq	R12	R12	R12	R12
R13	R13_fiq	R13_svc	R13_abt	R13_irq	R13_und
R14	R14_fiq	R14_svc	R14_abt	R14_irq	R14_und
R15	R15	R15	R15	R15	R15
CPSR	CPSR	CPSR	CPSR	CPSR	CPSR
	SPSR_fiq	SPSR_svc	SPSR_abt	SPSR_irq	SPSR_und

Fig 2.5: ARM registers in different modes

The registers in different modes have been shown in Fig 2.5. The registers R0 through R7 are accessible in all the modes of operation. The register CPSR is also common across the modes. Apart from that, each mode has got its own R13 and R14 registers, acting as stack pointer and link register. Among the remaining registers, R8 to R12 and R15 are common in all modes, excepting FIQ. The FIQ mode has its own set of R8 to R14 registers. It may be noted that the availability of this additional registers in FIQ helps in faster context switching during interrupts. Except the user mode, other modes contain a *saved program status register* (SPSR) that holds the value of the CPSR register before reaching this mode.

Instruction Sets

There are two instruction sets supported by the ARM processor.

- *ARM instruction set*. This is the standard 32-bit instruction set used by the ARM processor. The instructions may belong to one of the following categories – data processing, data transfer, block transfer, branching, multiplication, conditional, software interrupts. The individual categories have been elaborated next.
- *THUMB instruction set*. This is a compressed 16-bit instruction set. The THUMB instructions are converted to equivalent ARM instruction before execution. Though the performance suffers due to this, the resulting code density is better than most of the CISC processors. The decompression is carried out dynamically in the pipeline.

Data Types

The ARM instructions support six different data types, as follows.

- 8-bit signed and unsigned
- 16-bit signed and unsigned
- 32-bit signed and unsigned

For these data types, the ARM architecture supports both *little-endian* and *big-endian* formats. However, most of the ARM implementations realize the *little-endian* format.

2.3.2.1 Data Processing Instructions

ARM can perform 32-bit arithmetic operations, such as, addition, subtraction and multiplication. Apart from that, bit-wise logical operations are also supported. The results produced are 32-bit wide, excepting multiplication that can produce either 32-bit or 64-bit result. The instructions are of three-operand format. Out of them, the first operand and the result must be registers, while the second operand can be a register or an immediate value. As shown in Fig 2.2, the second operand comes over the B-bus, through a barrel shifter. The barrel shifter can be used to carry out a shift or rotation of the operand, if it is a register. The second operand can be a 32-bit immediate operand as well, specified as part of the instruction itself. However, since the instruction itself is 32-bit wide, not all immediate constants can be specified to be an operand. The following rule guides the permissible values of the immediate constants.

Immediate operand is a 32-bit binary number in which all 1's fall within a group of eight adjacent bit positions on a 2-bit boundary.

To state mathematically, for a 32-bit constant *n* to qualify as a valid immediate operand, it should be expressible in the following form,

$$n = i\ ROR\ (2 \times r)$$

where i is an 8-bit number between 0 and 255 while r is a 4-bit number between 0 and 15. ROR is the rotate right operation. Some example values of n are 255 (with $i = 255$, $r = 0$), 256 (with $i = 1$, $r = 12$) etc.

While executing a data processing instruction, the condition flags in the CPSR register may or may not get updated depending upon the instruction variant used. For example, for the addition operation, there are two instructions ADD and ADDS. While the ADD instruction does not affect the status bits of CPSR, ADDS affects those. The feature adds flexibility to the programmers as the status flags need not be checked immediately after the instruction that set them, some other intervening operations may be carried out via instructions that do not affect the status flags. Some example instructions of this category are noted next.

```
ADD R1, R2, R3            ;  R1 ← R2 + R3
ADD R1, R2, R3, LSL #3    ;  R1 ← R2 + (R3 × 8)
ADDS R1, R2, R3           ;  R1 ← R2 + R3 and set status flags
```

2.3.2.2 Data Transfer Instructions

These instructions are responsible for data transfer between CPU registers and memory locations. There are two types of such instructions, noted next.

- *Single register transfer* – used to transfer 1, 2 or 4 bytes of data between a register and a memory location.
- *Multiple register transfer* – used for transferring multiple bytes of data between a set of registers and memory locations.

Both types of data transfer use *base-plus-offset* addressing. The value in the base register is added to the offset to determine the memory address. The offset part may be available in another register or specified as an immediate value. The *auto-indexed* mode may be used in which apart from data transfer, the base register gets incremented by an offset. This is particularly useful for array access – the base register can be made to point to the next array item after accessing the current one. No separate instruction needs to be expended for the same. There can be two types of auto-indexing – *pre-indexing* and *post-indexing*, depending upon whether the base register update takes place before or after accessing the memory location.

The following are the single register transfer instructions supported by ARM.

- LDR, STR: Load, Store word

- LDRH, STRH: Load, Store half word
- LDRSH, STRSH: Load, Store signed half word
- LDRB, STRB: Load, Store byte
- LDRSB, STRSB: Load, Store signed byte

Some example instructions are as follows.

```
LDR R0, [R1]          ;  R0 ← Memory[R1]
LDR R0, [R1, -R2]     ;  R0 ← Memory[R1 – R2]
LDR R0, [R2, +4]      ;  R0 ← Memory[R2 + 4]
LDR R0, [R1, +4]!     ;  R0 ← Memory[R1 + 4], R1 ← R1 + 4
```

Little- vs Big-endian data representation

As noted earlier, for multibyte data representation, ARM supports both little-endian and big-endian storage formats. By definition, for little-endian representation, the least-significant byte of a word is stored in bits 0-7 of a memory word. On the other hand, for big-endian format, the most-significant byte of the word is stored in bits 0-7 of a memory word. For word transfer between CPU and memory, there is no difference in the transferred data in two formats. However, for byte or half-word transfers, the data actually transferred in the two formats differ from each other. Fig 2.6 illustrates the difference between the two representations. Here, the content of the register R0 has been stored at memory word pointed to by R1. Next, a byte pointed to by R1 has been loaded into the register R2. It can be noted that the content of the R2 register is different in the two cases.

For multiple register transfer operation, the instructions Load Multiple (LDM) and Store Multiple (STM) are available. These instructions can be used to transfer 1 to 16 register contents to or from memory. The addressing modes supported are similar to single register transfer. When the content of a set of registers is transferred to memory, the content of register with the lowest number is copied to the lowest memory address, irrespective of the order in which the registers are mentioned in the instruction. Similarly, when multiple registers are loaded from memory, the lowest memory address location is copied to the register with lowest number.

The multiple register transfer can be used effectively to

- Implement stack to save and restore contexts
- Moving large block of data across memory regions

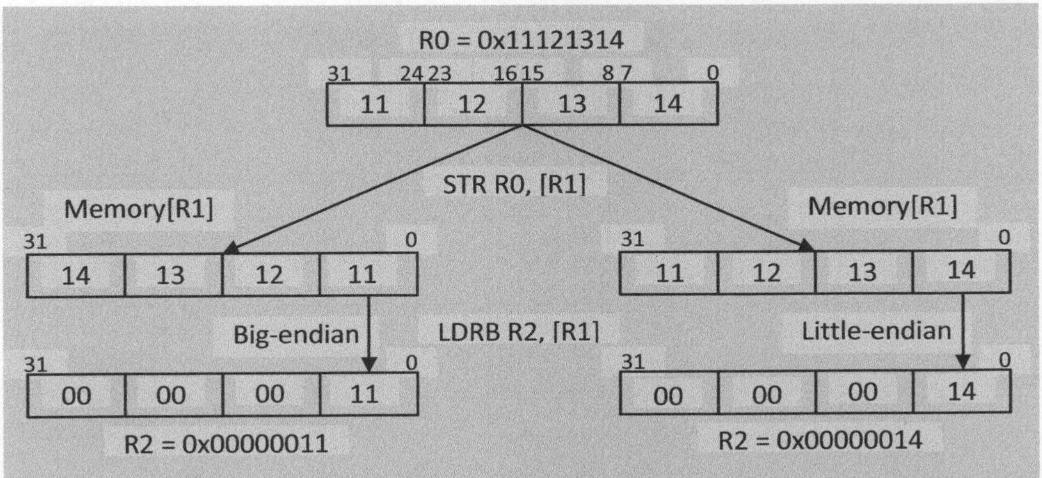

Fig 2.6: Little-endian vs Big-endian representation

Stack operation

Though in conventional processors stack is implemented by the processor designers themselves, in ARM, the stack implementation is left to the user programs. Stack is primarily used to realize subprogram calls and returns along with parameter passing. Leaving the stack implementation to the user program leverages the users with the following options.

- *Full stack vs. Empty stack.* In a stack implementation, the programmer may decide to make the stack pointer to point to the latest filled entry of the stack (called a *full stack* implementation) or to the immediate empty slot where the next item may be stored (called an *empty stack* implementation).
- *Ascending stack vs. Descending stack.* In a descending stack implementation, after an item has been put into the stack, the stack pointer is decremented (stack descends towards the lower addresses). In ascending stack implementation, after an item has been put into the stack, the stack pointer is incremented so that the stack grows to the higher addresses.

ARM has different sets of instructions to realize the stacks based on above features. These instructions are derived from LDM/STM by post-fixing the stack type, as follows.

- LDMFD/STMFD – to implement a full descending stack
- LDMFA/STMFA – to implement a full ascending stack
- LDMED/STMED – to implement an empty descending stack
- LDMEA/STMEA – to implement an empty ascending stack

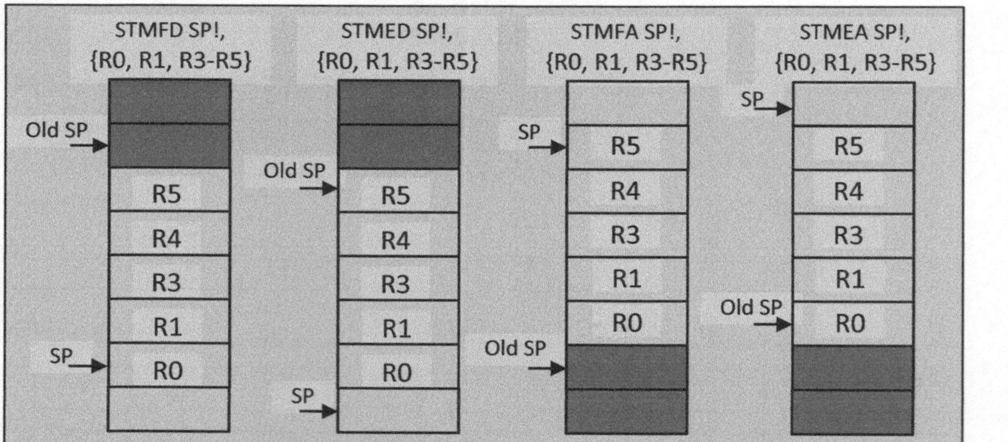

Fig 2.7: Stack implementations in ARM

Fig 2.7 shows some example stack implementations using the LDM/STM instructions. It may be noted that the lowest numbered register gets stored at the lowest memory address, irrespective of the relative ordering of registers in the instructions.

Block data movement

The LDM/STM instructions can be used to load/store multiple register contents using a single instruction. This facility can be utilized to transfer data from a source memory block to a destination memory block. Unlike the Intel architecture that allows direct transfers between the memory blocks, in ARM it has to be done in two phases. A set of registers need to be identified that can be utilized as intermediaries in this transfer process. If *k* number of registers participate in the transfer, first, 4*k* bytes of data is transferred from the source memory block to these *k* registers (using LDM instruction), which are then transferred to the destination block (using STM instruction). The process is repeated till all data in the source block are transferred to the destination. To enhance the transfer process, ARM has provided the following variants of the LDM/STM instructions to facilitate transfer even in the presence of overlapping between source and destination blocks.

- STMIA/LDMIA – Increment after transfer
- STMIB/LDMIB – Increment before transfer
- STMDA/LDMDA – Decrement after transfer
- STMDB/LDMDB – Decrement before transfer

The following code fragment transfers data from a source block pointed to by the register R12 to a destination block pointed to by the register R13. The end of the source block is pointed to by the register R14. The registers R0 to R11 are used as the intermediary ones. Thus, in one LDM/STM instruction, 48 bytes of data can be transferred.

```
Loop:   LDMIA R12!, {R0-R11}
        STMIA R13!, {R0-R11}
        CMP R12, R14
        BNE Loop
```

2.3.2.3 Multiplication Instructions

The ARM architecture possesses an explicit multiplier implementing Booth's multiplication algorithm. Using this module, following multiplication operations can be carried out – integer multiplication with 32-bit result, long integer multiplication with 64-bit result, multiply accumulate operation (useful to implement signal processing applications, such as, digital filtering). The specific instructions are MUL (integer multiplication), SMULL (signed 64-bit result), UMULL (unsigned 64-bit result), MULA (multiply accumulate), SMLAL (signed multiply accumulate 64-bit result), UMLAL (unsigned multiply accumulate 64-bit result). The following are a few examples of multiplication instructions.

```
MUL R0, R1, R2          ;  R0 ← R1 × R2
MULA R0, R1, R2, R3     ;  R0 ← R1 × R2 + R3
```

The following points should be noted about the execution of the multiplication instructions.

1. The destination register cannot be the same as the source register.
2. Register R15, which is Program Counter, cannot be used for multiplication.
3. In the Booth's multiplication algorithm, one cycle is needed for each pair of bits. An additional cycle is required to start the instruction. Thus, for 32-bit data, a total of 17 cycles are needed. However, in the implementation, the multiplication continues till the source register content does not become all zeros or all ones. In that case, the multiplication operation terminates to save execution time. This is known as *early-termination*.

2.3.2.4 Software Interrupt

The software interrupt instruction in ARM is of the form "SWI #*n*", where *n* is a 24-bit value identifying the service needed. The instruction is used to switch to the supervisor mode of execution from the user mode. In the execution of SWI instruction, the CPU branches to a vectored location identified in the exception handler table (discussed later). The exception handler routine can analyse the value of *n* and determine the action to be performed. It is important to note that for all values of *n*, the CPU branches to the same exception handler. This is a marked difference from the Intel family of processors in which each software interrupt instruction is handled by a different handler routine. Also, the typical value of *n* for Intel processors is a 8-bit quantity. Thus, in ARM, the number of such services is much larger (2^{24}, compared to 2^{8} for Intel). These services are typically utilized by the operating system designers to provide OS services.

2.3.2.5 Conditional Execution

In a significant departure from the other existing processors, ARM allows each instruction to be executed conditionally. For this, each instruction may have a condition prefixed to it. The instruction, though fetched and decoded by the processor, will be executed only if the condition specified is met by the current values of N, Z, C, V flags of the CPSR register. In case the condition is not satisfied, the instruction becomes equivalent to 'no operation'. The conditions identified in the instructions are as follows.

Condition	Code	Meaning	Condition	Code	Meaning
0000	EQ	Equal	0001	NE	Not equal
0010	HS/CS	Unsigned higher or same	0011	LO/CC	Unsigned lower
0100	MI	Negative	0101	PL	Positive
0110	VS	Overflow	0111	VC	No overflow
1000	HI	Unsigned higher	1001	LS	Unsigned lower or same
1010	GE	Greater or equal	1011	LT	Lower
1100	GT	Greater	1101	LE	Less or equal
1110	AL	Always	1111	NV	Reserved

Some examples of conditional execution are noted next.

```
EQADD R0, R1, R3           ; R0 ← R1 + R3 only if the zero flag is set

EQADDS R1, R2, R3, LSL #3  ; R1 ← R2 + (R3 × 8) only if the zero flag is set, and set
                             the status flags
```

2.3.2.6 Branch Instructions

There are two major branch instructions in ARM.

1. *Standard branch instruction "B"*. The execution of this instruction takes the processor to a target address specified in the instruction.
2. *Branch with link instruction "BL"*. Execution is similar to B, however, the PC+4 value is saved in the link register R14. The instruction can be used to implement subprogram calls. At the end of subprogram execution, the value from R14 can be copied to R15 for a return to the instruction following the original call.

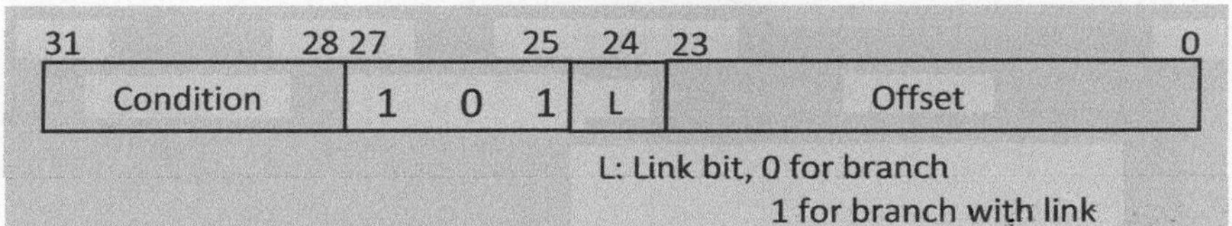

Fig 2.8: Format of branch instruction

The branching policy is to have a relative branch with respect to the current program counter (PC) value. In this relative branching, the target address is specified as offset from the current value of PC. During execution, the offset part is added with PC so that the PC now points to the targeted instruction. The offset is a signed 26-bit number, making the target to be located within ±32MB from the current location. Conditional branches are formed by specifying the condition codes with the instruction. The format of branch instruction has been shown in Fig 2.8. For B instruction, the L-bit is 0, for BL it is 1. It may be noted that though the actual offset for branch is 26-bit, in the instruction only 24 bits are stored. Since the instructions are always word aligned (32-bit wide), the least significant two bits of the address of any instruction are also zeros. Thus, in the difference computed, these two bits are also zero and hence are not stored in the instruction. During execution, the 24-bit offset specified in the instruction is left shifted by two bits to get 26-bit offset with two least significant bits 0. This shifted offset is added with the PC to get the target address.

Another class of branch instruction is called 'branch with exchange', denoted as 'BX' or 'BLX'. These are similar to the instructions 'B' and 'BL' respectively, excepting that the BX/BLX instruction also result in changing the instruction set from ARM to THUMB or vice versa.

2.3.2.7 Swap Instruction

As noted previously, the load/store instructions in ARM can perform only one memory access in a single instruction. However, for implementing synchronization primitives, the operating system designers need memory read and write operations within a single instruction. The swap instruction is an exception in this regard. It is an atomic operation in which a memory read is followed by a write operation. The instruction moves bytes/words between registers and memory locations. The format of the instruction is,

SWP Rd, Rm, [Rn]

SWPB Rd, Rm, [Rn]

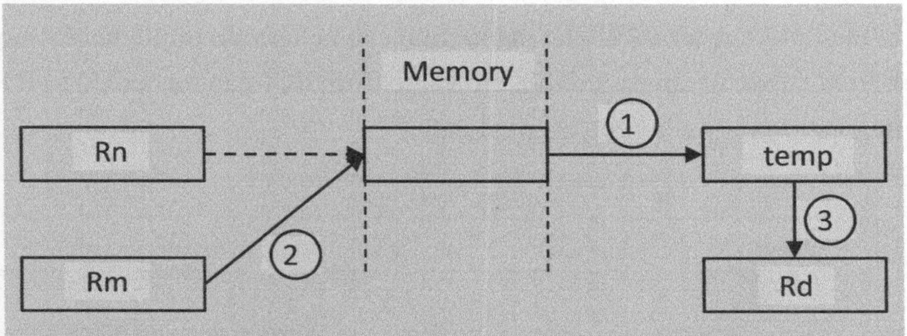

Fig 2.9: Execution of swap instruction

In execution of the instruction, first the content of the memory location pointed to by Rn is copied to a temporary location. Next, the content of register Rm is copied into the memory location pointed to by Rn. Finally, content of the temporary memory location is copied into the register Rd. Thus, if the registers Rm and Rd are same, the instruction effectively exchanges the content of this register with the memory location pointed to by Rm. Fig 2.9 shows the sequence of operations in the swap instruction.

2.3.2.8 Instructions Modifying Status Registers

The status registers CPSR and SPSR can be modified only indirectly and that also in the privileged modes. The instructions are as follows.

- MSR – to move content of CPSR/SPSR register to a selected general purpose register.
- MRS – to move content of a selected general purpose register to CPSR/SPSR register.

2.3.2.9 THUMB Instruction Set

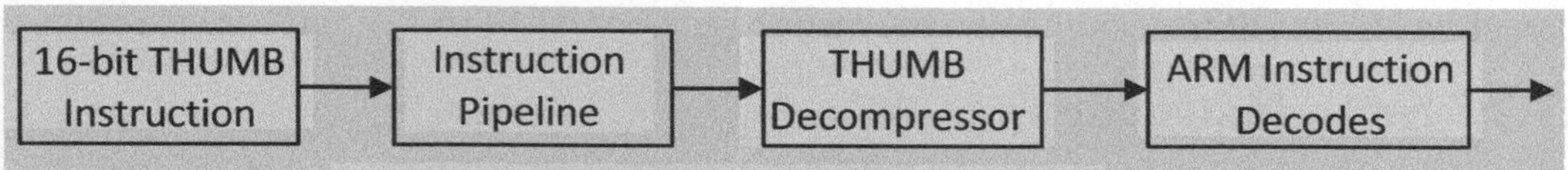

Fig 2.10: THUMB instruction processing

The THUMB instruction set contains compressed 16-bit instructions. Assuming that the memory word size is 32-bit wide, one memory word access gives two instructions to the CPU. However, the THUMB instructions are not executed directly. Rather, such an instruction is first converted to its equivalent 32-bit ARM instruction which is then executed by the CPU. The situation has been explained in Fig 2.10. It may be noted that the switching between the ARM and the THUMB instruction sets can be done by executing a BX/BLX instruction. The major differences in THUMB instructions, compared to ARM are as follows.

1. Excepting branch, all THUMB instructions are executed unconditionally.
2. The instructions have unlimited access to the registers R0-R7 and R13-R15. Only a few instructions can access the registers R8-R12.
3. The instructions are more like conventional processors. For example, the PUSH and POP instructions are back for stack operations. A descending stack is implemented with the stack pointer hardwired to R13.
4. No MSR/MRS instructions are supported.
5. The number of SWI calls are restricted to 256 from 2^{24}.
6. On reset or on exception, the processor enters into ARM instruction mode.

The THUMB instruction set provides several advantages over the ARM instruction set, particularly for resource constrained (in terms of area, memory requirement, power requirement etc.) embedded system designs. The THUMB code requires on an average 30% less space, compared to ARM code. However, THUMB instructions require decompression before execution. If the memory is organized as 32-bit words, the ARM code is 40% faster than THUMB. On the other hand, if the memory is organized as 16-bit words, THUMB code is around 45% faster than the ARM code. The savings come from the reduction in the number of memory accesses needed for THUMB code. The maximum benefit of THUMB comes from the power savings angle. THUMB code uses upto 30% less power than ARM code, making THUMB the choice for low-power consuming simple embedded system designs. To make a compromise between the performance and power consumption, in a typical embedded system, the speed-critical operations should be coded in ARM instruction set with the program being hosted in 32-bit on-chip memory. On the other hand, for non-critical routines, THUMB instruction set should be used with 16-bit off-chip memory.

2.3.3 Exceptions in ARM

Exceptions are raised during the CPU operations under different conditions. The sources of exceptions in ARM processor are the following – processor reset, attempt to execute an undefined instruction, software interrupt, instruction fetch failure (fetch abort), data fetch failure (data abort), IRQ (normal interrupt), FIQ (fast interrupt). On occurrence of any of these exceptions, first the processor switches to privileged mode. The current value of PC (R15) + 4 is saved into the link register R14. Current CPSR is saved onto the SPSR. The IRQ interrupt gets disabled. In the case of FIQ exception, the FIQ interrupt also gets disabled. Next, the program counter is loaded with the exception vector address noted next.

Exception type	*Mode*	*Vector address*
Reset	Supervisor	0x00000000
Undefined instruction	Undefined	0x00000004
Software interrupt	Supervisor	0x00000008
Prefetch abort	Abort	0x0000000C
Data abort	Abort	0x00000010
IRQ	IRQ	0x00000018
FIQ	FIQ	0x0000001C

It may be noted that the vector address 0x00000014 has not been used and is missed to ensure backward compatibility. Also, the FIQ interrupt has been assigned the highest address, so that, the corresponding service routine can start from that address itself. This eliminates the requirement of further jump instruction from the vector address to the interrupt service routine, saving the interrupt response time.

2.4 Digital Signal Processors

In the last section, we have seen the structure of ARM microcontrollers, predominantly used in designing embedded systems. Many of such embedded system applications interact with nature and works with analog signal as input and output. Typical examples of such signals are image and speech. These signals need special processing to extract the core information, before being processed digitally by the processor. Though general-purpose processors can be used, a special class of processors, called *Digital Signal Processor* (*DSP*) have been designed to cater to the signal processing computations efficiently. In general, DSPs provide low-cost, high performance and low-latency solutions. The power requirement is also less, limiting the battery size and making them more suitable for mobile applications.

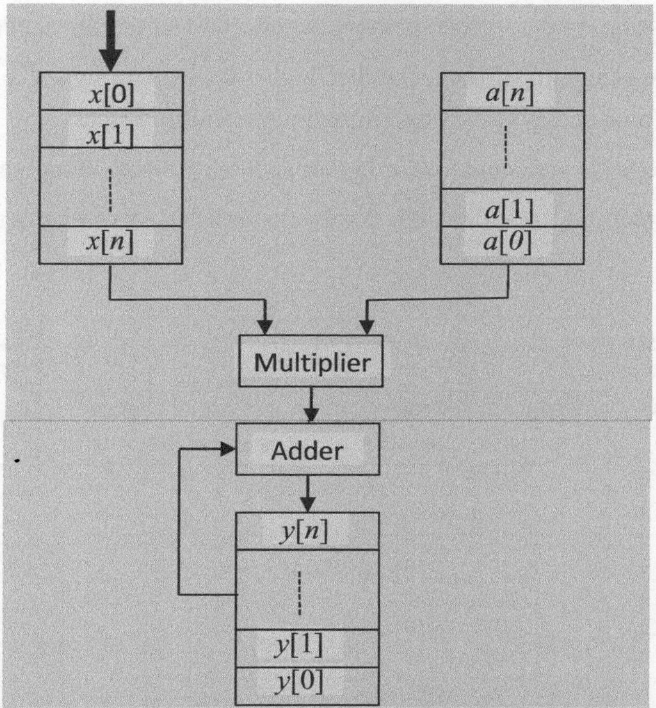

Fig 2.11: Typical multiply-accumulate unit in DSP

DSPs are microprocessors optimized to carry out the signal processing tasks. A typical such signal processing task is the *Finite Impulse Response* (*FIR*) filtering operation. The FIR filter has input signal *x*, output signal *y* and a finite set of filter coefficients a_0, a_1, a_2, …. The nth output $y[n]$ of the filter is given by,

$$y[n] = a_0x[n] + a_1x[n-1] + \cdots + a_nx[0]$$

The coefficients a_0, a_1, … a_n form the kernel of the filter. The filtering operation is computationally intensive with a number of multiplication and addition operations proportional to the size of the kernel. Time required in the filtering operation may become crucial, particularly for real-time applications. To carry out this type of repetitive multiplication and addition operations, the DSPs often contain a *multiply-accumulate* (MAC) unit in their architecture. A typical MAC structure has been shown in Fig 2.11.

2.4.1 Typical DSP Architecture

DSP architectures are tuned towards the efficient realization of high throughput signal processing tasks. The salient features of a DSP are as follows.

1. Ensure high-speed data access through the usage of high-bandwidth memory architecture, special addressing modes, direct memory access (DMA) facilities, and so on.
2. Usage of MAC unit, pipelining, parallel high speed operations via VLIW (Very Large Instruction Word) and SIMD (Single Instruction Multiple Data).
3. Contains extra-wide accumulator for higher accuracy during computation.
4. Special architectural facilities like hardware assisted zero-overhead looping, shadow registers etc.

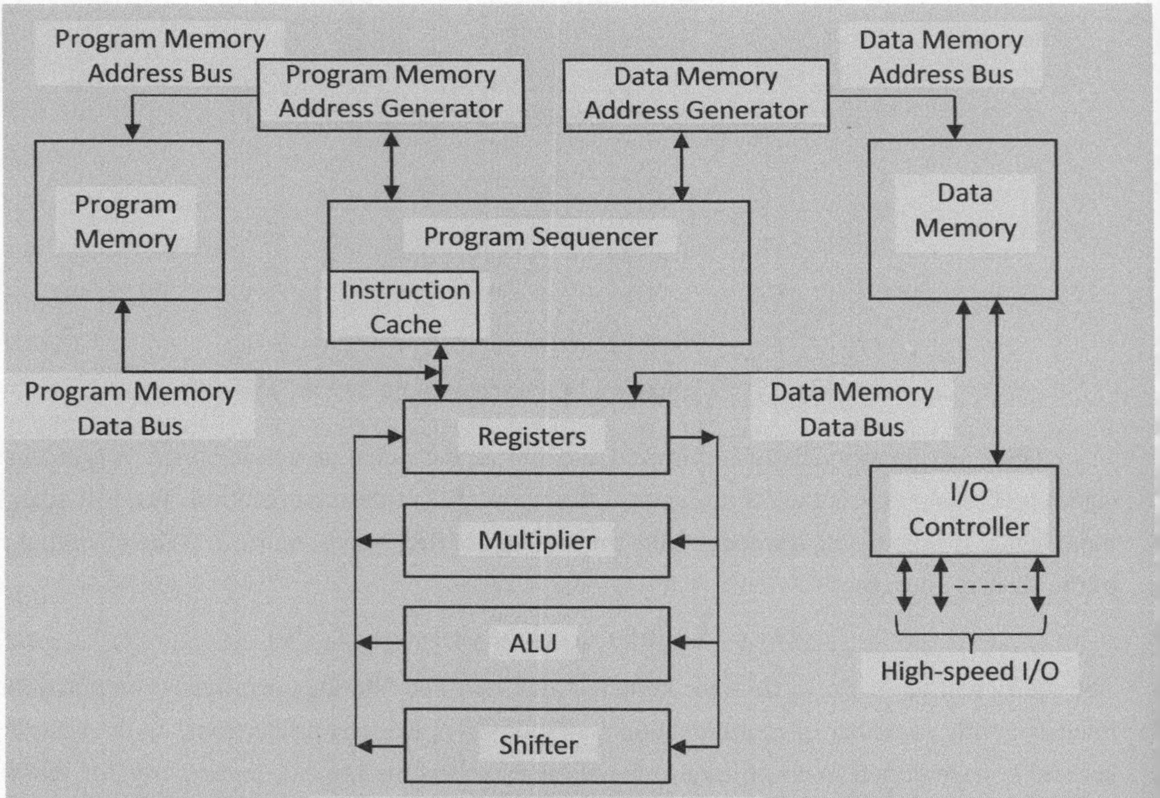

Fig 2.12: Typical DSP Architecture

The internal modules of a typical DSP architecture has been shown in Fig 2.12. One important feature of this architecture is the presence of *Address Generation Units* (*AGUs*). These units can work in parallel, independent of the main datapath operations. Once configured, the AGUs can operate in the background producing addresses to prefetch instructions and data operands. The datapath of the processor contains a large number of registers along with one or more instances of functional modules, such as, multiplier, ALU and shifter. Some important features of the DSP architecture are noted in the following.

1. **Bit-reversed addressing:** Many of the DSP algorithms work with a buffer full of data. With the arrival of the next data, the buffer is adjusted to accommodate the most recent one while discarding the oldest one. If organized as a *linear buffer*, this essentially requires shifting all the older data items to create space for the newest one. The operation is time consuming. An alternative to this is to keep data in a *circular buffer*. In a circular buffer, instead of moving the data items through the buffer locations, a pointer is moved through the data. This also needs the pointer to jump to the other end of the buffer, once it has reached one end of the buffer. If implemented in software, this requires checking the pointer value at every update of it. *Bit-reversed addressing* provides hardware support so that the pointer value need not be checked in software. In normal pointer arithmetic, the carry propagates to the left causing the value to grow till the highest number is reached. In bit-reversed arithmetic, the carry propagates to the right. Carries from the rightmost bit are ignored.

   An example of bit-reversed addressing is as follows. Assume that the buffer size is 8 while an index register has been set to 4. Further, assume that the buffer starts at memory address 0x100. The following table shows the addresses computed in successive increment operations in steps of the values of index register. The three least significant bits of result at each step have been noted. At each increment step, a unique address has been generated, reaching the same address after eight increments.

Address (Hex)	*3 LSBs*	*Comment*
0x100	000	
0x104	000 + 100 = 100	
0x102	100 + 100 = 010	Carry propagated to right
0x106	010 + 100 = 110	
0x101	110 + 100 = 001	

Address (Hex)	*3 LSBs*	*Comment*
0x105	001 + 100 = 101	
0x103	101 + 100 = 011	
0x107	011 + 100 = 111	
0x100	111 + 100 = 000	Carry falls off the right side

2. **VLIW architecture:** VLIW stands for *Very Large Instruction Word.* In VLIW architecture, a number of instructions are executed in parallel by multiple execution units present in the processor. The instruction word is much larger, so that multiple instructions can be issued simultaneously. Such DSPs are called *multi-issue* DSP. Multiple, non-conflicting instructions are executed simultaneously. The scheduling of instructions is determined at compile-time, rather than runtime. This makes the execution time predictable. However, this requires high memory bandwidth, as the instructions executing simultaneously will need number of operands from memory. Power consumption also goes up. Due to the scheduling complexity, assembly language programming for DSP is generally not recommended, rather the programmers are encouraged to write their programs in high-level language and use optimizing compiler specific to the DSP chip to get efficient implementation.

3. **SIMD architecture:** *Single Instruction Multiple Data* provides data-level parallelism. A single instruction is applied on a number of data sets to produce output in parallel, enhancing performance. To ensure the availability of a good number of such parallel operations, *loop-unrolling* is often employed. For example, consider the *for*-loop,

$$for\ j = 1\ to\ 5\ do\ a[j] = b[j] + c[j]$$

The loop when unrolled, gives rise to the following set of five statements that can be executed in parallel.

$$a[1] = b[1] + c[1]$$

$$a[2] = b[2] + c[2]$$

$$a[3] = b[3] + c[3]$$

$$a[4] = b[4] + c[4]$$

$$a[5] = b[5] + c[5]$$

4. **Fixed-point vs. Floating-point DSP:** The fixed-point DSPs usually represent real-numbers in 16-bits. They are relatively cheap. On the other hand, floating-point DSPs are costly and use minimum 32-bit representation for the real-numbers. The precision of floating-point numbers is much higher than the fixed-point numbers. This provides better *signal-to-noise* ratio in the case of floating-point numbers.
5. **Saturation arithmetic:** This is a special technique to handle overflow and underflow situations in DSP. In standard binary arithmetic, in case of an overflow or underflow, the wrap around value is returned. For example, if the numbers 0111_2 and 1001_2 are added, the result is a 5-bit number 10000_2. If the register is only 4-bit wide, the content becomes 0000_2. In saturation arithmetic, a value is returned which is as close as possible to the actual result. For example, for the previous case, it returns the value 1111_2. The strategy is particularly useful for audio and video applications. Humans cannot possibly distinguish between the true value and the largest value that can be represented in such signals. This also prevents generation of exceptions in many real-time situations. For example, generation of non-zero values prevent a possible division-by-zero fault.
6. **Large accumulator register:** DSPs generally utilize an accumulator register that is 2-3 times larger than the word size. This helps in taking care of quantization noise accumulation. In repetitive calculations, errors get accumulated in successive operations. Thus, larger accumulator can help in avoiding the round-off noise.
7. **Zero overhead loops:** Any loop execution consists of the following components – initialization, termination check, loop body, loop index updation. Out of these, the loop body is the only part that serves the computational requirement of the problem. The other parts are aptly called *overheads*. In a general processor, instructions are to be used to code these overhead parts also, over and above the loop body. In DSPs, often hardware support is provided to implement the overhead parts. When supported by hardware, no instruction is spent for coding the overhead parts – hardware takes care of all such operations. Thus, zero overhead loops help in faster execution of application code.

2.4.2 Example DSP – C6000 Family

In this section we shall look into the C6000 series of DSPs from Texas Instruments. These DSPs have been used extensively in applications involving audio and video processing, medical imaging, robotics etc. The family contains fixed-point variants C64x and C64x+, floating/fixed-point DSP cores C67x/C67x+, updated versions C674x and C66x. The devices can be efficiently programmed in C/C++ with optimizing compilers provided by Texas Instruments. Fig 2.13 shows the C6000 DSP core structure. It has the following components.

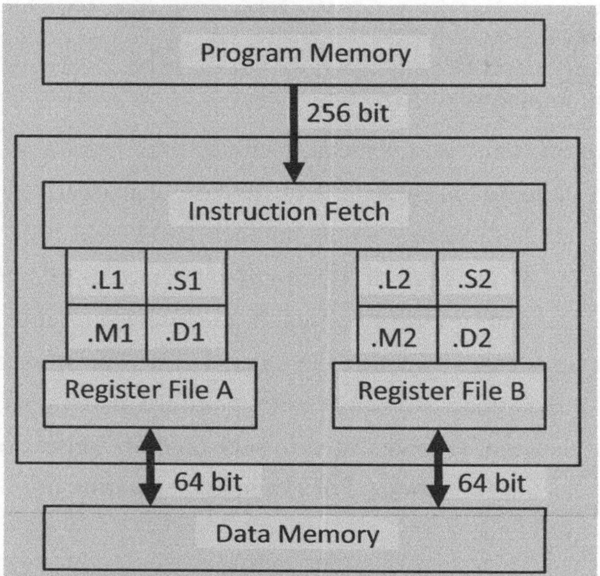

Fig 2.13: C6000 DSP architecture

1. *Eight parallel functional units*. Due to the presence of eight such units, upto eight instructions without data dependency can be executed in parallel. The data path elements are noted next.
   - *.D* (*.D1* and *.D2*) – these modules can handle data load and store operations.
   - *.S* (*.S1* and *.S2*) –handle shift, branch and compare operations.
   - *.M* (*.M1* and *.M2*) –perform multiplication.
   - *.L* (*.L1* and *.L2*) – these modules handle logic and arithmetic operations.
2. 32, 32-bit registers in each side *A* and *B*. *A* side has registers *A0-A31*, *B* side *B0-B31*.
3. Program and data memory to hold instructions and data.
4. 256-bit wide internal program bus, capable of loading 8, 32-bit instructions simultaneously.
5. Two 64-bit internal data buses allowing *.D1* and *.D2* to fetch data from data memory.

The standard Fetch-Decode-Execute cycle has been divided further into a number of sub-stages. This creates further balancing between the pipelined stages and thus enhancing performance of the DSP. The sub-stages are as follows.

1. The Fetch stage has been divided into four sub-stages.
   - *Program Address Generate* (*PG*) – updates the program counter
   - *Program Address Send* (*PS*) – Address sent to memory
   - *Program Access Ready Wait* (*PW*) – Wait for the instruction to arrive from memory
   - *Program Fetch Packet Receive* (*PR*) – Packet containing 8, 32-bit instructions received
2. The Decode stage is divided into two sub-stages.
   - Instruction Dispatch (DP) – Assign instructions to functional units
   - Instruction Decode (DC) – Decoding of instructions
3. The Execute stage may get divided into sub-stages ranging over E1 to E10, depending upon the instruction being executed.

This refinement of pipeline stages enhances the performance of the processor. To augment the process further, *software pipelining* strategies are used. In software pipelining, multiple instructions belonging to different iterations of loop body are executed in parallel. It may be noted that such instructions should not have any data dependence between them. Considering the complexity of the processor architecture, it is difficult for the users to write assembly language program code and optimize it, exploiting the available features. To alleviate this problem, the compiler provided by Texas Instruments need to be used to get optimized program realization.

2.5 Field Programmable Gate Array – FPGA

The embedded system platforms that we have discussed so far, use software to run on some processors, such as, general-purpose microprocessors, microcontrollers, DSPs etc. Though augmentations have been done via parallelism and pipelining, program fetch, data fetch and execution may take time, not affordable in many real-time and speed-critical applications. For such cases, it is necessary to have a full hardware implementation to achieve the desired performance level. In this direction, an Application-Specific Integrated Circuit (ASIC) may be tried out. However, the ASIC design has the problems of long time-to-market and high design cost. Unlike software implementations, an ASIC cannot be modified very easily. *Field programmable* devices serve the intermediary roles. Such devices can be programmed at the user-site, thus reducing the design time. The realizations are hardware based, thus operates at a much higher speed than the software implementations. Though the achievable speeds are much less, compared to ASIC, the re-programmability of these devices make them popular for embedded system implementation. Some of the important field programmable devices are as follows.

- *Programmable Logic Array* (*PLA*). It contains two programmable logic planes – an AND-plane and an OR-plane. The structure is suitable for two-level combinational logic realization with the AND-plane generating the product terms and the OR-plane performing the OR operation.
- *Programmable Array Logic* (*PAL*). Similar to PLA, however, only the AND-plane is programmable, OR-plane connections are fixed.
- *Programmable Logic Device* (*PLD*). Also referred to as CPLD (Complex PLD), it contains arrays of simple programmable devices like PLA/PAL etc. in a single chip, along with some memory elements (flip-flops).
- *Field Programmable Gate Array* (*FPGA*). These are also high capacity programmable logic devices. Compared to CPLDs, the number of logic resources in an FPGA chip is much high. Individual logic blocks in FPGA may have narrower inputs while the blocks in CPLD have wider inputs. The number of sequential elements (that is, flip-flops) is also more in FPGA.

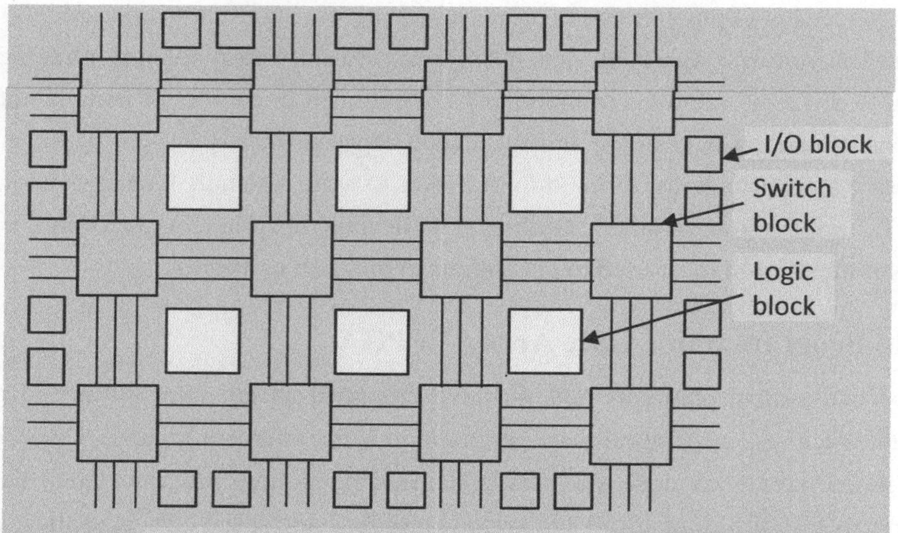

Fig 2.14: Generic FPGA architecture

Due to their high logic capacity, FPGAs have turned out to be instrumental in shifting the digital design paradigm from ASIC hardware to reprogrammable FPGA chips with much lower cost and added ease of design modification. A generic FPGA structure has been shown in Fig 2.14. It primarily consists of an array of logic blocks. Individual logic blocks can be programmed to perform different Boolean functions. Apart from the combinational elements, a logic block contains one or more flip-flops that can be used in conjunction to realize sequential logic. Interconnect links run in parallel between rows and columns of the logic blocks, throughout the chip. Connections from a logic block to its adjoining interconnection links and between the interconnection links, are also programmable. Programmable switches are present at the junction of interconnect rows and columns to establish such connections. Along the periphery of the chip, I/O blocks are put, capable of accepting inputs from the environment or producing output to the environment.

2.5.1 Programming the FPGA

As noted earlier, the FPGAs are user programmable. There are two types of FPGAs, as far as the programmability is concerned – *reprogrammable* and *one-time programmable*. The reprogrammable FPGAs can be programmed several times to realize different logic functions. On the other hand, one-time programmable devices can be programmed only once. The trade-off between the two comes in terms of properties of the switches (size, on-resistance, capacitance etc.) and associated cost. Commonly used reprogrammable FPGAs are based on static RAM (SRAM) switches. As shown in Fig 2.15, each programmable point in the chip is controlled by a SRAM bit. On reset, the FPGA chip loads the configuration program, controlling all the programmable points, from an off-chip memory to the on-chip memory. Thus, changing the configuration program changes the entire logic function realized by the FPGA chip. FPGAs belonging to *Xilinx*, *Plassey*, *Algotronix*, *Concurrent Logic*, *Toshiba* etc. use SRAM as the programming technology.

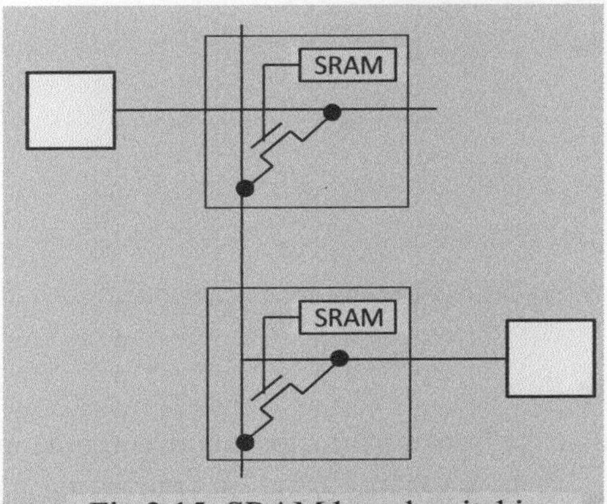

Fig 2.15: SRAM based switching

Among the one-time programming technology, the most common one is based on *antifuse*. Antifuse devices are originally open-circuit, offering very high resistance. However, on applying a voltage of 11-20V across the terminals, the resistance becomes very low, establishing electrical contacts. These devices are very small and thus require much less space compared to five-transistor SRAM bits. However, it has disadvantages – large size of programming transistors and the one-time programmability feature. Fig 2.16 shows the structure of an antifuse. FPGAs from *Actel*, *Quicklogic*, *Crosspoint* etc. use antifuse as the programming technology.

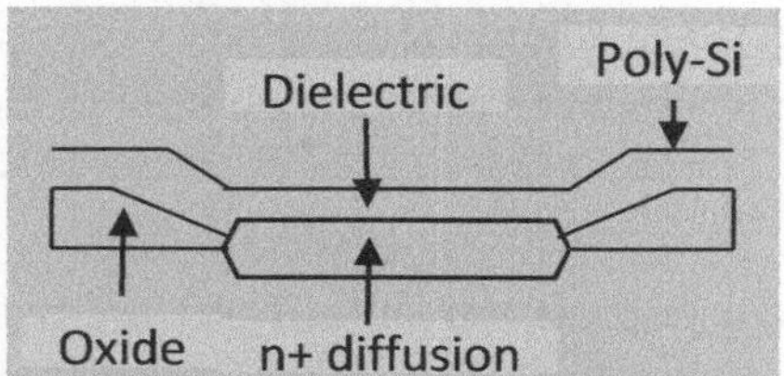

Fig 2.16: Antifuse structure

Some FPGA devices (from *Altera*, *Plus Logic*, *AMD*) use floating-gate transistor based programming technology. The device contains a floating gate and a control gate in the transistor. By applying a high voltage between the two gates, the transistor can be disabled. The process induces additional charge into the floating gate, raising the threshold voltage. On the other hand, UV light or electrical signal can be used in order to remove extra charges from the floating gate, reducing the threshold voltage of the transistor. Thus, floating-gate technology provides re-programmability like SRAM with the additional advantage that no external memory is needed to store the configuration program of the FPGA chip. Fig 2.17 shows the floating-gate concept.

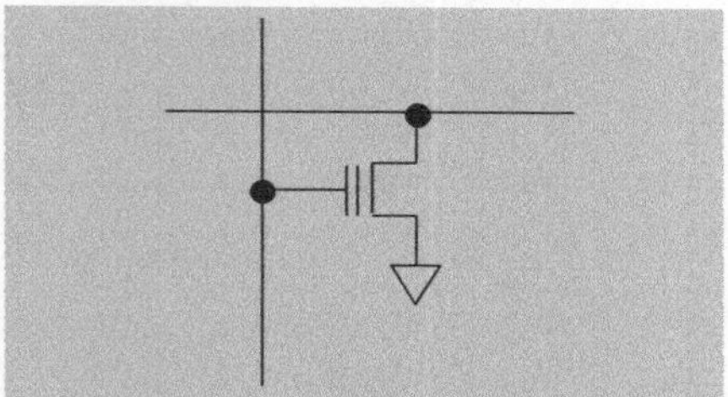

Fig 2.17: Floating-gate transistor

2.5.2 FPGA Logic Blocks

Logic blocks are used to realize the Boolean functions (both combinational and sequential). A large variant of logic block structures are available across the FPGA devices. The logic blocks vary in number of inputs/outputs, area consumed, logic function realized and so on. The range of logic blocks can be broadly classified into two categories – *fine grain* and *coarse grain*.

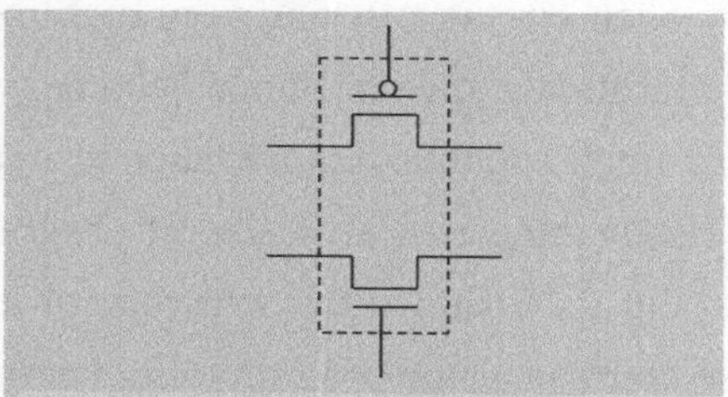

Fig 2.18: Crosspoint logic block

1. *Fine Grain Logic Block*: Fine grain logic blocks are very simple in structure, consuming very small area. A number of such logic blocks need to be interconnected to realize the desired logic function. A typical example of this type of logic blocks is from *Crosspoint*. It consists of a transistor pair, controlled by an input variable. The structure of the logic block has been shown in Fig 2.18.
2. *Coarse Grain Logic Block*: A coarse grain logic block can hold good amount of logic functionality within a single block. FPGAs belonging to *Xilinx* and *Actel* are a few examples of this category. It may be noted that complexity of such blocks vary significantly across the manufacturers.

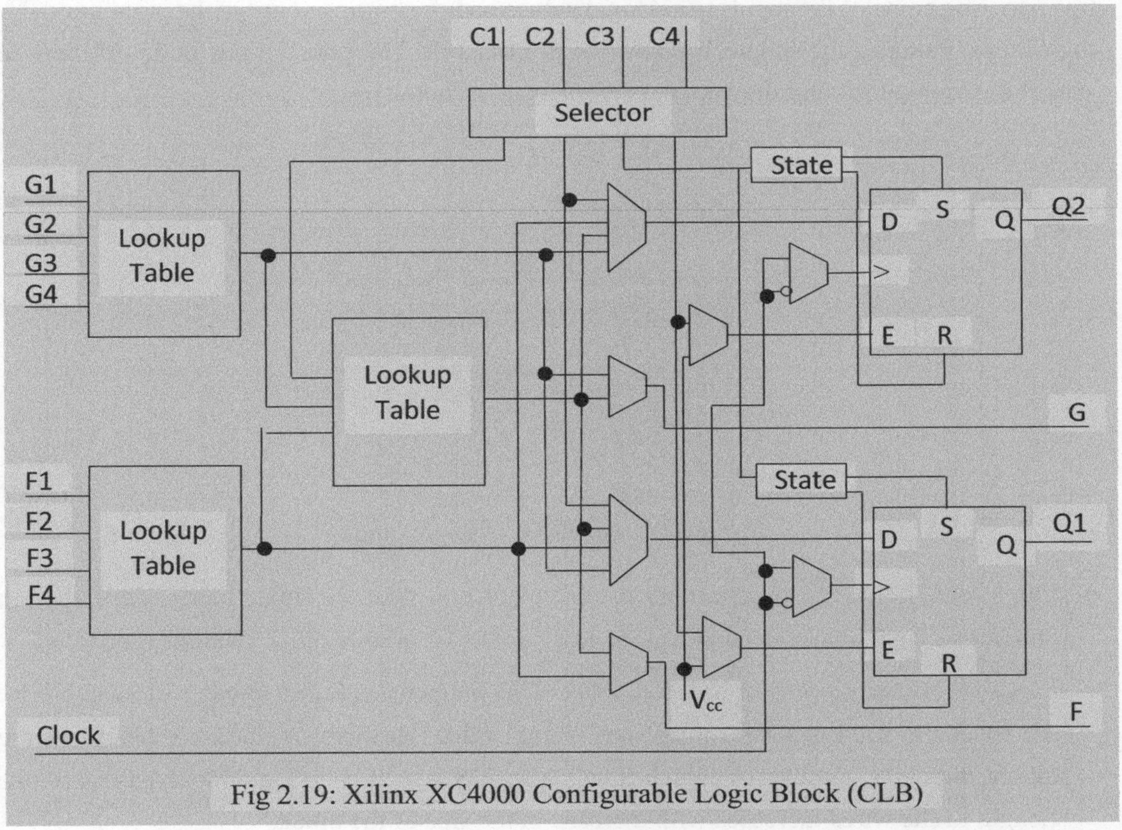

Fig 2.19: Xilinx XC4000 Configurable Logic Block (CLB)

Fig 2.19 shows the logic block of Xilinx FPGA XC4000. As it can be observed, the structure is quite complex, named as *Configurable Logic Block* (*CLB*). A CLB is based upon *Look-Up Tables* (LUTs). An LUT consists of one-bit SRAM based memory. A CLB contains two 4-input LUTs and one 3-input LUT. A *k*-input LUT can realize any combinational logic function of upto *k* variables. The total number of such functions is 2^{2^k}. The overall CLB can realize two 4-input Boolean functions or one 5-input Boolean function. Apart from the combinational part, a CLB also contains two flip-flops. The structure makes it very convenient to realize sequential logic functions. The advanced versions of Xilinx FPGAs can realize more complex functions. For example, a *Virtex-6* CLB can be configured to function as a 6-input LUT or two 5-input LUTs. It also contains 156-1064 dual-port block RAMs (depending upon family), each capable of storing 36Kbits of information.

Another example of coarse grain logic block is Actel's ACT1, shown in Fig 2.20. It is based on multiplexers. Three 2:1 multiplexers are connected in a tree-like fashion with four data inputs and four control signals. Several logic functions of upto eight variables can be realized by restricting some of the inputs to set logic values and/or shorting some of the input lines. This logic block, though quite simple, has low overhead as well. There are definite trade-offs between size of the logic block and the system performance, as noted next.

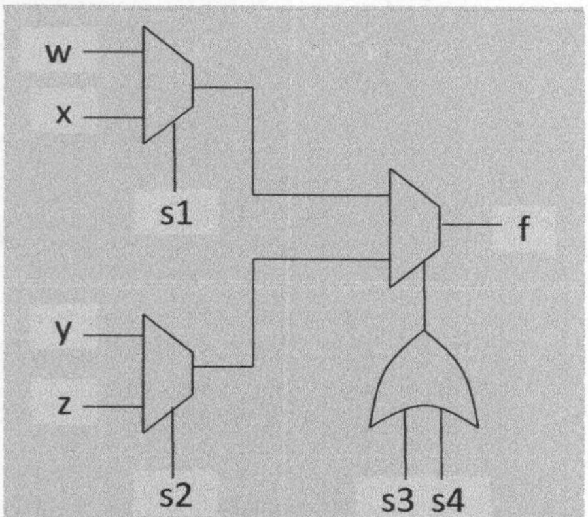

Fig 2.20: Actel ACT1 logic block

- Large logic block can realize more complex function within a single block. Thus, the total number of logic blocks needed may be less. However, a large block requires more area.
- Large blocks may result in reduced delay. This happens as lesser number of switch boxes are needed to route a net carrying some signal value. However, with larger block, average fanout increases, number of switches may also increase as each logic block has more pins. Length of the wires increases with increase in the size of the block.

2.5.3 FPGA Design Process

A typical design process for FPGAs has been shown in Fig 2.21. The FPGA vendors come up with an *Integrated Development Environment* (IDE) that can be utilized to enter the design, perform simulation and realize the logic in terms of resources available in the target FPGA chip. The design process consists of the following steps.

1. *Design Entry*. This is the first step in the overall process. The design can be entered at schematic-level (consisting of predesigned library modules and interconnections) or at a behavioural level (via languages like VHDL, Verilog). Design synthesis is needed to convert a behavioural description into a netlist of library components. Since a schematic entry is already in the form of a netlist, such translation is not needed for them.
2. *Behavioural Simulation*. A simulation is necessary to ensure correct functionality of the entered design, both for schematic and behavioural level.

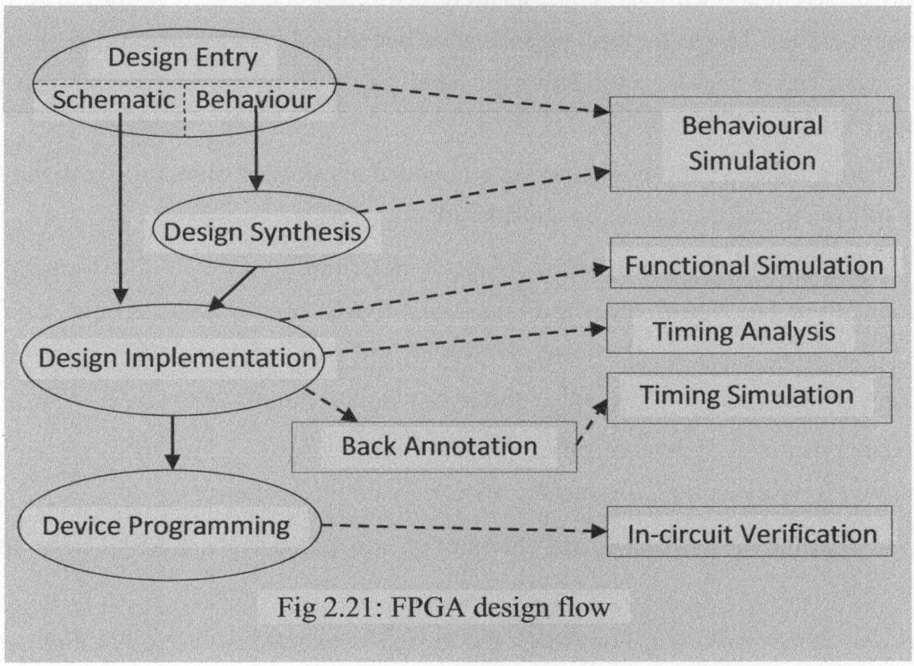

Fig 2.21: FPGA design flow

3. *Design Implementation*. This step implements the generated netlist for the target device. A functional simulation is performed to ensure functional correctness of the implementation. Detailed place-and-route is performed to implement the design onto target device. Timing analysis is carried out to identify the delays of different nets in the implementation. Delays are back-annotated onto the design and the design is passed through timing simulation. This step can identify the timing violations (set-up and hold time violations) in the implementation.
4. *Device Programming*. This stage generates the final configuration program for the FPGA device. The configuration program may be downloaded onto a memory that is read at the time

of power up (for SRAM based FPGAs). For antifuse based FPGAs, the configuration program is used as the burning pattern of fuses to realize the system functionality. In-circuit verification modules are often provided by the FPGA vendors to debug the downloaded configuration program.

2.6 Application Specific Integrated Circuit – ASIC

In the last section we have seen the features of FPGA and its usage in hardware based system realization. Compared to software implementation, the FPGA implementation of a system offers much enhanced performance. However, an FPGA chip is generic in nature that can be programmed for realizing different applications. Thus, its architecture is not completely optimized towards any particular application. To get the best performance benefits, dedicated integrated circuit chips are necessary, tailor-made for the application in hand. Such chips are called *Application Specific Integrated Circuits* (*ASICs*).

To take a decision about whether an embedded application should be realized as an ASIC or not, the following points need to be considered.

- *Volume*. The quantity of production plays a determining role in the decision for ASIC implementation. The *Non-Recurring Engineering* (*NRE*) cost of ASIC is quite high, compared to other hardware/software platforms. However, the unit cost for ASIC is pretty low. Thus, ASIC may be a good option for high-volume production requirements.
- *Customization*. Level of customization is quite high for ASIC. Thus, to fit an implementation perfectly with the system requirements, ASIC may be the best option.
- *Efficiency*. For the most efficient realization of an embedded system, ASIC is the alternative to be followed.
- *Budget and Time-to-Market*. For ASIC, the design time and cost are quite high, compared to other alternatives. As embedded systems are time-constrained, ASICs are more cost-effective in large quantities, though they incur higher initial cost and longer time-to-design.

2.6.1 ASIC Design Flow

The ASIC design process is quite complex and includes a number of iterative steps. A large number of CAD tools are utilized to convert a specification into a final chip. The major steps in the process are as follows.

1. *Specification*. This step captures the intended functionality of the system. The desirable features of the system, in terms of its area, performance and power requirements are noted.

2. *Design Entry*. This step creates a high-level description of the system, typically in some hardware description language, such as, VHDL and Verilog. The system functionality is verified via *functional simulation*.
3. *Synthesis*. The high-level design description is next synthesized into a netlist of library components. The resulting description is often called to be at *Register Transfer Level* (*RTL*).
4. *Partitioning*. The RTL description, particularly the complex ones, are next partitioned into a number of smaller components. This enhances the block-by-block optimization of the design and also promotes design reuse.
5. *Design for Test* (*DFT*) *Insertion*. This step introduces additional hardware into the circuit to enhance its testability. The components inserted typically include scan-chains, Built-In-Self-Test (BIST) module etc.
6. *Floorplanning*. This step plans the layout of the chip on the actual silicon floor. Provisions are made to create space for functional blocks, I/O pads, power distribution network etc. Signal integrity and thermal management issues are taken into consideration.
7. *Placement*. This step finalizes the places for the circuit components onto the silicon floor.
8. *Clock Tree Synthesis*. It creates and places the network to distribute clock signals to the required pins of different modules in the chip. All sequential elements should get the clock signal with a minimum jitter.
9. *Routing*. It plans the connectivity between the modules and decides how the signal lines be taken through the silicon floor, satisfying timing requirements, reducing signal interferences and decreasing the necessary signal power.
10. *Final Verification*. This step checks the satisfaction of design rules regarding the minimum feature size (of transistors), spacing, metal density etc. Timing verification is performed to guarantee the compliance with signal propagation delays.
11. *GDS II*. This is the final layout of the chip, called *Graphical Data Stream Information Interchange* (*GDS II*). At foundry level, this data is used by the semiconductor manufacturers to produce the final ASIC. After the chip has been fabricated, each unit goes through unit-level testing to check its operation. The good chips are kept while the defective ones are rejected.

2.7 Embedded Memory

Memory plays a vital role in the design and associated achievable performance of any embedded system. It serves as the physical storage for input and output data. The intermediate data generated by the program are also stored in the memory. The program itself is kept in memory in the form of instructions. Embedded memory may be of different types. A classification of memory modules used in embedded systems has been shown in Fig 2.22. The two major memory groups are (i) *primary memory* and (ii) *secondary memory*. The primary memory consists of *Read-Write memory* and *Read-Only memory*. The commonly used Read-Write memories can be of two types – *Static* and *Dynamic*. The Static memories include SRAM and NVRAM. The dynamic memories can be SDRAM and DDR. The Read-Only memories may be either programmable or fused (one-time usage). The programmable category includes EEPROM, EPROM and Flash (NAND, NOR, 3D). The fused ones are PROM and Masked ROM. The secondary memory is created using SSD, Hard Disk, Magnetic Tape and CCD. In the following a brief overview of the major memory alternatives has been noted.

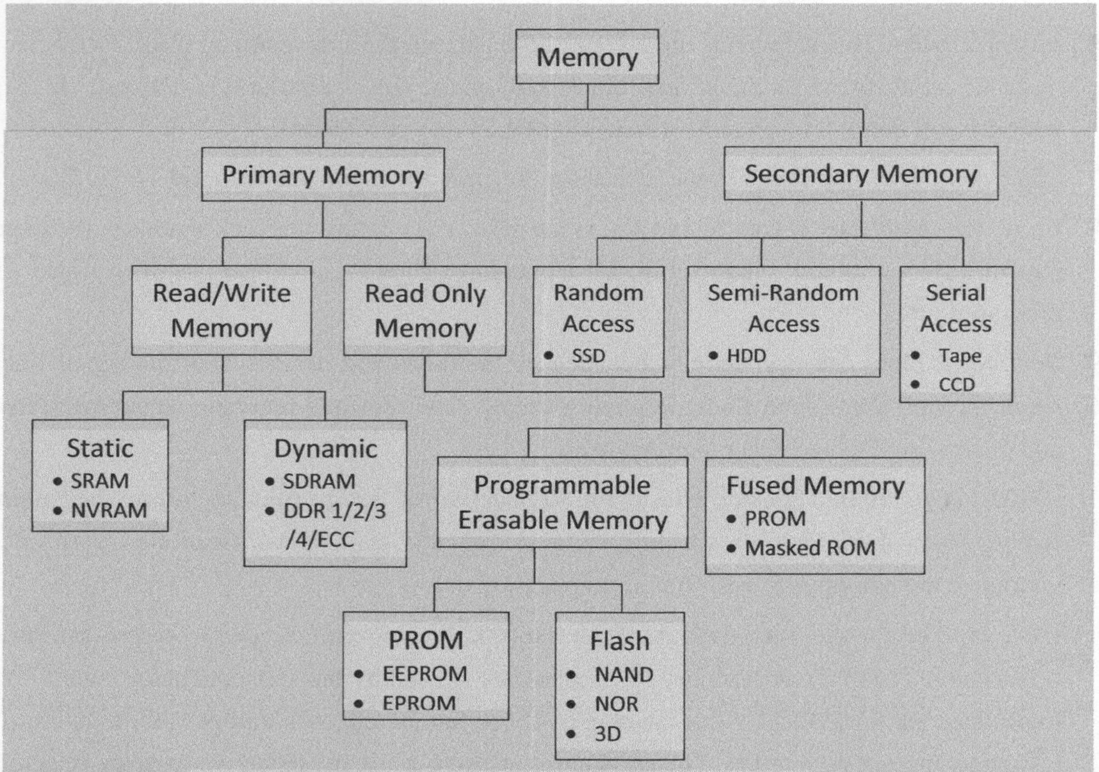

Fig 2.22: Memory modules in embedded systems

1. *Static RAM*. Static RAM or SRAM is a volatile memory that uses a latching mechanism to store information bits. Individual cell structure consists of six transistors forming two back-to-back CMOS inverters. It is expensive compared to other memory alternatives like DRAM.

However, it is quite fast and typically used in Cache and internal registers of processors. The structure of a typical SRAM cell has been shown in Fig 2.23.

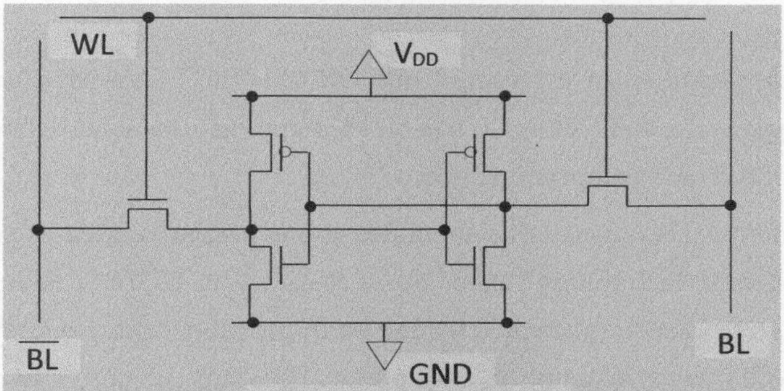

Fig 2.23: SRAM cell

2. *Non-Volatile RAM*. Non-Volatile RAM or NVRAM retains its data even when the power is switched off. The initial NVRAMs used the floating-gate MOSFET transistors to realize EPROM and EEPROMS. However, these devices require the write operation to be done in blocks only, precluding the true random-access feature. An alternative to this is *Ferroelectric RAM* (*FeRAM*) that uses a ferroelectric material to store information via polarization of its atoms. Other two emerging technologies of NVRAM are *Magneto-resistive RAM* (*MRAM*) and *Phase Change Memory* (*PCM*). The fast reading and writing capabilities of NVRAM can be used for Cache memory and high-performance computing systems.

3. *Dynamic RAM*. Dynamic Random Access Memory or DRAM stores each information bit in a memory cell consisting of a tiny capacitor and a transistor. The structure has been shown in Fig 2.24. The charge stored in the capacitor gradually leaks away, requiring periodic rewriting of data bits. The process is known as *memory refresh*. Due to its small size, DRAM has very high density with much reduced cost per bit, compared to SRAM. DRAM is typically used to realize main memory in computing systems. The most common variants of DRAM are as follows.

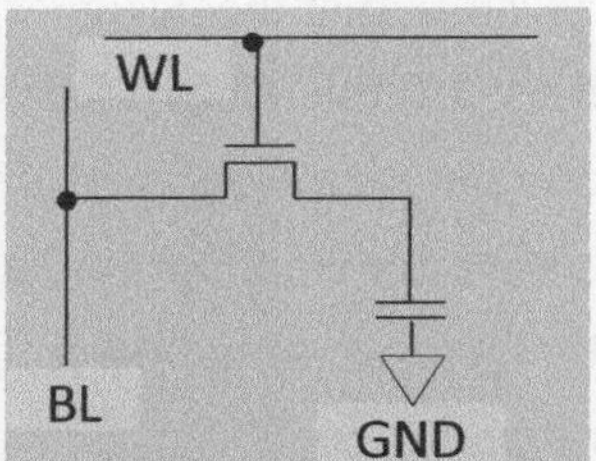

Fig 2.24: DRAM cell

- *SDR*, *DDR*, *DDR2*, *DDR3* and *DDR4*. Single Data Rate (SDR) is the oldest DRAM type. Double Data Rate (DDR) DRAMs support high speed transfer. DDR2 is faster than DDR but consumes more power. DDR3 and DDR4 are faster than their previous versions and also consume less power than predecessor.

- *SDRAM*. Synchronous DRAM (SDRAM) works with a clock signal to synchronize with other system components. It provides faster data transfer compared to the asynchronous DRAM.
- *ECC DRAM*. The Error Correcting Code DRAM (ECC DRAM) checks for errors in data transfer process, as well. Thus, it is useful for applications where the correctness of stored and transmitted data is a prime concern.

4. *Flash*. Flash memory is non-volatile in nature and is primarily used as secondary storage and ROM. Its solid-state technology makes *Solid State Drive* (*SSD*) a faster alternative to *Hard Disk Drive* (*HDD*). The storage capacity can be in the range of few Gigabytes (GB) to several Terabytes (TB). Power consumption is also low. The flash memories work on the principle of floating-gate transistors. There are two types of flash memories – NAND and NOR. The NAND flash has high memory density and high capacity. It is typically used in memory cards, USB drives and SSD. On the other hand, NOR flash memory cells are attached in a parallel manner, giving faster reading speed, compared to NAND. There is a 3D Flash memory with density higher than NAND flash and is used in high-capacity SSDs. However, the storage capacity and life-span of flash memory are often less than Hard Disks.

2.8 Choosing a Platform

After looking into the range of alternatives available to realize an embedded system, a pertinent question that the designer needs to sort out is which of these be used for the application in hand. In most of the embedded systems, one of the following two options are picked up to get the computation done – a microcontroller or a microprocessor. Microcontrollers become a natural choice for small, portable embedded systems. The choice of a particular microcontroller is guided by its processing power, OS support, interface or I/O pins, and availability of advanced high data-rate interface.

In case the microcontrollers cannot provide the required computational performance, the next choice is to go for microprocessors. They have much enhanced computational capabilities, however, require additional memory and interfacing chips to be connected to it to build the full system. Some important questions pertaining to the selection of a microprocessor are as follows.

- Whether the system will run on battery power.
- Types of interfaces needed.
- Peripheral devices to be connected.

- Type of tasks to be performed.
- Pin count – with larger pin count, connectivity to the microprocessor becomes complex in terms of both area and power requirements.

While exploring the microprocessor alternatives, it is advisable to look into the digital signal processors as well, particularly for signal processing dominated applications.

The options discussed so far are software solutions for embedded systems. For systems performing lots of data crunching and/or requiring large number of peripherals, the hardware options need to be judged as well. This is particularly true for real-time applications that need to respond to the events within a deadline. For such systems, the next alternative platform to explore is FPGA. Again, there are large number of alternatives available. The least cost alternative may be chosen that satisfy the system requirements. For an application, entire part of it may not be equally critical. The parts requiring time-bound computations may be put in hardware, whereas, non-critical parts may be realized in software. If the FPGAs also fail to meet the performance goals for the system, ASIC implementation becomes the final alternative. Here also, the target technology node (for example, 180nm, 90nm, 32nm and so on) decides the area, delay and power consumption of the system. An embedded system designer can weigh all the software and hardware options suitable for a system and proceed with the least cost solution, satisfying the constraints imposed by the requirement analysis.

UNIT SUMMARY

Processors are needed in embedded systems to carry out the computations. Large number of alternatives are available, ranging from the most generic one to completely customized solutions, to be chosen as an embedded processor. For small-to-medium sized embedded systems, microcontrollers often provide ideal solution due to their single-chip architecture having processor, memory and other peripheral interfaces on the same chip. Among the available microcontrollers, ARM has been used extensively in low-power, high performance embedded applications. For signal processing tasks, Digital Signal Processors provide low-cost solutions. Special architectural features of DSPs can be exploited to enhance signal processing. Beyond software, an embedded system may be realized in hardware. FPGA and ASIC form two alternatives here. FPGAs are semi-custom in nature and can be programmed to realize a desired computation. The feature of programmability also aids in design debugging. However, for highly time-critical applications,

FPGAs may not be able to meet the performance goals. For such cases, an ASIC may be designed that is fully customized towards the application. ASIC design may target one or more of the features – area, delay and power to be optimized in the design process. Apart from computation, storage of information is also an important issue. Several technologies including SRAM, DRAM, NVRAM, SDRAM, Flash, magnetic/optical disk, SSD etc. are available for use as embedded memory. A detailed understanding of all these alternatives for computation and storage available to the designer, paves the way for efficient embedded system design.

EXERCISES

Multiple Choice Questions

MQ1. ALE signal in ARM is

(A) Input to the processor (B) Output from the processor

(C) Bidirectional (D) Configurable

MQ2. Suppose the contents of registers R1, R2, R3 and R4 in an ARM processor are 1, 2, 3 and 4 respectively. Following two instructions are executed in sequence.

STMFD SP!, {R1, R3, R4, R2}

LDMFD SP!, {R4, R1, R3, R2}

The contents of the registers R1, R2, R3 and R4 will be

(A) 1, 3, 4, 2 (B) 3, 1, 2, 4

(C) 1, 2, 3,4 (D) 4, 3, 2, 1

MQ3. In ARM, conditional execution is supported in the instruction set

(A) ARM (B) THUMB

(C) Both ARM and THUMB (D) A programmable manner

MQ4. The registrar used as program counter in ARM is

(A) R12 (B) R13 (C) R14 (D) R15

MQ5. An ARM processor writes the 32-bit number 22292F3FH into memory and then reads a byte from the same address. The value read in big-endian convention will be

(A) 22H (B) 29H (C) 2FH (D) 3FH

MQ6. Number of software interrupts in ARM processor is

(A) 1 (B) 24 (C) 2^{24} (D) 2^{20}

MQ7. ARM processor supports

(A) Big-endian format (B) Little-endian format

(C) Both Big- and Little-endian format (D) None of the other options

MQ8. Which of the following is NOT a criterion in choosing a microcontroller?

(A) Power consumption (B) Speed

(C) Memory capacity (D) None of the other options

MQ9. Status word bit in ARM identifying THUMB mode of execution is

(A) T (B) N (C) Z (D) None of the other options

MQ10. In ARM, between FIQ and IRQ, which one has higher start address of the exception handler?

(A) FIQ (B) IRQ

(C) Either may be higher (D) Both may have same address

MQ11. Which register in ARM is always the stack pointer?

(A) R12 (B) R13 (C) R14 (D) None of the other options

MQ12. Multiply-accumulate unit is a feature of

(A) ARM (B) DSP (C) FPGA (D) None of the other options

MQ13. In bit-reversed addressing, for arithmetic operations, carry is generated from

(A) MSB (B) LSB

(C) Either MSB or LSB (D) None of the other options

MQ14. Number of instructions in a word in VLIW is

(A) One (B) Two (C) Many (D) None of the other options

MQ15. Number of instructions executed at a time in SIMD is

(A) One (B) Two (C) Many (D) None of the other options

MQ16. Signal-to-Noise ratio can be better for DSP

(A) Floating-point (B) Fixed-point

(C) Both Floating- and Fixed-point (D) None of the other options

MQ17. For 4-bit operations with saturation arithmetic, the value at overflow is

(A) 1111 (B) 0000 (C) 1000 (D) 0001

MQ18. Number of functional units in C6000 DSP is

(A) 2 (B) 4 (C) 6 (D) 8

MQ19. Software pipelining is a feature of

(A) ARM (B) DSP (C) FPGA (D) None of the other options

MQ20. Which of the following is not reprogrammable?

(A) SRAM (B) Antifuse (C) Flash (D) All of the other options

MQ21. Number of functions realizable by a 2-input LUT is

(A) 2 (B) 4 (C) 8 (D) 16

MQ22. Between FPGA and ASIC, delay of a net will be high in

(A) FPGA (B) ASIC (C) Both (D) None of the other options

MQ23. Refreshing is needed for

(A) SRAM (B) DRAM

(C) SRAM and DRAM (D) None of the other options

MQ24. Flash memory used in SSD is of type

(A) NAND (B) NOR

(C) Both NAND and NOR (C) None of the other options

MQ25. MRAM is of type

(A) SRAM (B) DRAM (C) NVRAM (D) None of the other options

Answers of Multiple Choice Questions

1:A, 2:C, 3:A, 4:D, 5:A, 6:C, 7:C, 8:D, 9:A, 10:A, 11:D, 12:B, 13:B, 14:C, 15:A, 16:A, 17:A, 18:D, 19:B, 20:B, 21:D, 22:B, 23: B, 24: A, 25: C

Short Answer Type Questions

SQ1. How does an embedded processor architecture differ from a generic processor?

SQ2. State the modification in ALE signal of ARM compared to x86.

SQ3. How does the R15 register in ARM differ from program counter in other processors?

SQ4. Explain if the number 56 can be specified as an immediate operand in ARM.

SQ5. How does software interrupt handling in ARM differ from x86?

SQ6. How does BX/BLX instructions differ from B/BL?

SQ7. How is the FIQ interrupt processed faster than IRQ?

SQ8. State the difference between VLIW and SIMD.

SQ9. Explain the concept of zero-overhead looping.

SQ10. How does ASIC differ from FPGA?

SQ11. Explain why refreshing needed for DRAM but not for SRAM and Flash.

Long Answer Type Questions

LQ1. Draw and explain the functional diagram of ARM7 processor.

LQ2. Enumerate the operating modes of ARM.

LQ3. Enumerate the architectural features available in DSP compared to generic processors.

LQ4. How does bit-reversed addressing help in realizing circular buffers?

LQ5. Distinguish between the programming technologies used in FPGAs.

LQ6. Enumerate the steps involved in ASIC design.

LQ7. State the alternative memory technologies available to be used in embedded system.

KNOW MORE

Looking back into the history, TMS1000 was the first microcontroller reported in the year 1971, developed by Texas Instruments. This was followed by Intel 4004. ARM version1 was introduced in the year 1985. The first digital signal processor is TMS5100, introduced by Texas Instruments in the year 1978. The first commercially viable FPGA is XC2064 from Xilinx, introduced in the year 1985. It had 64 CLBs, each with two three-input lookup tables. Each of these alternatives, along with ASIC, has advanced significantly over the years. ARM has come up with different versions, of which ARM7, ARM9 and ARM11 are the notable ones. Beyond ARM11, the ARM architectures have developed into three distinct categories – Cortex-A, Cortex-R and Cortex-M. Cortex-A series is for application processors targeted to be typically used in mobile computing, smart phones, energy-efficient high-end servers etc. Cortex-R series is for real-time processors. These can be used for real-time applications, such as, hard-disk controller, automotive power train, base-band control in wireless communication etc. Cortex-M series is for microcontrollers, targeted towards deeply embedded applications, such as, sensors, MEMs, IoT. The processors in this series include M0, M0+, M1, M3m M4, M7.

REFERENCES AND SUGGESTED READINGS

[1] S. Chattopadhyay, "Embedded System Design", PHI Learning, 2023.

[2] "ARMv7-M Architecture Reference Manual", ARM Limited, 2006-2010.

[3] K. Varghese, NPTEL course on "Digital System Design with PLDs and FPGAs".

[4] S. Saurabh, NPTEL course on "VLSI Design Flow: RTL to GDS".

[5] Yifeng Zhu, "Embedded System with ARM Cortex-M in Assembly Language and C", E-Man Press LLC, 2017.

[6] J.W. Valvano, "Embedded Microcomputer System: Real Time Interfacing", Brooks/Cole 2000.

Dynamic QR Code for Further Reading

1. S. Chattopadhyay, "Embedded System Design", PHI Learning, 2023.

2. K. Varghese, NPTEL course on "Digital System Design with PLDs and FPGAs".

3 Interfacing

UNIT SPECIFICS

Through this unit we have discussed the following aspects:

- *Features of Serial Peripheral Interface (SPI) protocol;*
- *Operation of Inter Integrated Circuit (IIC) interface ;*
- *Overview of RS-232 family protocol;*
- *Interfacing devices through Universal Serial Bus (USB);*
- *Operation of IrDA interface;*
- *Overview of Controller Area Network (CAN);*
- *Features of Bluetooth wireless interface;*
- *Operation of Digital-to-Analog and Analog-to-Digital converters;*
- *Interfacing of subsystems through PCIe and AMBA bus;*
- *Overview of user interface design.*

The overall discussion in the unit is to give an overview of interfacing standards commonly followed in embedded system design. It is assumed that the reader has a basic understanding of device interfacings and digital design.

A large number of multiple choice questions have been provided with their answers. Apart from that, subjective questions of short and long answer type have been included. A list of references and suggested readings have been given, so that, one can go through them for more details. The section "Know More" has been carefully designed so that the supplementary information provided in this part becomes beneficial for the users of the book. This section mainly highlights the advanced processors supporting many of the interfacing standards discussed in the unit. The designer may choose these processor for the ease of system implementation.

RATIONALE

This unit on interfacing makes the readers familiar with the typical interfacing standards followed while connecting peripheral devices to an embedded processor. A processor used for embedded system is expected to possess the traditional interfaces such as RS-232 for serial communication, Universal Serial Bus (USB) for incorporating plug-and-play features. However, apart from them, many other interfaces have been designed typically for embedded applications. Two such very simple interfacing standards are Serial Peripheral Interface (SPI) and Inter Integrated Circuit (IIC). Both the standards require minimum hardware and simple protocols. Another very important standard is Controller Area Network (CAN) that can operate in highly noisy environment like automobiles. It uses an arbitration-free mechanism with assigned message priorities. Two important converters, digital-to-analog and analog-to-digital, are used in realization of embedded applications interacting with the environment. Depending upon the cost and performance metrics, the designer may choose one or other type of converters available in the market. It is often necessary to connect a number of peripheral systems to the processor, over a bus. For this purpose, the desktop computers may use PCIe (Peripheral Component Interconnect Express) bus, apart from USB. An embedded system designer has similar choice. For microcontroller based System-on-Chip type embedded system design, Advanced Microcontroller Bus Architecture (AMBA) has come up as the standard. AMBA possesses a hierarchy of buses with varying performance parameters. For human interaction with embedded applications, user interface design is of utmost importance. Most such devices contain an LCD touchscreen panel that may be either resistive or capacitive in nature. The goal is to make the user experience for the embedded application satisfactory. This unit takes the reader through all these interfacing standards to equip them with the capability to choose the appropriate one to connect devices to the system.

PRE-REQUISITES

Digital Design, Computer Architecture

UNIT OUTCOMES

List of outcomes of this unit is as follows:

U3-O1: Interface devices using SPI, I^2C protocols

U3-O2: Enumerate features of RS-232 family

U3-O3: Interface devices using USB protocol

U3-O4: List the features of CAN protocol

U3-O5: State the operating principle of IrDA and Bluetooth

U3-O6: Enumerate different types of DACs and ADCs

U3-O7: State the features of subsystem buses and user interfaces

Unit-3 Outcomes	*EXPECTED MAPPING WITH COURSE OUTCOMES (1- Weak Correlation; 2- Medium correlation; 3- Strong Correlation)*			
	CO-1	*CO-2*	*CO-3*	*CO-4*
U3-O1	1	3	-	-
U3-O2	1	3	-	-
U3-O3	1	3	-	-
U3-O4	2	2	-	-
U3-O5	1	3	-	-
U3-O6	1	3	-	-
U3-O7	1	3	-	-

3.1 Introduction

Embedded systems interact with the environment through various types of sensors and actuators. These devices differ significantly from those commonly found in general computing platforms. A desktop computer typically contains devices like keyboard, display, mouse, printer etc. The devices are mostly connected to the processor via interfaces like USB, serial/parallel communication ports and Bluetooth. To the contrary, an embedded system may have many non-conventional devices connected to it. For example, a climate-control system may have a few temperature and humidity sensors. While designing a sensor, the primary concern is to sense the physical parameter and convert into electrical signals. Transportation of this electrical equivalent to a processor (located at a close or distant place) may not be given adequate importance. As a result, it is imperative to have some very simple interfacing strategy to be followed. At the same time, the communication must be reliable.

The requirement has given rise to a number of simple to moderate complexity interfacing standards for embedded hardware. The traditional communication standards like RS232, USB, Bluetooth are definitely used in embedded system design. However, a number of other standards have been introduced from time-to-time by the industry, to be used in embedded applications. Some such interfaces include *Serial Peripheral Interface* (*SPI*), *Inter-Integrated Circuits* (*IIC*,I^2C), *IrDA*, *Controller Area Network* (*CAN*) etc. SPI and I^2C are synchronous communication protocols with the hardware requirement of only four and two signal wires, respectively. The CAN protocol can be used in highly noisy environment of automobiles. Analog-to-digital and digital-to-analog converters form a part of many embedded systems. Many of the embedded appliances interact with human beings. For this, special attention must be given to the user interface design to ensure good user experience. In the following, the device interfacing standards targeted to embedded processors and their associated issues have been elaborated.

3.2 Serial Peripheral Interface

Serial Peripheral Interface (*SPI*) is a synchronous communication protocol that can transfer data serially between a *master* and one/more *slave* devices. It is a low-cost interface developed by Motorola targeting simple communication technique between microcontrollers and peripheral chips. SPI is also known as a *four-wire* interface as it has only four signal lines connected between the master (processor) and the slave (peripheral). Fig 3.1 shows the four signals used in the protocol. The signal lines are as follows.

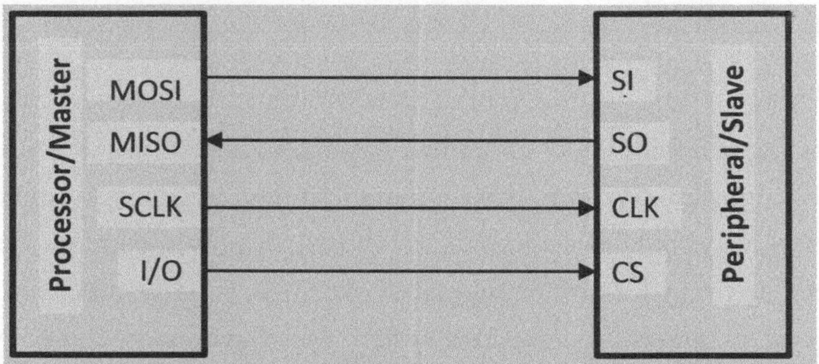

Fig 3.1: The SPI Interface

- MOSI – Master Out Slave In
- MISO – Master In Slave Out
- SCLK – Serial Clock
- CS – Chip Select

The roles of these signals are depicted by their names. The data bit from master to slave device traverses through MOSI. On the other hand, the bit from slave to master travels via MISO. The serial clock signal SCLK is the synchronizing clock provided by the master and used by the slave. The chip select signal CS acts to select the slave device to which master wants to communicate. The CS signal is particularly useful in multi-slave environment. For example, Fig 3.2 shows the situation in which a master device selectively communicates with one of its three slave devices. The slave device to interact with the master is selected via the *Slave Select* (*SS*) signal from the master.

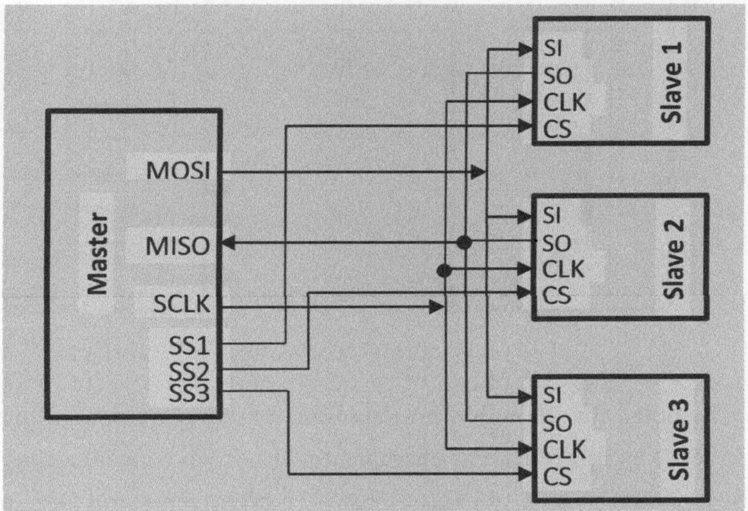

Fig 3.2: Connecting Multiple Slaves in SPI

Data transfer in SPI is effectively an exchange of data between the master and the slave via MOSI and MISO signal lines. The master and the slave contain one 8-bit register each. These data registers act as serial shift registers. The contents of these registers are exchanged serially to facilitate data transfer. The data transfer is initiated when the master/processor writes a byte to its SPI data register. Bits are transmitted serially over the MOSI line to the SPI data register of the slave, one bit per clock cycle. Simultaneously, the bits from the SPI data register of slave device are transmitted serially over the MISO line to reach the SPI data register of the master. The process has been explained in Fig 3.3. It may be noted that the data exchange can be restructured to perform only read or only write by the master.

- *Read Operation*: Master writes a dummy byte to its data register. This in turn, initiates transfer of the content of data register of slave to the data register of the master. The master can then transfer the content of its SPI data register to one of its internal registers.
- *Write Operation*: The master writes the intended byte to its SPI data register. As a result, the content of this register gets transferred to the SPI data register of the slave. Simultaneously, the previous content of the SPI data register of slave reaches the SPI data register of the

master. As master intended to do only a write operation, the content available now in its SPI data register is simply ignored by the master.

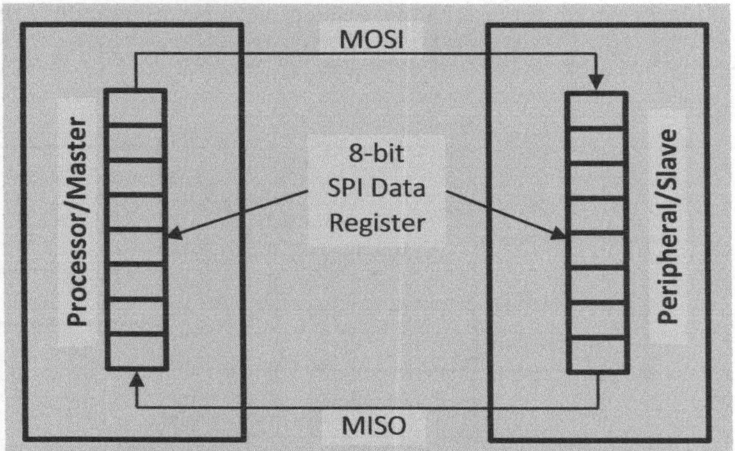

Fig 3.3: Data transfer through SPI Interface

It may be noted that though 8-bit data transfer is most common in SPI, other word sizes are also used in some applications. For example, touch-screen controllers and audio codecs use 16-bit words, many DACs and ADCs follow 12-bit word structure. Among the popular microcontrollers, AVR ATmega series processors provide SPI communication. Some common example peripherals having SPI interface are as follows.

- *Analog-to-Digital Converters* (*ADCs*): *LTC2452* – an ultra-tiny, differential, 16-bit delta-sigma ADC.
- *Touch Screen*: *SX8652* – low power, high reliability controller for resistive touch screen with supply voltage range of 1.65V to 3.7V.
- *EEPROM*: *25XXX* series with densities varying from 128 bits to 512 kilobits, low-power EEPROM with built-in write protection.
- *Real-time Clock*: *DS3234* – low-cost, highly accurate real-time clock.
- *Memory Card*: *MMC* and *SD* cards.

3.3 Inter-Integrated Circuit

Inter-Integrated Circuit (*IIC, I^2C*), also known as *Two-Wire Interface* (*TWI*) is a simple, cheap, bus-based communication protocol. This is ideally suitable for small-scale embedded systems. Two wires are used to form the I^2C bus, devices are connected to the bus in a multidrop fashion. The bus is bidirectional with a speed of 100-400 kbps. The two wires are called,

- *SDA* – Serial Data
- *SCL* – Serial Clock

The bus has an open-drain configuration, pulled to V_{DD} when idle. Fig 3.4 shows one system in which several master and slave devices have been interfaced.

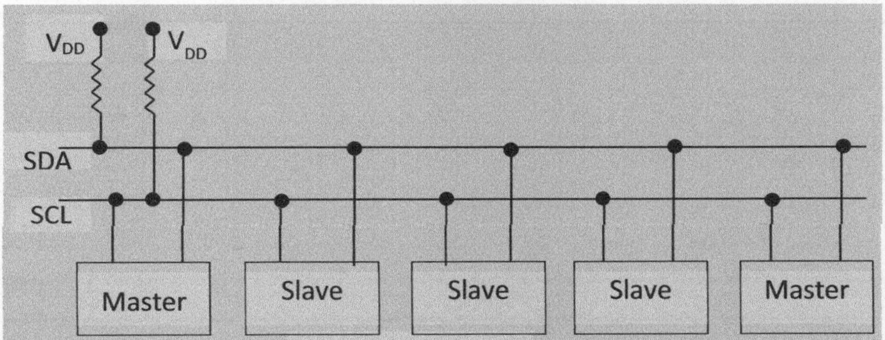

Fig 3.4: I^2C wires

A master device can start the communication by first pulling SDA to low, followed by SCL to low. These transitions in SDA and SCL lines from high to low indicate a START condition for communication. With SCL low, SDA transits to the first valid data bit. The rising edge of SCL samples the data bit at destination. Data bit in SDA must remain valid as long as SCL remains high. SDA transits to the next data bit after SCL becomes low. The STOP condition is indicated by SCL becoming high, followed by SDA becoming high. After transmitting 8 bits, the master releases SDA and gives an additional pulse on SCL. The slave acknowledges the receipt of the byte by pulling SDA low. In this way, multiple bytes can be transmitted with acknowledgement for each byte transfer. If the receiver is unable to accept more bytes, the transmission can be aborted by the receiver by pulling SCL low. Each device has a unique 7-bit address. Thus, upto 128 devices can be connected to an I^2C bus. The first byte transmitted by the master contains this 7-bit slave address along with a *direction* bit. If the direction bit is 0, it indicates a write operation by the master – the slave receives subsequent bytes from the master over the bus. On the other hand, the direction bit being 1 indicates a read operation, in which the slave starts sending subsequent bytes onto the bus, to be read by the master. Fig 3.5 shows a timing diagram for the I^2C operation.

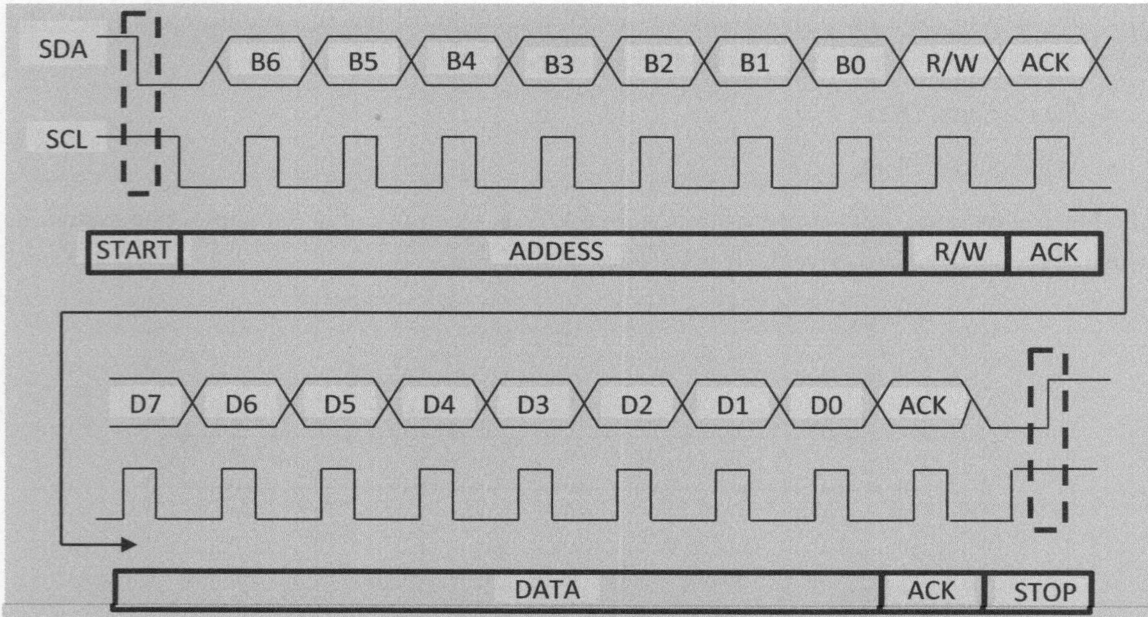

Fig 3.5: Timing diagram for I²C communication

Some example devices with I²C interface are as follows.

- *Temperature Sensor*: *LM75* with a temperature range of -55°C to +125°C.
- *Pressure Sensor*: *BMP085* with pressure range 300 to 1100 hPa, low-power, low-noise device.
- *Analog-to-Digital Converter*: *AD7992* – a 12-bit ADC with 2μS conversion time, 2 analog input channels.
- *EEPROM*: *PCA94S08* with 8 kbit storage.
- *Real-time Clock*: *PCA8565* with low-power CMOS real-time clock and calendar.

Compared to SPI, I²C needs fewer signal lines – individual slave select signals are not required in I²C. Instead of that, I²C uses in-band addressing – the first communicated byte itself identifies the slave device. Slave acknowledgement is also available in I²C. This proves the existence of the addressed device. However, SPI communication is full-duplex, whereas I²C is half-duplex in nature. The word size for communication in I²C is fixed to 8 bits, whereas in SPI, higher word sizes may be used. SPI can operate to provide data rate of 10-100 Mbps while I²C can provide 400 kbps in fast mode and 3.4 Mbps at high-speed mode. SPI is more suitable for applications working with long data streams – not just word addressed locations. Some such examples include

DSPs, ADCs, DACs etc. I^2C provides better support for multi-master environment with flow control.

3.4 RS-232

RS-232 is one of the oldest serial communication standards dating back to 1960s. Devices can communicate serially over a cable length of upto 25m at data rates upto 38.4 kbps. The original specification document has undergone several revisions over the years. EIA RS-232 was introduced in 1960. The versions A, B and C of it came up in the years 1963, 1965 and 1969 respectively. It has been renamed as TIA standards later. Accordingly, TIA-232 D, E and F have come up in 1986, 1991 and 1997 (with revision in 2012), respectively.

In RS-232, data bits are transmitted at voltage levels with respect to local grounds only. This gives rise to an *unbalanced interface*. The communication is asynchronous. Unlike SPI, there is no synchronizing clock running between the communicating devices. The protocol is quite simple, justifying its demand for use over the decades, even though several other serial communication protocols have come up. In order to send a 0-bit, the driver output is a signal in the range +5V to +15V. On the other hand, for transmitting a 1-bit, the corresponding voltage range is -5V to -15V. At receiver, a signal in the range +3V to +15V is taken as 0, while a signal in the range of -3V to -15V is considered as 1. A logic1 is called a *space* while a logic 0 is called a *mark*. The protocol is meant for connecting a Data Terminal Equipment (DTE) to a Data Communication Equipment (DCE). While a computer may be an example DTE, a modem can be considered as a DCE.

3.4.1 Handshaking

Due to the absence of synchronizing clock, flow control of information becomes a concern for RS-232 communication. Additional flow control mechanisms need to be utilized to prevent data overloading at the receiver. Handshaking methods are used to solve the overloading problem. RS-232 supports three different handshaking strategies, as noted next.

1. *Software handshaking*: Software implementation of handshaking protocol saves the hardware area and reduces the number of additional signal lines. Data transmission over telephone lines is a typical example of software handshaking. The protocol used is known as *Xon/Xoff*. In this protocol, control characters are embedded into the data stream and sent along the data lines. The *Xon* command starts the transmission while *Xoff* stops it. To embed into the ASCII charcter stream, character with code 17 has been taken for *Xon* and 19 for *Xoff*. As soon as the receiver

is ready to receive further data, it sends a *Xon* character to start transmission. The receiver can send a *Xoff* character to stop transmission.

2. *Hardware handshaking*: The strategy is superior to software based handshaking. The connection pattern has been shown in Fig 3.6. As can be noted in the figure, the *Request To Send* (*RTS*) of *Data Terminal Equipment* (*DTE*) needs to be connected to the *Clear To Send* (*CTS*) pin of *Data Communication Equipment* (*DCE*). The line *Data Terminal Ready* (*DTR*) of DTE is connected to the *Data Set Ready* (*DSR*) of DCE and vice versa. For initiating the transmission, DTE sets RTS ON. Once DCE becomes ready for communication, it puts CTS ON. The DTE responds by making DTR ON and the line remains ON as long as data is being transmitted.

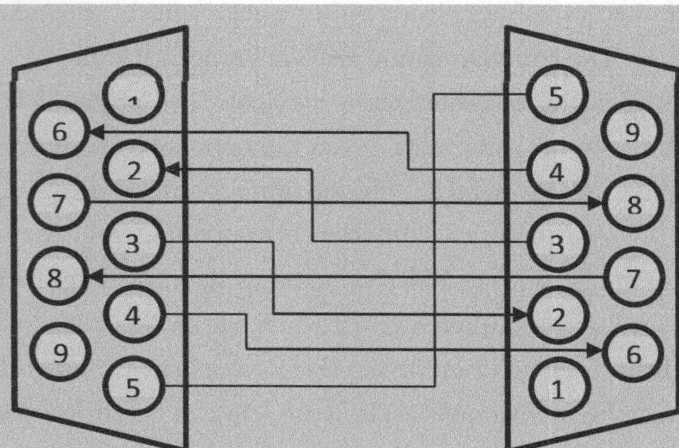

Fig 3.6: 9-Pin Connector in RS-232

3. *Combined hardware software handshaking*: In the combined policy, both the hardware connectivity and software control via *Xon*/*Xoff* character transmission are implemented for flow control.

3.5 Universal Serial Bus – USB

Universal Serial Bus (*USB*) is a standard evolved for plug-and-play type interfacing between processors and peripherals. It enables devices to connect to each other, transfer data and also share a power source. While many of the older interfacing standards need some special efforts (right type of cable and connectors, manual parameter setting and so on) to make two devices talk to each other, USB provides a uniform interfacing strategy. It uses single, standardized interface socket and permit improved plug-and-play feature technically known as *hot-swapping* of devices. USB can also provide power to low power consuming devices, eliminating the necessity of additional external power sources for them. Many of the USB devices can be used without installing the manufacturer specific *device driver* software.

3.5.1 USB Versions

USB comes in different versions with varying data transfer rates. The version USB 1.1 was released in 1998, supporting data rate upto 12 Mbps. It used Type-A and Type-B connectors (going to be outdated with the introduction of Type-C connectors). This version was primarily used for connecting computer peripherals like keyboard and mouse. USB 2.0 was released in the year 2000, having the maximum data transfer rate of 480 Mbps. It used Type-A, Type-B, Mini-USB and Micro-USB connectors. The standard is backward compatible with USB 1.1 and can be used to connect to more sophisticated peripherals like printers and external hard drives. In 2008, USB 3.0 was released with the maximum data rate of 5 Gbps. It is backward compatible with USB 2.0 and USB 1.1. Typical use cases involve large file transfers, high-resolution media and data-intensive applications. Type-A, Type-B and Micro-USB connectors are supported. USB 3.1 was introduced in two generations – Gen 1 in 2013 and Gen 2 in 2015. Gen 1 supports transfer rate upto 5 Gbps while Gen 2 supports upto 10 Gbps. USB 3.1 is typically used in high-performance storage devices, video transfer, fast charging etc. It is backward compatible with previous USB versions, the connectors can be of Type-A, Type-B, Micro-USB or Type-C. USB 3.2 was also released as two generations – Gen 2×1 in 2017 supporting transfer rate upto 10 Gbps and Gen 2×2 in 2019 supporting upto 20 Gbps. It is backward compatible with previous USB versions with Type-A, Type-B and Type-C connectors. Apart from that, it also supports Thunderbolt 3 alternate mode over USB-3. USB4 was released in 2019 with two versions – USB4 20 (supporting upto 20 Gbps) and USB4 40 (upto 40 Gbps). Only Type-C connectors are supported. It has the ability to dynamically allocate bandwidth between data and video.

3.5.2 USB Connection and Operation

USB network has a tiered-star topology with a root hub located at a host. Additional hubs may connect to the root hub or intermediary hubs forming a tree structure, subject to a limit of five levels of tiers. Devices may be connected to the hubs at any level. A USB host may contain several host controllers with each host controller having one or more USB ports. As per USB standard, upto 127 devices (including hubs) can be connected to a single host controller. Fig 3.7 shows the typical structure of USB hubs and devices connected in a tiered-star topology. A single USB device may contain several logical devices within it. These sub-devices are referred to as *device functions*.

For example, a webcam may have a microphone integrated with it along with the camera, thus containing two logical sub-devices – video device function and audio device function.

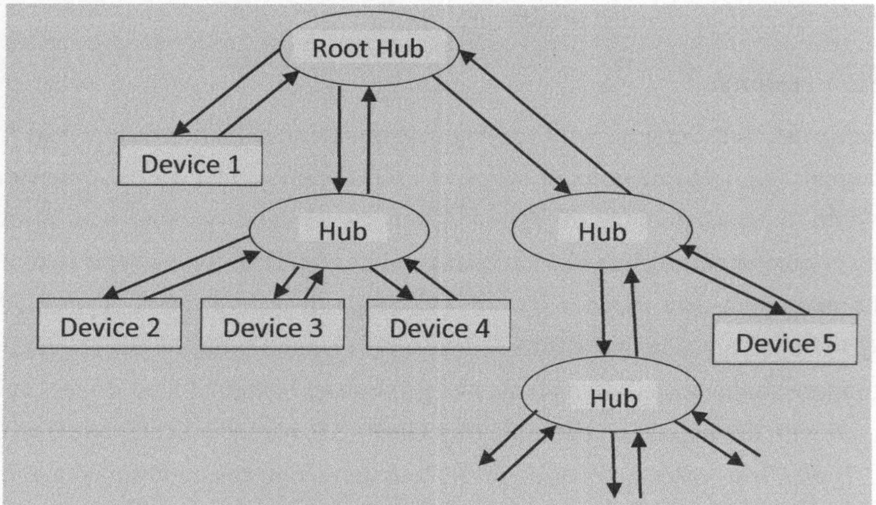

Fig 3.7: Tiered-star USB tree structure

Connection and disconnection of a device to a USB network get detected by the host automatically. To ensure this, the host regularly polls the hubs to get their status. If a new device has been plugged-in to a hub, the hub informs the host about its change in state. The host in turn issues command to enable and reset the port. In response, the device is expected to provide information about itself to the host. The received information is used by the host operating system to determine the associated software driver to be used for the device. When a device is unplugged from a hub, at next polling, the hub informs the host accordingly about its change of state. The host removes the device from its list of available devices. This process of automatic detection and identification of devices by USB host is called *bus enumeration*.

There are four types of data transfer in USB, as noted next.

1. *Control transfer*. It is used to configure the bus and return status information.
2. *Bulk transfer*. It is an asynchronous, bidirectional data transfer strategy.
3. *Isochronous transfer*. It is used for moving time-critical data to an output device. The transfer is unidirectional without any error check. Many audio and video devices use this mode of transfer.
4. *Interrupt transfer*. It is used to receive/transmit data at regular intervals – 1 to 255 ms. The transfer is designed for devices that need to send/receive data infrequently but with a guaranteed minimum service period and retrial on failure.

3.5.3 USB Device Classes

The devices with USB support can be grouped into some pre-defined *device classes*. A device may be a full-custom one requiring its full-custom device driver, or may belong to one of these classes. A class defines the expected behaviour and interface descriptors, so that for all such devices belonging to a class, a single device driver may be used. The operating system designer has to take special care to implement such generic device drivers. The commonly available device driver classes have been listed in Table 3.1.

Table 3.1: USB device classes

Class	*Purpose*
Audio	Audio and music devices
Chip/Smart Card Interface	Smart card devices
Common class	Generic devices
Communication	Modems, Telephones, Network interfaces
HID	Human interface devices – keyboard, mouse
Hub	USB hub
IrDA	Infrared devices
Mass storage	Hard disks, CD, DVD
Monitor	Computer monitor
Physical interface device	Joystick and similar devices
POS terminals	Cash register
Power	Power control or monitoring
Printer	Printers
Imaging	Scanners, cameras

3.5.4 USB Physical Interface

The physical interface of USB can be divided into two parts – cable and connector. The cable is shielded and data are transmitted over a twisted pair differential data cable having 90 ohm ±15% impedence. The transmitted signal levels are as follows.

- USB 1.1: 0.0 – 0.3V for low, 2.8 – 3.6V for high.
- USB 2.0: ±400 mv.
- USB 3.0: ±500 mv.

The interface has four wires (upto USB 2.0) or nine wires (USB 3.0 and beyond). Table 3.2 shows the wires along with colour coding. Pins 1 to 4 are common in all USB versions, 5 to 9 are specific for USB 3.0 onwards.

USB has two connection types.

- *Upstream connection*. This is the connection from device back to host/hub.
- *Downstream connection*. This connection is from host out to the device.

Table 3.2: USB wires in interfaces

Pin	*Colour*	*Signal Name*		*Description*
		Type-A	*Type-B*	
1	Red	VBUS		Power
2	White	D-		Differential data line
3	Green	D+		Differential data line
4	Black	GND		Power ground
5	Blue	STDA_SSRX-	STDA_SSTX-	Superspeed transmitter differential data line
6	Yellow	STDA_SSRX+	STDA_SSTX+	Superspeed transmitter differential data line
7	Shield	GND_DRAIN		Signal ground
8	Purple	STDA_SSTX-	STDA_SSRX-	Superspeed receiver differential data line
9	Orange	STDA_SSTX+	STDA_SSRX+	Superspeed receiver differential data line
Shell	Shell	Shield		Connector metal

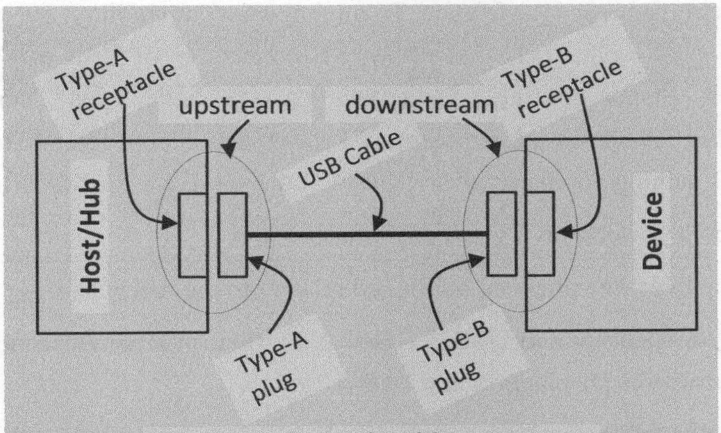

Fig 3.8: USB cable with connectors

The connection pattern has been shown in Fig 3.8 Assuming USB 1.1or USB 2.0 communication, USB cable possesses an upstream connection at host end and a downstream connection at device end. For upstream connection, Type-A connectors are needed while the downstream connection needs Type-B connectors. The cable possesses Type-A plug at host end (upstream) and Type-B plug at device end (downstream). To connect to the plugs, the host/hub contains a Type-A receptacle while the device contains a Type-B receptacle. As discussed later, the size of Type-A and Type-B connectors ensure that the USB cable cannot be connected wrongly, even by a layman.

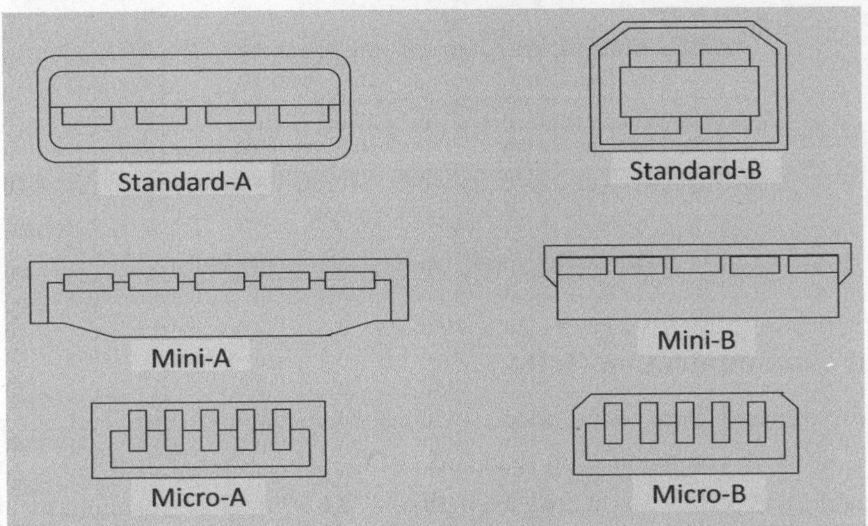

Fig 3.9: Type-A and Type-B connectors

The USB connectors are designed to be robust with electrical contacts protected by adjacent plastic tongue. The entire connection assembly is further protected by an enclosing metal sheath to ensure protection from electromagnetic interference. To minimize incompatibility, by specification, USB connectors have low tolerance. Type-A and Type-B connectors of USB can be of one of the following categories – Standard, Mini and Micro. On the other hand, Type-C connector is only of a single structure. Fig 3.9 shows the structure of Type-A and B connectors. However, the USB Type-C connector is gaining popularity over Type-A and Type-B for the following reasons.

- It is capable of both power delivery and data transmission.
- Connector is flippable – the plug can be flipped relative to the receptacle.
- Supports USB 2.0, USB 3.0 and USB 3.1 Gen 2. Further, in Alternate mode, it can support third-party protocols like DisplayPort and HDMI.
- The devices are allowed to negotiate appropriate level of power flow through the interface.

The Type-C connector has 24 pins, the corresponding pin layouts of receptacle and plug have been shown in Fig 3.10.

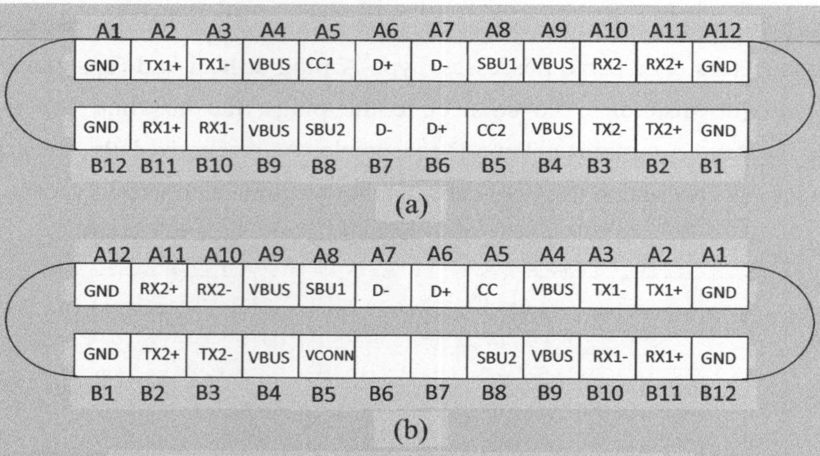

Fig 3.10: USB Type-C (a) Receptacle (b) Plug

3.6 Infrared Communication (IrDA)

IrDA stands for *Infrared Data Association* – a consortium of more than 150 companies that developed the infrared communication standard. IrDA uses infrared LEDs to communicate between computers and peripherals at a wavelength of 870 ± 30nm. It is a medium for short-range, low-power, high data rate connection with low-cost transceivers. Due to short range, the spectral region of IrDA communication is virtually unlimited and unregulated world-wide. The infrared signals can penetrate glass, but not other opaque mediums. This restricts the communication to a room only.

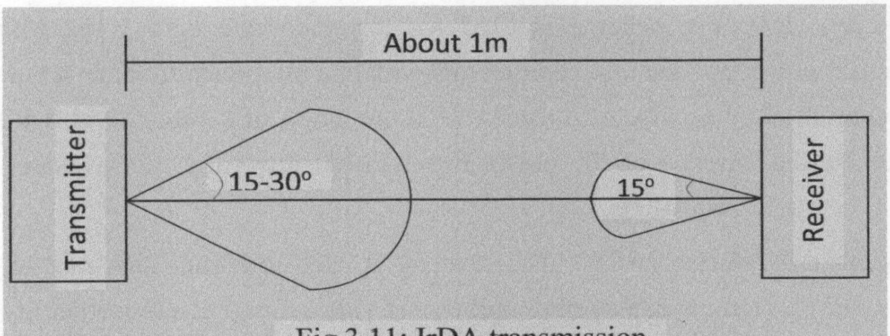

Fig 3.11: IrDA transmission

A directed infrared beam is used for communication from the transmitter to the receiver. This is a *line-of-sight communication* with transmitter beaming out its transmission at 15-30° either side of the line-of-sight. The viewing angle of the receiver is 15° either side of line-of-sight. The distance between transmitter and receiver is at least 1m, typically going upto 2m. The transmission policy has been shown in Fig 3.11. With the maximum surrounding illumination of 10 klux (daylight), the *Bit Error Ratio* (*BER*) is 10^{-9}. Devices start communicating at 9600 bps which may be negotiated, without user intervention, for higher and lower data rates. IrDa is suitable for point-to-point and even point-to-multipoint communication and is popular with portable devices like notebook, handheld computer, digital camera.

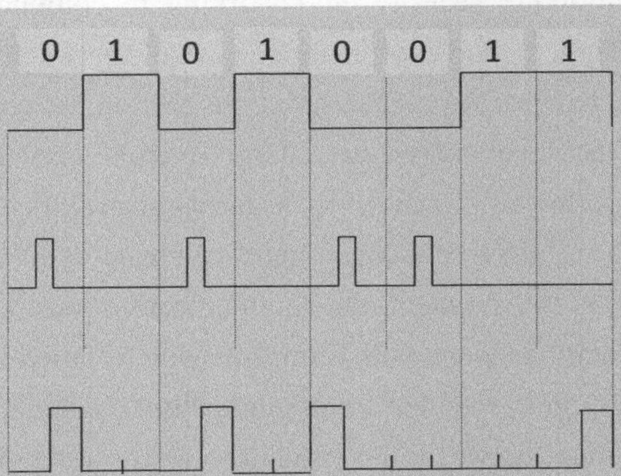

Fig 3.12: IrDA encodings (a) Data bits "01010011", (b) RZ coding (c) 4PPM coding

IrDA uses two different bit encoding schemes depending upon the rate of transmission. The schemes are as follows.

- *Return-to-Zero* (*RZ*). The scheme is used for low data rate upto 1.152 Mbps. In this, a transmission frame is divided into subintervals with one bit transmitted per subinterval. A logic 0 bit is represented by a pulse of duration 3/16 the width of a subinterval, while a logic 1 is represented by the absence of the pulse. Fig 3.12(b) shows the transmission of bit pattern "01010011" using RZ encoding.
- *Pulse Position Modulation* (*PPM*). The strategy is used at higher data rate of 4 Mbps, also denoted as *4PPM*. Here, a data symbol duration (*Dt*) is defined that is further divided into four equal-length time slices, called *chips* or *cells* (*Ct*). A data symbol contains a pulse at exactly one of its four cells and represents two bits of information. Corresponding to the information bits "00", pulse is put at cell 1. This makes the data symbol "1000". Similarly for information bits "01", "10" and "11", the data symbols are "0100", "0010" and "0001", respectively. Fig 3.12(c) shows the transmission of bit pattern "01010011" using *4PPM* encoding.

3.7 Controller Area Network (CAN)

Controller Area Network (*CAN* or *CAN-bus*) is a networking protocol primarily used in automotive electronics to facilitate devices communicate in a highly noisy environment. Automotive contains a large number of electronic components (engine management system, ABS braking, active suspension, lighting, air conditioning, security etc.) working in conjunction with mechanical components. When a car is moving, a good coordination is needed between the modules, resulting in large number of message exchanges. A point-to-point connection between the modules can be an ideal networking solution, however would need large amount of wire. A low-cost digital network is the alternative to be followed. Considering all mechanical and electrical components on board, the 12V power supply to the electronic components can have ±400V transients. In order to ensure proper data transfer in this environment, the communication must be noise immune, have error detection and correction facilities along with retransmission of failed packets.

CAN provides an effective solution to the above communication challenges. It uses a broadcast, differential, serial bus connection between the modules (also called device units). Data is transmitted using an automatic arbitration-free mechanism. Transmission follows a *carrier-sense, multiple-access* protocol with *collision detection* and *arbitration on message priority* (*CSMA/CD+AMP*). Before starting a transmission, a node has to wait for a prescribed period of bus inactivity. Each message has an identifier field that contains a pre-programmed priority noted in its identifier field. In case multiple devices transmit simultaneously, the one transmitting more number of *dominant bits* wins, thus asserting its higher priority. The node with lower-priority message senses the same, backs off and waits for the bus to become idle. A '0' is taken as the dominant bit over '1' as recessive. The physical bus is thus an open-collector, wired-AND connection. If one node transmits a dominant bit (0) and another a recessive bit (1), the device transmitting the dominant bit wins and its transmission continues, while the other device backs off. Thus, higher priority messages are never delayed. The allocation of message IDs is very important – each ID must be unique and has to be assigned by considering its priority.

The CAN bus structure has been shown in Fig 3.13. Two lines, CANH and CANL constitute the differential pair terminated by 120Ω resistance to avoid reflection. Each node connected to the CAN bus has the following components.

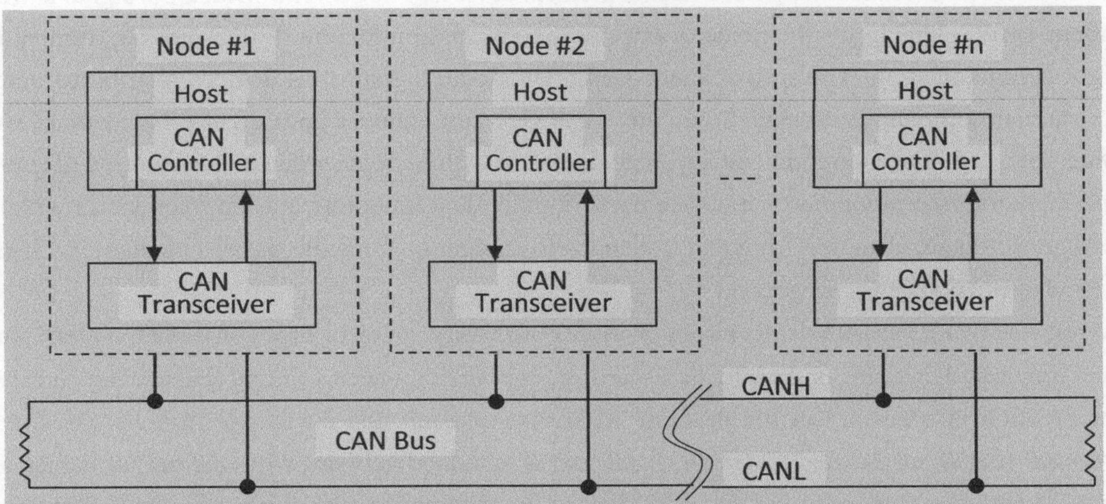

Fig 3.13: CAN bus structure

- *Host Processor*. This is responsible for determining the type of messages received and their meanings. It also performs the task of transmitting messages from the node.
- *CAN Controller*. It is responsible for the operation of transmitting and receiving messages. Received bits are read from the bus till the complete message is available. It then interrupts the host processor asking it to collect the message. For sending a message, the host processor stores it in the CAN controller which is then transmitted serially through the bus.

- *Transceiver*. It is responsible for adapting the bus signal levels to that expected by the CAN controller. It contains protective circuitry for the CAN controller. On the transmitter side, it converts the signal level of the CAN controller to that of CAN bus.

CAN bus can transmit at a rate of 1 Mbps over a network length of 40m having a maximum of 30 nodes. Upto 500m distance can be covered at a lower data rate of 125 kbps.

3.8 Bluetooth

This is a standard for small, cheap, wireless communication, typically used between devices like computers, printers and mobile phones. It was originally introduced by Ericsson and quickly adopted by large number of companies. Bluetooth transmits data through low-power radio waves at a frequency of 2.45 GHz (typically 2.40 to 2.4835 GHz). This frequency band is internationally reserved for use of industrial, scientific and medical devices. The power of Bluetooth signal is weak (about 1mW). This limits the range of Bluetooth transmission to 10m. It does not require line-of-sight communication. The walls cannot stop a Bluetooth signal, thus devices distributed across rooms can communicate using Bluetooth. A device can connect upto eight other devices over Bluetooth, at a time. Communications do not interfere with each other due to the adoption of *spread spectrum frequency hopping* – a device uses 79 individual randomly chosen frequencies within a designated range, changing from one frequency to another on a regular basis. Transmitters change frequencies 1600 times per second.

As soon as two Bluetooth devices come within a proximity, an electronic conversation takes place deciding whether there is data to be shared or one device needs to control the other. No user intervention is necessary in the process. After conversation, the devices form a *Personal Area Network* (*PAN*), also called a *piconet*. A piconet is an adhoc network with one master device and upto seven slave devices. Another 255 devices may remain as inactive or *parked*. The initial communication between two Bluetooth devices is called *pairing* or *bonding*. It may be protected by a 6-digit numeric *passkey* to be entered by at least one of the device users.

3.9 Digital-to-Analog Converter (DAC)

Embedded systems interact with its environment. Unlike the digital world, the signals in the environment are mostly analog in nature. The control signals produced by an embedded processor are digital bits that need to be converted to analog electrical quantities (voltage, current etc.). The *Digital-to-Analog Converters* (*DACs*) perform this second job – the digital data is converted into an analog signal. Fig 3.14 shows the schematic of a DAC. There are two architectures commonly used in DAC design – *Weighted Resistors* method and *R-2R Ladder Network* method. An overview of the two architectures have been presented in the following.

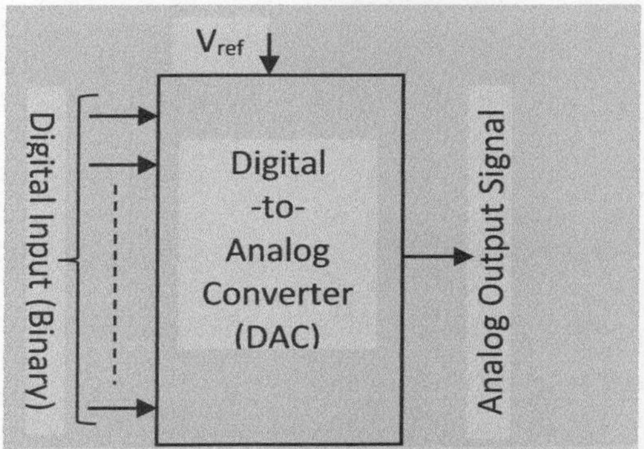

Fig 3.14: Digital-to-Analog Converter

1. *Weighted Resistors DAC*. Fig 3.15 shows the schematic of a 4-bit *Weighted Resistor DAC*. The digital input bits $b_3b_2b_1b_0$ control the switches in the connection pattern of weighted resistors. Contribution of a bit gets consideration only if the corresponding bit value is 1. All such contributions get summed up via a summing op-amp module. It may be noted that the resistors are weighted based on the weights of the bits in the digital input. The output V_o of the op-amp is given by,

$$V_o = \frac{R_o}{R}\left(b_3 + \frac{b_2}{2} + \frac{b_1}{4} + \frac{b_0}{8}\right) V_{ref}$$

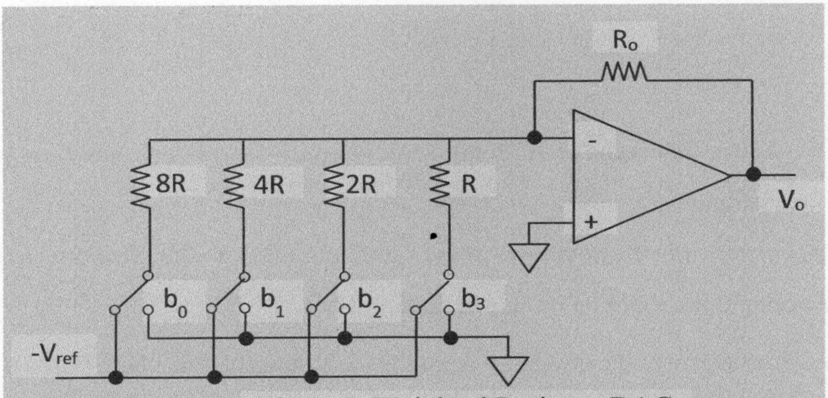

Fig 3.15: Weighted Resistors DAC

A major drawback with the approach is its scalability. With increasing number of bits in the digital input, the required range of resistor values become large, the accuracy also suffers.

2. *R-2R Ladder Network DAC.* Fig 3.16 shows the schematic of a 4-bit DAC using *R-2R Ladder* circuit. Using circuit analysis, it can be shown that the output voltage V_o for the summing amplifier is given by,

$$V_o = \frac{1}{2}\left(b_3 + \frac{1}{2} b_2 + \frac{1}{4} b_1 + \frac{1}{8} b_0\right) V_{ref}$$

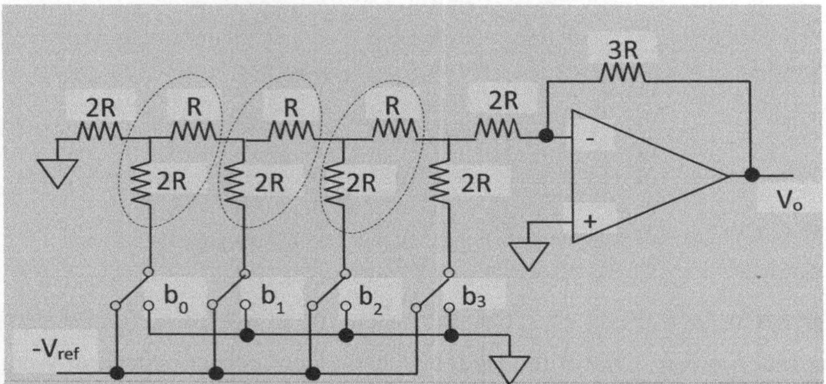

Fig 3.16: R-2R Ladder Network DAC

3.9.1 DAC Performance Parameters

The following are the important parameters determining the performance of a DAC.

1. *Resolution.* It is defined as the change in output voltage corresponding to the smallest input change (that is, change in the least significant input bit). It can also refer to the number of bits the DAC can handle. For an *n*-bit DAC, the resolution can be expressed in either of the following two forms.
   - $\frac{1}{2^n - 1} \times 100\%$
   - $\frac{V_{FS}}{2^n}$, where V_{FS} is the DAC's full-scale output voltage corresponding to the maximum binary input.
2. *Relative Accuracy.* It is the deviation of the actual output from the ideal one, as a fraction of the full-scale voltage. It should be no worse than $\pm\frac{1}{2}$ LSB.
3. *Linearity.* This measures the deviation from the ideal straight-line behaviour of the DAC output. The error should be no more than $\pm\frac{1}{2}$ LSB. When all input bits are zero, the output voltage gives the *offset error* for the DAC.

4. *Monotonicity.* A DAC is said to be monotonic if the output voltage increases every time with the increase in input code.
5. *Settling Time.* This is the time needed by the DAC for the output to switch and settle within $\pm\frac{1}{2}$ LSB when input changes from all 0s to all 1s. It should be less than the half of the data arrival rate.

3.10 Analog-to-Digital Converter (ADC)

An ADC converts an analog signal to its digital equivalent that can be read and processed by the processor. A schematic representation of an ADC has been shown in Fig 3.17. A block diagram depicting the stages of analog to digital conversion has been shown in Fig 3.18. The input analog signal is continuous in both amplitude and time, while the final digital output signal is discrete in both amplitude (binary format) and time. The stages in between have signals with various properties, as shown in the diagram. The stages in the conversion process are as follows.

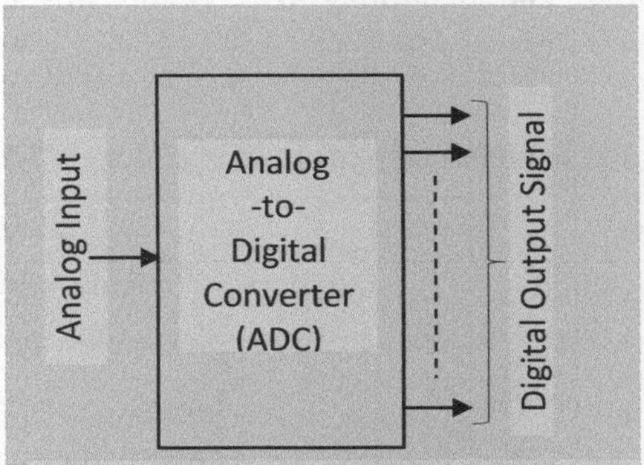

Fig 3.17: Analog-to-Digital Converter

1. *Sample.* The analog input signal is sampled at certain frequency to obtain the instantaneous amplitude values to be converted to digital form. As the analog signal is a continually time varying one, the ADC can convert only the values at sampling instances into digital equivalents. As per the Nyquist Criteria, if the highest frequency of analog signal is f, sampling should be carried out at a frequency more than $2f$.
2. *Hold.* This stage holds the analog signal sample at steady value so that the subsequent ADC stages can work on it and that the value does not change till the next sampling interval.
3. *Quantize.* The quantization process approximates the sampled analog signal amplitude to one of the few selected fixed values. Naturally, the process introduces an error, called quantization error/noise.

4. *Encoder*. This is the final stage of an ADC, converting the quantized analog signal into binary digits (bits).

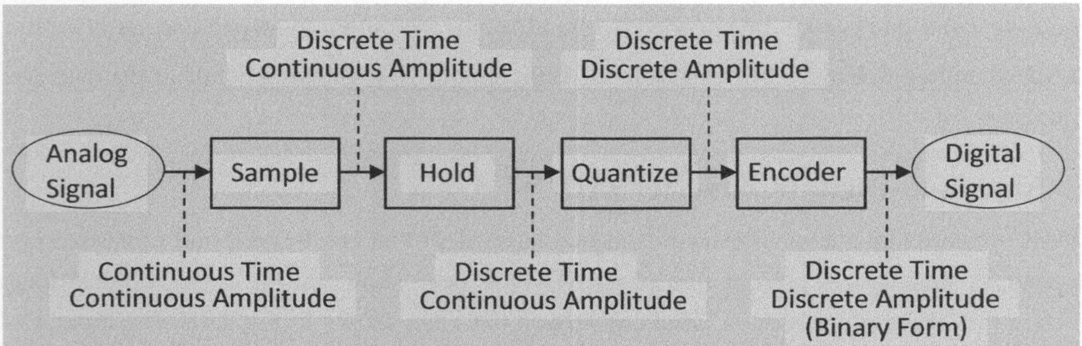

Fig 3.18: Stages in an ADC

The following are the most commonly used ADCs – *Delta-Sigma ADC*, *Flash ADC*, *Successive Approximation ADC*, and *Integrating ADC*. A comparison between their features has been shown in *Table 3.3*.

Table 3.3: Feature comparison of common ADC types

ADC Type		*Strength*	*Weakness*
Delta-Sigma		High resolution, relatively inexpensive	Relatively slow, not suitable for high bandwidth applications
Flash		Very fast	Large, expensive, high power consumption
Successive Approximation		Simple design	Not very fast, limited resolution, susceptible to noise
Integrating	Voltage-to-Frequency	Precise, inexpensive, high noise rejection	Low accuracy
	Single-Slope	Good resolution	Low accuracy
	Dual-Slope	Relatively slow	Good accuracy

3.10.1 Delta-Sigma (ΔΣ) ADC

The *ΔΣ converter* is fundamentally a single-bit sampling system. The converter samples the input signal multiple times following an *oversampling* technique. Naturally, the input signal must be slow enough to enable oversampling at a frequency f_S. Typically, f_S is hundreds of time faster than the desired data rate f_D at the output of the ADC. Individual samples are accumulated over time and averaged with other input-signal samples through a *digital decimation* filter. Fig 3.19 shows the block diagram of the internals of Delta-Sigma ADC. The modulator samples input signal at a very high rate into a one-bit stream. The digital decimation filter takes these sampled data and converts into a high-resolution, slower digital code.

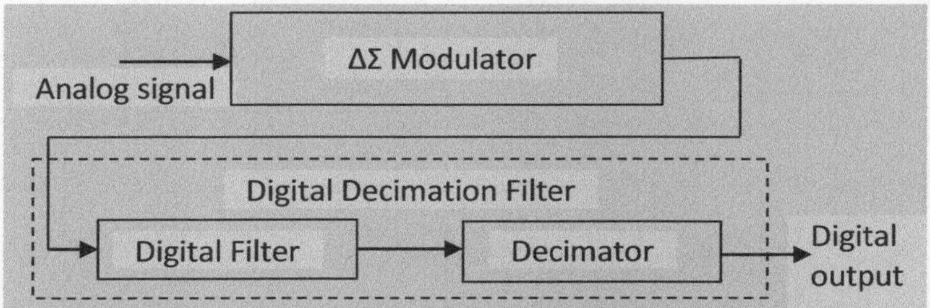

Fig 3.19: Delta-Sigma ADC

3.10.2 Flash ADC

Flash ADC, one of the fastest ADCs by architecture, is also called a parallel ADC. It contains a series of comparators, each one comparing an input signal with a given unique reference voltage. The outputs of the comparators are applied to the inputs of a priority encoder to produce the binary output. Fig 3.20 shows the structure of a 3-bit Flash ADC. It may be noted that the reference voltage V_{ref} has to be provided via a precision voltage regulator. The priority encoder generates the binary output corresponding to its highest order active input set to 1 by the comparators. The lower order active inputs are discarded by the converter. Thus, for the 3-bit ADC in Fig 3.20, if the outputs of the comparators are 0, 1, 1, 1, 1, 1, 1 from the highest to the lowest order, the priority encoder outputs "110".

Flash ADC is the most efficient ADC technology, in terms of speed. However, the comparator requirements grow exponentially with the increase in the number of output bits. Another practical advantage of Flash ADC is its capability to produce non-linear output. The resistors in the voltage-divider network can be adjusted for this purpose. If the resistors are of equal values (as in Fig 3.20), each successive binary counts correspond to the same amount of increase in analog signal. The resistors may be taken to be of different values to vary the increase in analog signal, thus incorporating non-linearity.

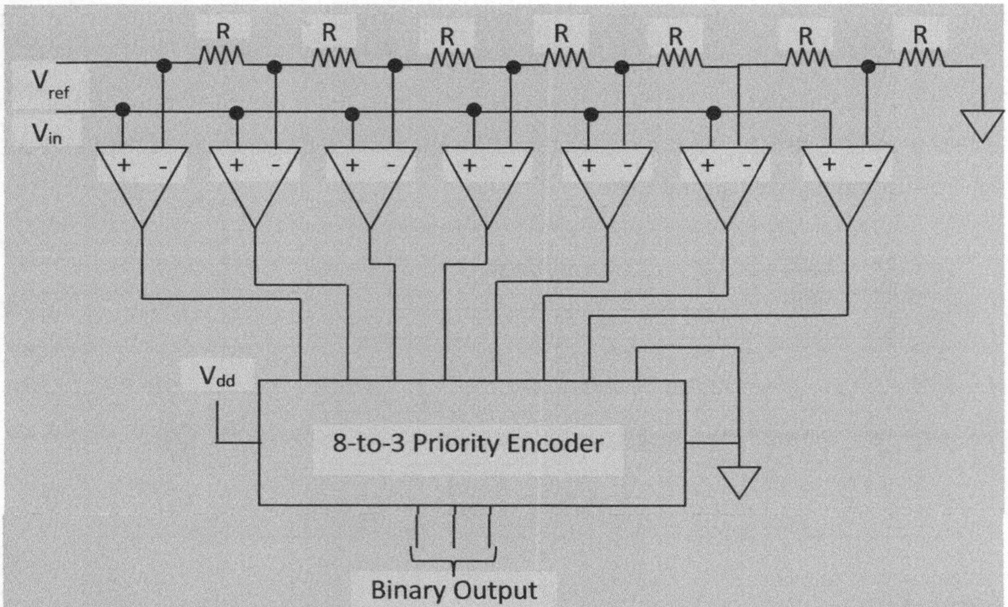

Fig 3.20: Flash ADC

3.10.3 Successive Approximation ADC

This ADC uses a mechanism similar to the *Binary Search* algorithm to determine the digital equivalent of an analog input voltage. It searches through all quantization levels to determine the digital bit values. Fig 3.21 shows a block diagram of the successive approximation ADC. It consists of the following modules.

1. *Sample-and-Hold*. It acquires and holds the input voltage samples for conversion.
2. *Comparator*. It compares the analog input with the output of an internal DAC. The result is fed to a *Successive Approximation Register* (*SAR*).
3. *Successive Approximation Register* (*SAR*). This provides an approximate digital code corresponding to the input voltage, to the internal DAC.
4. *Digital-to-Analog Converter* (*DAC*). Supplies the comparator with an analog voltage, equivalent to the digital output of the SAR.

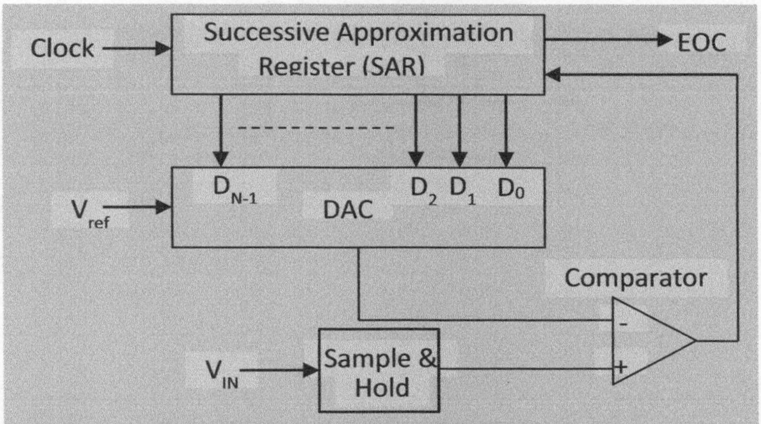

Fig 3.21: Successive Approximation ADC

To start the conversion process, the MSB of SAR is set to 1, all other bits 0. Accordingly, DAC outputs an analog voltage $V_{ref}/2$. If this voltage exceeds V_{IN}, the SAR bit is reset, otherwise left as 1. The next bit of SAR is set then. The process continues in this way for each bit and determining its value, one bit at a time. The final content of the SAR is output as the digital count and the *end-of-conversion* (*EOC*) signal is activated to inform the same.

3.10.4 Integrating ADC

The block diagram of an *Integrating ADC* has been shown in Fig 3.22. It converts an unknown input analog voltage to its digital equivalent through an integrator. In the dual-slope implementation, first the unknown input voltage is applied to the integrator and the output is allowed to ramp up for a fixed *run-up* time, t_u. Next, a known reference voltage of opposite polarity is applied to the integrator and is allowed to ramp till output becomes zero. This is called *run-down* time t_d. Now, the input voltage is computed as a function of reference voltage, t_u and t_d, as noted next.

$$V_{IN} = -V_{ref}\frac{t_d}{t_u}$$

By adjusting the values of R and C, the times t_u and t_d can be varied. For higher resolution, longer integration times can be used. For faster conversion, the resolution can be sacrificed.

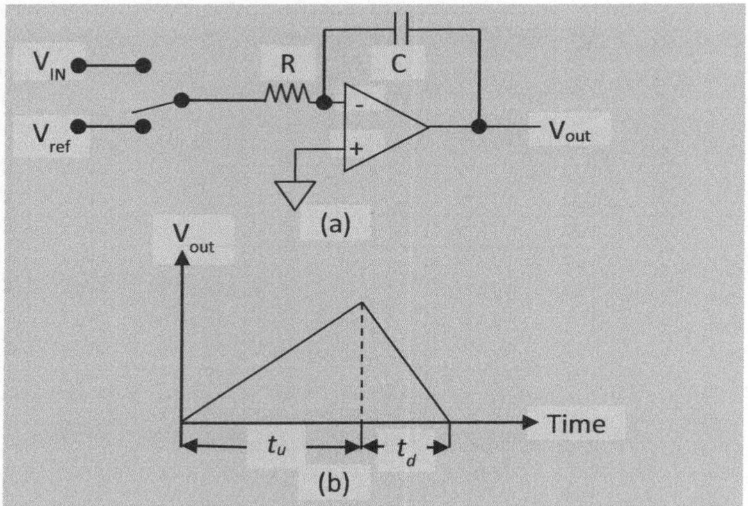

Fig 3.22: Integrating ADC (a) Circuit (b) Output voltage

3.11 Subsystem Interfacing

An embedded system design needs a number of electronic and electro-mechanical modules and devices to be connected to the processor. These include the memory devices forming memory subsystem, peripheral devices forming I/O subsystem etc. While the speed of operation of the processor is an important parameter determining the system performance, efficient access to the subsystems also plays an important role. As discussed in previous sections, devices may be attached using simple buses like USB, SPI, I^2C etc. However, even if there are memory chips and peripherals having these simple interfaces, a much more efficient parallel interface may be necessary to design high-performance embedded systems. Depending upon the desired bandwidth of communication, several bus standards have been introduced. Some of them are traditional interfaces like PCI (and its advanced version PCIe), some other are introduced typically for microcontroller based embedded system design, such as AMBA. The PCIe interface comes as slots available in the motherboard hosting the processor. Interface cards supporting PCIe standard can be inserted into a slot of suitable capacity. The corresponding device drivers are to be installed to start using the devices in the card. On the other hand, AMBA contains a hierarchy of buses with varying capacities. High bandwidth devices (like memory, DMA) may be connected to high speed bus while the slower peripheral devices may be grouped together and connected to a bus with lower speed. The AMBA protocol has been largely used in *System-on-Chip* (*SoC*) solutions for embedded system design. In the following an overview of PCIe and AMBA bus has been presented.

3.11.1 PCI Express Bus

Peripheral Component Interconnect Express (*PCIe*) bus is a high-speed serial computer expansion bus standard. This is primarily used as motherboard interface in personal computers to attach graphics cards, capture cards, hard disk drive adapters, Wi-Fi, Ethernet connections etc. represented as *end points*. Its predecessor PCI is a parallel bus standard. However, PCIe provides point-to-point serial connection between the host processor and the attached peripherals. The scheme has been shown in Fig 3.23. It improves the maximum bus throughput, lowers I/O pin count, reduces the foot-print, provides better scaling and advanced error reporting mechanism.

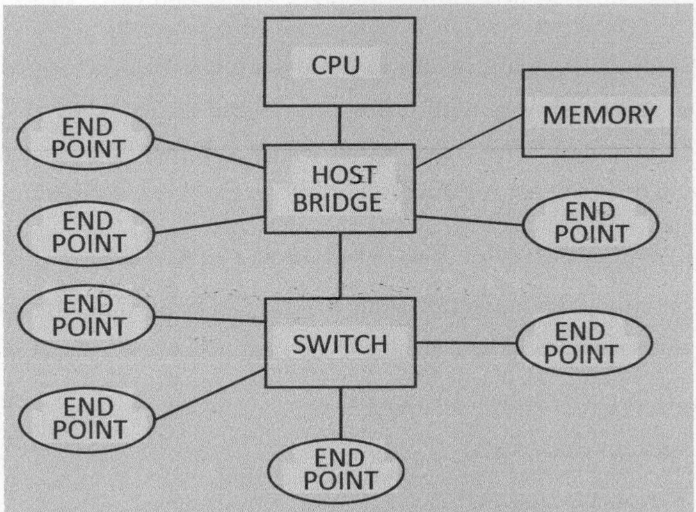

Fig 3.23: PCI Express bus connection scheme

An electrical interface of PCI Express is measured in terms of number of *lanes* contained in it. A lane correspond to a single send/receive line of data with traffic in both directions, a full-duplex communication. A PCIe link between two devices can have 1 to 16 such lanes in it. In case of a multi-lane link, packet data is striped across the lanes. Lane count is negotiated during device initialization. The standard defines link widths of *x1*, *x2*, *x4*, *x8* and *x16* lanes (link *xk* has *k* lanes in it). A lane consists of two differential signal pairs – one pair for receiving data and the other for transmitting. A PCI Express link structure has been shown in Fig 3.24. The latest version is PCIe 7.0, having a per lane transfer rate of 128 *Gigatransfers per second* (*GT/s*).

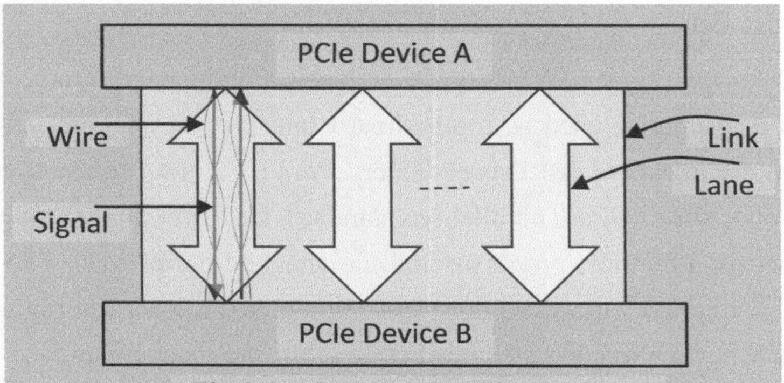

Fig 3.24: PCI Express link structure

PCIe bus slots are typically backward compatible with other types of PCIe slots. This makes it possible for the PCIe links with fewer lanes to use the same interface as PCIe links used for more lanes. The computer users may install a better device into an expansion slot and the corresponding device driver to get improved services on graphics, networking, storage etc.

3.11.2 Advanced Microcontroller Bus Architecture (AMBA)

AMBA defines an on-chip communication standard that can be used in microcontroller-based high-performance embedded systems. There are three distinct buses under the AMBA specification.

1. Advanced High-performance Bus (AHB)
2. Advanced System Bus (ASB)
3. Advanced Peripheral Bus (APB)

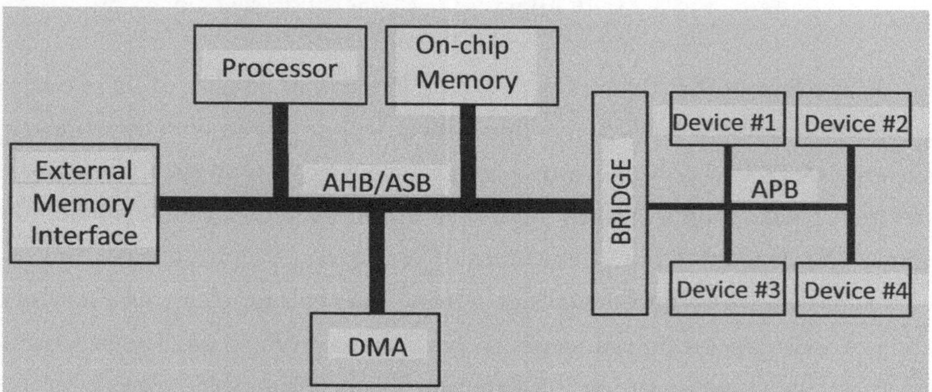

Fig 3.25: Typical AMBA based microcontroller platform

AHB is for interfacing high-performance system modules operating at high frequency. This forms the backbone bus of the system connecting processors, on-chip and off-chip memories etc.

AMBA ASB is an alternative to AHB, in which high performance features may not be essential. APB is used for connecting low-power peripherals. Fig 3.25 shows a typical AMBA based microcontroller platform in which three types of buses have been used to connect to the system modules. Table 3.4 shows a comparison between the features of the three standards.

Table 3.4: Comparison between AMBA standards

AMBA AHB	*AMBA ASB*	*AMBA APB*
• High performance • Pipelined operation • Multiple bus masters • Split transactions • Wide data bus	• High performance • Pipelined operation • Multiple bus masters	• Low power • Simple interface • Many peripherals

AMBA AHB: This constitutes a new generation high-performance, high clock-speed bus for synthesizable designs. The feature set includes burst transfers, split transactions, single-cycle and single-clock operations, and wider data bus (64/128) configuration. Typically high bandwidth peripherals (such as, internal memory, external memory interface) reside on AHB. The components in AHB are as follows.

1. *AHB Master*. It is responsible for initiating read/write operations. Only one bus master may be activated at a time.
2. *AHB Slave*. A slave responds to a read/write request within an address range.
3. *AHB Arbiter*. It selects a bus master to be active at a time instant. The arbitration protocol is fixed, however, different algorithms can be used.
4. *AHB Decoder*. It decodes the address bus for each transfer and provides select signal to the slave responsible for the transfer.

AMBA ASB: This has been the first generation AMBA system bus supporting features like burst transfer, pipelined transfer and multiple bus masters. Some common devices connected through ASB are *Direct Memory Access* (*DMA*), *Digital Signal Processor* (*DSP*) etc. The AMBA ASB system contains the following components.

1. *ASB Master*. The master is capable of initiating a read/write operation by providing address and control information. Only one bus master is active at a time.

2. *ASB Slave*. A slave device responds to the read/write operation requests from the master.
3. *ASB Decoder*. Performs address decoding, similar to the decoder in AHB.
4. *ASB Arbiter*. Ensures that there is only a single bus master at a time. It is otherwise similar to the AHB arbiter.

AMBA APB: In the AMBA hierarchy of buses, APB is used for minimal power consumption and reduced interface complexity. To AHB/ASB, APB is a local secondary bus encapsulated as a single AHB/ASB slave device. An *APB bridge* acts as the slave module that takes care of handshaking and control signal retiming. The interfaced devices are of low bandwidth and do not require high performance. The APB is much cheaper than the AHB or ASB. The bus is typically useful for interfacing simple register-mapped devices, very low power situation where clock cannot be globally routed and in grouping narrow bus peripherals to avoid loading of the system bus.

3.12 User Interface Design

User Interface (*UI*) is an essential component of embedded systems. It defines the means by which human beings interact with an embedded device. There are two important concepts in this interaction process – *User Interface* (*UI*) and *User Experience* (*UX*). The terms are often used interchangeably. However, UI refers to screens, buttons, toggles, icons and other visual elements available for interaction in an embedded system. While UX is the entire interaction with a product covering feeling of using the system. UI definitely impacts UX.

With the surge in Internet of Things (IoT) technology, many of the consumer electronics products are equipped with complex LCD (Liquid Crystal Diode) control screens. Some older such equipment used to possess LEDs, 7-segment displays, overlays etc. as user interfaces. To design a good user interface for embedded devices, it is required to have knowledge in UI/UX design process and the availability of platforms and libraries. The type of LCD screen device plays an important role in UI design. Such displays utilize *touch functionality*. There are two types of touch LCDs – *resistive* and *capacitive*. Resistive touch screens register the pressure applied on a touch. These screens are more durable but less responsive than capacitive screens. Resistive screens are duller in look than capacitive ones. To compensate for the poor responsivity, in resistive screens, the size of elements to be pressed are made large. The dragging operation is also difficult. On the other hand, capacitive screens, though brighter and higher in contrast, these are expensive and less robust than the resistive screens.

An embedded UI design consists of the following four steps.

1. *Determine users and needs*. The embedded system designer has to identify the target users and their requirements. For example, for medical devices, the UI should provide critical information,

such as, patient data, vital signs and alerts. On the other hand, for industrial applications, critical information are operational data and warnings.

2. *Ideation*. This involves generating alternate UI/UX designs. The following points need to be considered in more detail.
   - Navigation and organization of information.
   - Colour schemes and contrast.
   - Selection of font style and size.
   - Iconography and graphics,
   - Type of display.
3. *Prototype*. This is about creating a preliminary version of the interface. Prototyping tools can be used for the purpose. The step emphasizes on the following aspects.
   - Designing the navigation flow and interaction by the user.
   - Layout and composition of screen.
   - Iconography and typography.
   - Consistent design of interface elements.
4. *Test and evaluate*. This is the final stage in UI/UX design dealing with test and evaluation of the interface. Feedback from the users need to be collected and the suggestions are to be incorporated into the final design of UI.

UNIT SUMMARY

Interfacing plays an important role in the design and implementation of embedded systems. This is primarily due to the fact that such systems needs to interact with the environment via different types of devices, including sensors and actuators. These associated devices are primarily optimized towards their operational requirements, rather than incorporating standards used for processor interaction. As a result, unlike conventional computing systems, an embedded processor may need to support a large number of other interfacing techniques. In this unit, several such interfacing standards have been introduced. Among the simplest ones, the standards like SPI and IIC are very popular while connecting simple devices. For more complex interfaces, RS-232, USB can be used. The standard USB has evolved a lot to become the de facto choice for many system designers. To operate in noisy environment, like automobiles, the CAN protocol has been introduced. The interfaces IrDA and Bluetooth can be used for short-range point-to-point connections. For interacting with the analog environment, analog-to-digital and digital-to-analog converters are used. There are several categories of these converters varying in their performance and cost parameters. For system design, the modules may be connected through a bus. The standards PCIe and AMBA are used extensively for this purpose. Another very crucial issue to be looked after by the embedded system designers is the user interface design. The interaction through the user interface needs to provide good user experience.

EXERCISES

Multiple Choice Questions

MQ1. RS-232 communication is

(A) Balanced (B) Unbalanced

(C) Balanced or unbalanced (D) None of the other options

MQ2. With respect to RS-232, a computer is a

(A) DCE (B) DTE (C) DCE or DTE (D) None of the other options

MQ3. SPI protocol is

(A) Synchronous (B) Asynchronous

(C) Both synchronous and asynchronous (D) None of the other options

MQ4. Number of wires in SPI is

(A) 2 (B) 4 (C) 8 (D) 16

MQ5. Bit width of SPI data register is

(A) 8 (B) 16 (C) 32 (D) None of the other options

MQ6. In SPI, the master writes a dummy byte for the intended operation

(A) Read (B) Write (C) Both Read and Write (D) Compare

MQ7. An SPI operation can be

(A) Read (B) Write (C) Exchange (D) None of the options mentioned

MQ8. Number of wires in I^2C is

(A) 2 (B) 4 (C) 8 (D) None of the other options

MQ9. Maximum number of devices in I^2C is

(A) 4 (B) 16 (C) 64 (D) 128

MQ10. In idle condition, the SCL and SDA lines are

(A) Both low (B) Low, high (C) High, low (D) Both high

MQ11. In I^2C, SDA going low followed by SCL going low indicates

(A) Start (B) Stop (C) Tristate (D) None of the other options

MQ12. Communication in SPI and I^2C are

(A) Both half-duplex (B) Both full-duplex

(C) Half-duplex and full-duplex (D) Full-duplex and half-duplex

MQ13. USB4 supports speed upto

(A) 10 Gbps (B) 20 Gbps (C) 30 Gbps (D) 40 Gbps

MQ14. Connector type(s) supported by USB4 is/are

(A) A (B) B (C) C (D) All of the other options

MQ15. In USB cable upstream connection can be found in

(A) Host (B) Device

(C) Both host and device (D) None of the other options

MQ16. In USB cable downstream connection can be found in

(A) Host (B) Device

(C) Both host and device (D) None of the other options

MQ17. In RZ coding, presence of a pulse indicates bit

(A) 0 (B) 1 (C) Both 0 and 1 (D) Absence

MQ18. Number of pulse positions in a PPM data symbol is

(A) 2 (B) 4 (C) 8 (D) 16

MQ19. The dominant bit in CAN communication is/are

(A) 0 (B) 1 (C) Either 0 or 1 (D) None

MQ20. Frequency of Bluetooth communication is

(A) 2.45 GHz (B) 5 GHz (C) 3 GHz (D) None of the other options

MQ21. Size of passkey in Bluetooth is

(A) 4 (B) 2 (C) 6 (D) 3

MQ22. Major problem with weighted-resistor DAC is

(A) Resolution (B) Scalability (C) Linearity (D) Settling time

MQ23. Number of comparators for an 8-bit flash ADC is

(A) 7 (B) 8 (C) 255 (D) 256

MQ24. PCIe bus is

(A) Multidrop (B) Point-to-point

(C) Hierarchical (D) None of the other options

MQ25. Size of objects should be large in touchscreen of type

(A) Resistive (B) Capacitive (C) Inductive (D) All of the other options

Answers of Multiple Choice Questions

1:A, 2:B, 3:A, 4:B, 5:A, 6:A, 7:C, 8:A, 9:D, 10:D, 11:A, 12:D, 13:D, 14:C, 15:A, 16:B, 17:A, 18:B, 19:A, 20:A, 21:C, 22:B, 23: C, 24: B, 25: A

Short Answer Type Questions

SQ1. Enumerate the signals in SPI interface.

SQ2. How are the START and STOP conditions indicated in I^2C?

SQ3. Explain the DTE and DCE in RS-232 protocol.

SQ4. What do upstream and downstream connections mean in USB?

SQ5. Why is IrDA communication restricted to a room only?

SQ6. What is represented by Dt and Ct in IrDA?

SQ7. What is meant by dominant bit in CAN transmission?

SQ8. What is meant by the spread spectrum frequency hopping?

SQ9. Why is flash ADC considered to be the fastest?

SQ10. State the advantage of PCIe over PCI.

SQ11. How does ASB differ from AHB?

SQ12. Differentiate between UI and UX.

Long Answer Type Questions

LQ1. Explain the exchange, read and write operations in SPI.

LQ2. Draw the timing diagram and explain the operation of I^2C communication.

LQ3. Show the connection pattern between DTE and DCE in RS-232.

LQ4. Enumerate the USB connector types.

LQ5. Show the encoding of 8-bit pattern "10101011" using RZ and PPM schemes.

LQ6. Explain the arbitration policy of CAN.

LQ7. Explain the operation of weighted resistor and R-2R ladder type DACs.

LQ8. Explain the operation of delta-sigma, flash, successive approximation and integrating ADCs.

LQ9. Enumerate the structure of PCIe link.

LQ10. Show different bus structures in AMBA.

LQ11. State the user interface design steps for embedded systems.

KNOW MORE

Traditional microprocessors and microcontrollers do not support most of the interfacing standards discussed in this unit. However, in the recent times, many processors (mainly microcontrollers) have integrated those interfaces in their architecture itself. One of the oldest microcontrollers, 8051 supports serial communication protocol similar to RS-232. However, the signal levels are different. The 8051 uses 0V and 5V as the analog equivalents of digital bits. A chip named as MAX232 needs to be interfaced with 8051 to achieve the desired RS-232 operation. AVR ATmega microcontrollers possess SPI and I^2C interfaces. The chip HC-05 can be interfaced with the older processors like 8051 to realize Bluetooth communication in them. Many microcontrollers like ESP32 supports Wi-Fi communication. A wireless network processor CC3100 can be used to incorporate wireless communication in traditional processors.

REFERENCES AND SUGGESTED READINGS

[1] S. Chattopadhyay, "Embedded System Design", PHI Learning, 2023.

[2] "Serial Peripheral Interface User Guide", Texas Instruments.

[3] "A basic guide to I^2C", Texas Instruments.

[4] "RS232 Serial Communication Protocol: Basics, Working & Specifications", https://circuitdigest.com/article/rs232-serial-communication-protocol-basics-specifications, downloaded on 3rd October, 2024.

[5] "Introduction to Controller Area Network (CAN)", Texas Instruments.

[6] https://www.bluetooth.com, downloaded on 3rd October, 2024.

[7] "Data Converters", Texas Instruments, https://www.ti.com/data-converetrs/overview.html, downloaded on 3rd October. 2024.

[8] "PCIe Slots Explained: Types, Speeds and Uses in Modern Computers", https://www.hp.com, downloaded on 3rd October, 2024.

[9] "AMBA", https://developer.arm.com/Architectrures/AMBA, downloaded on 3rd October, 2024.

Dynamic QR Code for Further Reading

1. USB Complete – The Developer's Guide.

2. AMBA.

4 Real-Time System Design

UNIT SPECIFICS

Through this unit we have discussed the following aspects:

- *Classification of real-time tasks based on criticality and periodicity;*
- *Classification of scheduling algorithms;*
- *Task scheduling under Rate Monotonic Scheduling policy;*
- *RMS schedulability tests for periodic tasks;*
- *Task scheduling under Earliest Deadline First policy;*
- *Priority Inheritance Protocols including HLP and PCP;*
- *Other features of RTOS excepting scheduling;*
- *Illustration of features of commercial RTOS.*

The discussion in this unit gives an overview of system design commonly followed in real-time embedded systems. It is assumed that the reader has a basic understanding of generic operating systems and system software.

A large number of multiple choice questions have been provided with their answers. Apart from that, subjective questions of short and long answer type have been included. A list of references and suggested readings have been given, so that, one can go through them for more details. The section "Know More" has been carefully designed so that the supplementary information provided in this part becomes beneficial for the users of the book. This section mainly highlights the usage of RTOS in different real-time applications.

RATIONALE

This unit on real-time system design familiarizes the readers with the intricacies of large embedded system design having real-time interactions with the environment. The designed system, though running on a target processor only, is complex enough to have several interacting tasks. The tasks share the system resources and need to be scheduled at proper instants of time so that the application deadlines are met. Majority of these tasks are periodic in nature with its instances appearing at regular time intervals. Each instance has its associated deadline and must be completed within that time. Apart from those periodic tasks, the application may contain other tasks which are aperiodic in nature with the possibility of occurring at some arbitrary instants. All tasks may not be equally critical to impact the valid system operation. Thus, scheduling of real-time tasks becomes a very important issue. The schedulers may be clock-driven or event-driven, with the second being more powerful, in general. Scheduling policies are guided by task priorities, which may be static or dynamic in nature. Rate Monotonic Scheduling (RMS) is a prominent example of static priority guided event-driven scheduling policy, Earliest Deadline First (EDF) is based on dynamic priority. In real-time systems with shared resources, a high-priority task may sometimes need to wait for a low-priority task to release the required resources held by the low-priority task. This leads to priority inversion. Special resource allocation policies are used to tackle this problem. Several real-time operating systems are available for use in embedded system design. This unit enumerates all these aspects of real-time embedded system design and presents an overview of different algorithms and policies available. The designer may choose the most appropriate alternative for the desired system.

PRE-REQUISITES

Operating System, System Software

UNIT OUTCOMES

List of outcomes of this unit is as follows:

U4-O1: Distinguish between hard-, firm- and soft real-time tasks

U4-O2: Classify tasks based on periodicity

U4-O3: Perform Rate Monotonic Scheduling for a task set

U4-O4: Check if a set of tasks schedulable under RMS

U4-O5: Perform EDF scheduling of task set

U4-O6: Compare between the performances of RMS and EDF

U4-O7: Enumerate priority inheritance schemes

U4-O8: State the features of commercial real-time operating systems

Unit-4 Outcomes	EXPECTED MAPPING WITH COURSE OUTCOMES (1- Weak Correlation; 2- Medium correlation; 3- Strong Correlation)			
	CO-1	CO-2	CO-3	CO-4
U4-O1	3	2	3	-
U4-O2	2	2	3	-
U4-O3	1	2	3	-
U4-O4	1	1	3	-
U4-O5	1	2	3	-
U4-O6	1	1	3	-
U4-O7	1	2	3	-
U4-O8	1	1	3	

4.1 Introduction

In the previous few units, we have primarily discussed about the hardware platforms available for embedded system design. The alternatives in terms of processors and peripheral device interfacings have been enumerated. As noted in Unit-1, the complexity of embedded applications varies widely – from small, hand-held devices to highly computationally intensive ones like guided missile, avionics and telecom switches. For smaller applications, the software part happens to be small as well – no special mechanism may be needed to coordinate between the hardware components realizing the application. However, for the relatively complex embedded systems, only hardware based solution may be difficult and costly. A good amount of system functionality needs to be implemented in software. In such systems, a number of coordinating software tasks interact with the hardware to realize the desired system functionality. The coordination essentially leads to the scheduling of those interacting software tasks at proper time instants. Most of the embedded applications require time-bound system responses. Scheduling is dependent upon the properties of the tasks (like criticality, periodicity, and deadline). Ensuring the overall coordination between such processes may not be very simple. A special piece of system software, called *operating system* (*OS*) is needed for the purpose. Operating system takes care of managing the underlying hardware and provides a platform to the embedded system designer. Applications are mostly real-time in nature, having continuous interaction with the environment, it is very important that the operating system supports the handling of real-time tasks. This is a significant departure from the conventional operating systems that primarily attempt to maximize the system throughput and resource utilization. To understand the intricacies of real-time embedded system design, it is essential to first look into the features of real-time tasks and the scheduling policies commonly followed.

4.2 Types of Real-Time Tasks

The real-time tasks can be considered to belong to one of the following three categories.

- Hard real-time tasks
- Firm real-time tasks
- Soft real-time tasks

4.2.1 Hard Real-Time Tasks

A *hard real-time* task must produce its result within a specified time limit, also called its deadline. Missing the deadline implies that the task as well as the system have failed. An example of such a system can be a plant consisting of several motors along with sensors and actuators. The plant controller senses various conditions through sensors and issues commands through the actuators. It is necessary that the controller responds to the input signals in a time-bound fashion. That is, on the occurrence of some event, the response from the controller should come within a pre-specified time limit. Examples of such signals may be inputs from fire-sensor, power-sensor, etc. Another example can be a single (or a set of) robot(s) that performs a set of activities under the coordination of a central host. Depending upon the environment, a robot may need to take some instantaneous decisions, for example, on detecting an obstacle on its path of movement, the robot should find a way out to avoid a collision. A delay in the detection and reaction process may result in a collision, causing damage to the robot.

A very important feature of tasks in a hard real-time system is its *criticality*. Failure of a task to finish computation within its deadline will have a catastrophic effect on the system. Many of the hard real-time tasks are *safety-critical*. This is particularly true for the medical instruments monitoring and controlling the health of a patient. In a safety-critical system, even if a task fails, it should not cause any damage to the environment in which the application system is working. For example, in health-care system, even if some monitoring task fails, it should not cause harm to the patient. However, all hard real-time systems need not be safety-critical. For example, in a video game, missing a deadline is not that severe.

As far as scheduling of hard real-time tasks is concerned, we have to honour the deadline. Unlike in ordinary operating systems in which we try to complete tasks as early as possible to maintain a high throughput, there is no gain in finishing a hard real-time task early. As long as the task completes within the specified time limit, the system runs fine.

4.2.2 Firm Real-Time Tasks

In comparison to hard real-time tasks, a firm real-time task is expected to be completed within an associated deadline. However, failure to meet the deadline by the task is not counted as a system failure. Due to late arrival or delay in computation, it may only be required to discard some of the results. To illustrate it further, consider the streaming operation in a video conferencing. Video frames are sent over a network. Depending upon the characteristics of the network, arrival of some frames may be delayed, out-of-order or some frames may even be lost. However, the video quality, though degraded may still be accepted with a tolerance. Here, the failure to meet deadlines does not mark a total system failure.

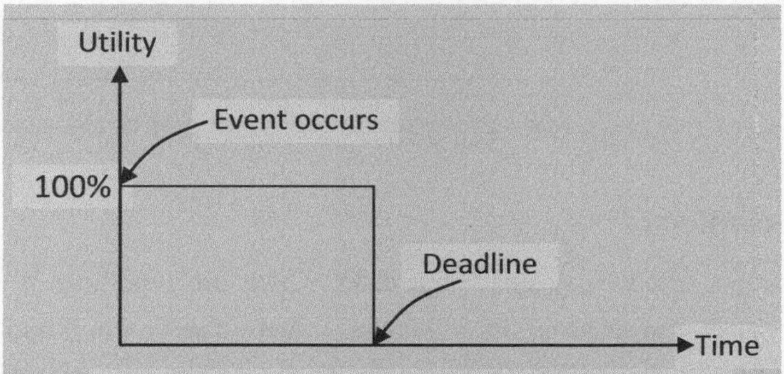

Fig 4.1: Result utility in firm real-time systems

In firm real-time tasks, results made available after the deadline are of no value and are thus discarded. Fig. 4.1 shows the situation in which after the occurrence of the event, the response has an utility of 100% till the deadline. Beyond deadline, utility is zero and the computed result is discarded.

4.2.3 Soft Real-Time Tasks

Some real-time tasks can be categorized as soft real-time ones. Such tasks have their deadlines. However, it is only expected that the task completes within the deadline. If the task does not complete within the deadline, the system is not labeled as failed, neither the outputs are discarded. However, with the passage of time, the utility of the result drops, as shown in Fig. 4.2.

To illustrate soft real-time tasks, consider the railway-reservation system. In this system, it is not mandatory that the booking request process should complete within a fixed deadline. It is only expected that the average time for processing be small. Even if the processing of a particular ticket request takes some additional time, the system is acceptable. The booking requester does not reject the ticket altogether. Web-browsing is another soft real-time task. Here also, after typing the URL, it is quite common to wait for some time for the page to get loaded. However, even if it takes slightly more time, the system does not fail, neither the page loaded gets discarded. We do not consider it as an exception if the process takes slightly longer time.

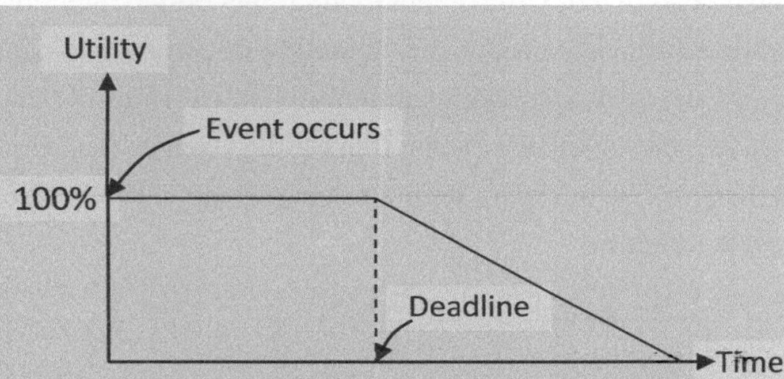

Fig 4.2: Result utility in soft real-time systems

4.3 Task Periodicity

Embedded systems often carry out some tasks which are repetitive in nature. Based on the periodicity property, the tasks in an embedded system can be classified into one of the three categories – *Periodic*, *Aperiodic* and *Sporadic*. The repetitive activities of an embedded system are carried out by the periodic tasks. For example, a temperature monitoring system needs to get the values from the temperature sensors at regular intervals of time. A conveyor belt used for transportation of materials in a plant has the periodic tasks of putting and removing items on the belt. Any system design needs to ensure that such task instances are scheduled at proper time instants and completed within their respective deadlines. However, the system generally has some other tasks which are not periodic in nature – the tasks may or may not have their deadlines. Accordingly, the importance attached to their scheduling have to be decided. In the following, the task classification based on periodicity has been presented.

4.3.1 Periodic Tasks

A task is designated to be periodic if it repeats itself regularly at certain fixed time intervals. A periodic task T_i is characterized by four factors – *phase* (φ_i), *deadline* (d_i), *execution time* (e_i) and *periodicity* (p_i). Individual occurrences of a periodic task are called its *instances*. The time instant at which the first instance of a task arrives, is called its *phase*. Relative to the instant of occurrence of a task instance, the time by which it must be completed, is called its *deadline*. The worst case time requirement to carry out a task is called its *execution time*. It may be noted that the execution time must be less than the deadline of the task. *Periodicity* defines the time interval at which the successive instances of a task repeats. A periodic task is thus represented by the four-tuple $< \varphi_i, d_i, e_i, p_i >$. Fig 4.3 shows the behavior of periodic tasks. Most of the real-time tasks in an embedded system are periodic in nature. The four parameters of such tasks could be computed beforehand. While designing an embedded system, scheduling of such task instances need to be carried out carefully, so that proper resources are available for timely completion (before deadline) of them. In many cases, the deadline of a task instance is taken to be same as the periodicity of the task. This may be acceptable as no further instances of the task can arrive in between.

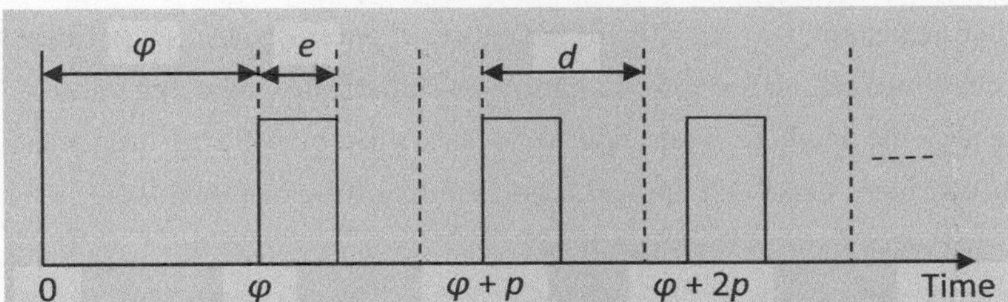

Fig 4.3: Periodic task behaviour

4.3.2 Sporadic Tasks

An instance of a sporadic task can come at any time instant. However, the occurrences of two successive instances are separated by a minimum time duration. A sporadic task can be represented by a three-tuple $< e_i, g_i, d_i >$. Here g_i represents the minimum time gap between two successive instances. The other two parameters e_i and d_i have similar meanings as for periodic tasks. The interrupts to an embedded processor (generated internally or externally) are some examples of sporadic tasks. Depending upon the source of the task, the criticality level may vary. For example, a fire-alarm may be treated as a sporadic task. It is very critical and thus needs to be handled within its deadline. On the other hand, an interrupt generated from an I/O device is not that critical. Behavior of a sporadic task has been enumerated in Fig 4.4.

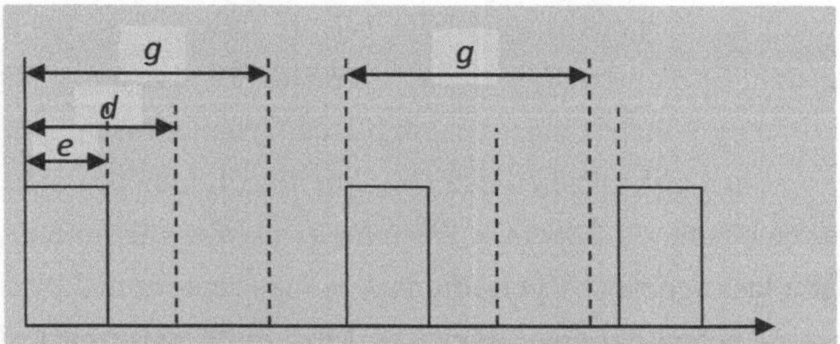

Fig 4.4: Sporadic task behaviour

4.3.3 Aperiodic Tasks

Similar to sporadic tasks, aperiodic tasks can also arrive at any random time. However, for this type of tasks, there is no guarantee that the next instance will not arrive before a guaranteed minimum time gap. In an extreme case, successive instances of aperiodic tasks may arrive at consecutive time instants as well. Due to the nature of aperiodic tasks, aperiodic tasks cannot have associated deadlines which are tight in nature. A statistically expected value or an average value can be utilized as the deadline. Thus, aperiodic tasks must be soft real-time ones. As the successive instances of aperiodic tasks can appear at consecutive time instants, there is a high possibility of some of its instances to miss their deadlines.

Railway-reservation system is an example of a typical aperiodic task. Due to the simultaneous booking operations over a large number of counters and terminals, there is no fixed gap between the two requests reaching the server. The deadline requirement is also not stringent, it is only expected that the booking requests have a small average response time.

4.4 Task Scheduling

Task scheduling is the process of determining the order of execution of ready task instances in a system. In a real-time embedded system, the important tasks are predominantly periodic in nature. Hence, the scheduling algorithms/policies primarily work with the problem of executing the periodic tasks, such that, they meet their deadlines. Many such scheduling algorithms possess some additional rules to take care of the sporadic and aperiodic tasks whose occurrences cannot be predicted.

A scheduling algorithm creates a *schedule* for a given set of tasks. It assigns time-frames and resources to the instances of individual tasks. A schedule is considered to be *valid* if it assigns at most a single task to a processor at each point of time, no task instance gets scheduled before its arrival, the precedence constraints between the tasks are met, and the resource constraints are honoured. A valid schedule may or may not be acceptable by the system designer as it may not honour the deadlines of all task instances. A valid schedule meeting all deadlines is said to be *feasible*.

The quality of a schedule is identified by the resulting processor utilization. For a task, its processor utilization is defined as the fraction of processor time used by the task. If the periodicity of a task be p_i and execution time e_i, its processor utilization u_i is given by the ratio e_i/p_i. The processor utilization of a task correspond to the fraction of time for which the processor is used by it. For overall processor utilization, resulting from a set of *n* tasks is defined as,

$$U = \sum_{i=1}^{n} \frac{e_i}{p_i}$$

Ideally, the processor utilization should be 100%. However, it may not be possible to have a feasible schedule with 100% processor utilization meeting deadlines of all periodic tasks. The scheduling algorithms attempt to generate feasible schedules with high processor utilization.

Operating system invokes the scheduling algorithm to decide upon the ready task to be executed next by the processor. The invocation instants of the scheduling algorithm are called *scheduling points*. Based upon the scheduling points and the task selection policy, the scheduling algorithms can be classified into the categories shown in Fig 4.5. The algorithms can be broadly classified into the following three categories – *Clock driven scheduling*, *Event driven scheduling* and *Hybrid scheduling*.

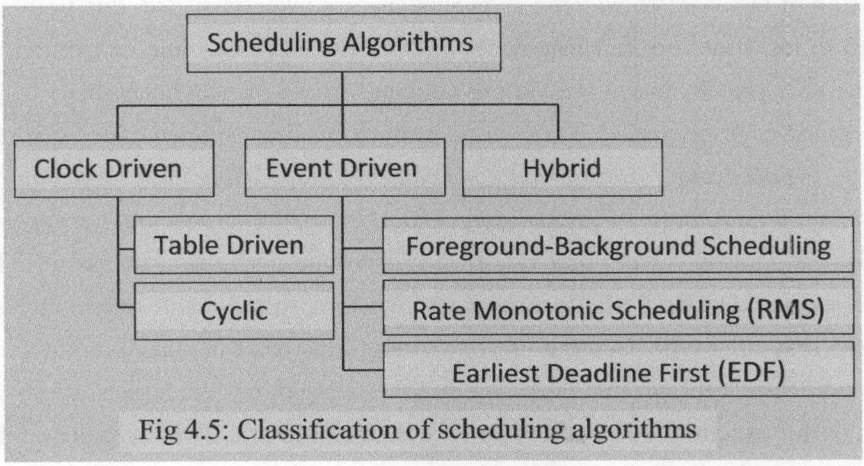

Fig 4.5: Classification of scheduling algorithms

1. *Clock driven scheduling*. These schedulers work in synchronism with a clock/timer that generates periodic interrupts. The interrupts act as the scheduling points at which the decision

is taken about the next task to be executed till the next scheduling point. The schedulers maintain a precomputed table of tasks to be executed at each scheduling point. Due to the usage of such precomputed table, these schedulers are also called static schedulers. The clock driven scheduler design is quite simple, however, the major drawback of this type of schedulers is their inability to handle aperiodic and sporadic tasks, as their exact arrival times cannot be predicted, which implies that their scheduling points cannot be determined. This type of schedulers are therefore known as static schedulers. There are two popular clock driven schedulers – *Table driven* and *Cyclic*. A *Table driven* scheduler maintains a table of tasks to be scheduled at each clock instant. The scheduler is invoked at each clock interrupt, its interrupt service routine consults the table to schedule the task earmarked in the table. A Cyclic scheduler works in terms of major and minor cycles (also called frames). The major cycle is determined by taking the *least common multiple* (*LCM*) of periodicity of all tasks and is divided into a number of fixed sized frames. In a frame, only one task gets scheduled. The frame boundaries constitute the scheduling points, thus reducing the number of interrupts to the processor.

2. *Event driven scheduling*. A fundamental problem with any clock driven scheduling policy is its inability to handle large number of tasks. The LCM of the periods becomes a large number, making it difficult to determine a proper frame size for the task set. In each frame, some processor time is wasted to run the scheduler, which is treated as scheduling overhead. Also, the sporadic and aperiodic tasks cannot be handled efficiently. These problems can be alleviated to a large extent by the use of event driven schedulers. In these schedulers, the arrival and completion of tasks are considered as events and are taken as scheduling points. Priorities are assigned to tasks and/or their instances. The priority may be static or dynamic in nature. As with any other priority based scheduling policies, arrival of a higher priority task will preempt a running lower priority task. Three important scheduling policies have been reported in this category – *Foreground Background scheduling*, *Rate Monotonic scheduling* (*RMS*) and *Earliest Deadline First* (*EDF*) *scheduling*. Out of these, the *foreground background scheduling* policy is very simple. The periodic real-time tasks of the application are assigned higher priority than the aperiodic tasks. Periodic tasks run in the foreground, while others including non-real-time tasks may run in the background. The background tasks are taken up for execution only if there is no pending foreground task. At any scheduling point, the highest priority pending task is taken up for execution. The other two schedulers RMS and EDF are more complex and have been discussed separately in the following.

4.5 Rate Monotonic Scheduling

Rate monotonic scheduling (RMS) is a static-priority-based event-driven scheduling algorithm. It works for periodic tasks. Priority assignment is *static* in the sense that priorities are assigned to individual tasks before the system starts operating. All instances of a task get the same priority. Priorities are assigned to the tasks based on their periodicity values. A more frequent task (that is, more instances reaching the system within a time window) is assigned higher priority than a relatively less frequent one. Periodicity value being low indicates that the operating system has got less slack time to schedule the task instances before their corresponding deadlines. The schedule is preemptive – arrival of a higher-priority task instance will preempt any lower-priority task currently being executed.

The RMS algorithm is based upon the theory of rate monotonic analysis (RMA). RMA uses a simple model of the system as follows.

1. There is a single CPU to run all processes – no task parallelism.
2. Context switching time is ignored.
3. Different instances of a task need same and constant execution time.
4. All tasks are independent of each other.
5. Deadline of any instance of a task occurs at the end of its period.

RMA Theorem: *Given a set of periodic tasks to be scheduled using a pre-emptive priority scheduling, assigning priorities, such that the tasks with shorter periods have higher priorities, yields an optimal scheduling algorithm.*

The term *rate monotonic* refers to the fact that tasks with higher rates of occurrences will be assigned monotonically higher priorities. The optimality criteria states that if a schedule meeting all the deadlines exists with fixed task priorities, then the rate-monotonic approach will also definitely identify a feasible schedule. To illustrate, let us consider the problem of assigning static priorities to a set of *n* tasks to identify at least one assignment under which all task instances are guaranteed to meet their deadlines. A brute force search for the same will evaluate all *n*! possible priority assignments and check for their feasibility. The presence of RMA theorem and its optimality property ensures that one need not do that exercise, rather, assign priorities in the order of task periodicities. If the task set is having a feasible schedule under static priority assignment, this priority assignment will also result into a feasible schedule. We shall consider Example 4.1 to illustrate the RMS further.

Example 4.1: Table 4.1 lists a set of three tasks P1, P2 and P3 with periodicity values 3, 5 and 15 time units, respectively. The corresponding execution times are 1, 2 and 3 time units. The tasks are to be scheduled using the RMS policy. Looking into the periodicity values, the tasks are assigned priorities P1 > P2 > P3.

Table 4.1: Example tasks

Task	Execution time	Period
P1	1	3
P2	2	5
P3	3	15

Fig 4.6 shows a schedule for this set of tasks. As the LCM of the periodicities of the three tasks is 15, from 15th time instant the schedule repeats itself. To start with, it has been assumed that at time instant 0, one instance each of the three tasks have arrived to the system. Later instances of P1 come at time instants 3, 6, 9, 12 and so on. Such occurrences of all the three tasks have been shown in the figure. Among three ready tasks at time 0, P1 has the highest priority, hence it gets scheduled. Once the P1 instance is over at time instant 1, the waiting instance of P2 gets scheduled. It executes for full 2 time units. At time instant 3, the next instance of P1 has arrived. Even though P3 is waiting is waiting at this point, the newly arrived instance of P1 gets chance to execute, by virtue of its higher priority. At time instant 4, there is no waiting instance of P1 and P2. Thus, P3 gets scheduled for a single time unit. At time instant 5, the newly arrived instance of P2 preempts the running lower priority task P3. The process continues. At time instant 14, no task is ready for execution and the processor remains idle. Thus, the set of tasks can be scheduled in RMS principle.

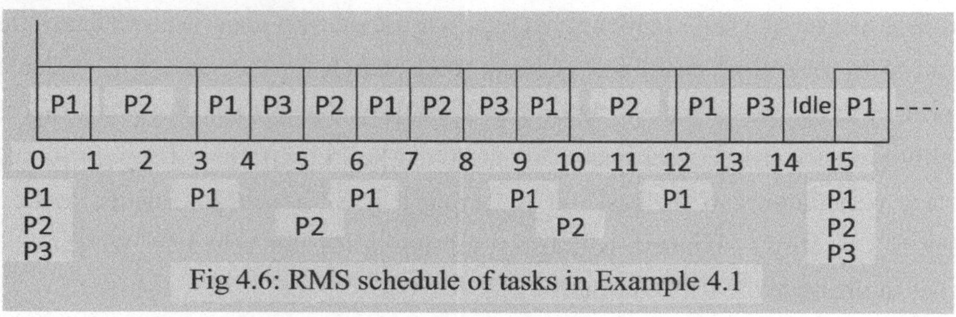

Fig 4.6: RMS schedule of tasks in Example 4.1

4.5.1 Schedulability in RMS

A fundamental issue with RMS is to decide whether a given set of tasks is schedulable following the RMS policy. A brute-force method is of course to assign the priorities as per the policy and draw a pert chart for tasks getting scheduled at various time-instants and looking for deadline misses. Checking the pert chart upto the LCM of task periodicities, if all tasks have met their respective deadlines, then the task set is definitely schedulable under RMS. However, the process may be tedious, particularly if there are large number of tasks and the LCM value is large. In the following, we shall look into necessary and sufficient conditions for a set of tasks to be definitely schedulable under the RMS policy, none of them missing their deadlines.

1. *Necessary condition*: Sum of CPU utilizations of individual tasks should be less than or equal to 1. That is,

$$\sum_{i=1}^{n} \frac{e_i}{p_i} = \sum_{i=1}^{n} u_i \leq 1$$

   For the task set of Example 4.1,

$$\frac{1}{3} + \frac{2}{5} + \frac{3}{15} = 0.93 \leq 1$$

   Thus the set of tasks satisfy the necessary condition.

2. *Sufficiency condition*: As per the theory developed by *Liu* and *Leland*, a set of n real-time periodic tasks is definitely schedulable under RMS policy if,

$$\sum_{i=1}^{n} u_i \leq n(2^{1/n} - 1)$$

   The number of tasks in Example 4.1 is 3. Putting the value of $n = 3$ in the above inequality with left-hand side representing CPU utilization (sum of CPU utilizations is 0.93), we need,

$$0.93 \leq 3(2^{1/3} - 1) = 0.78$$

   The condition cannot be satisfied. Thus, the sufficiency condition is not met by the task set. However, as shown earlier, the tasks can be scheduled using RMS policy.

   As per the sufficiency condition, the maximum achievable CPU utilization is given by,

$$\lim_{n \to \propto} n(2^{1/n} - 1)$$

   Applying *L'Hospital's* rule, it can be shown that the value of the expression is 0.692. This implies that the maximum achievable utilization is 69.2%. For any set of tasks with utilization exceeding this value fails the sufficiency test. However, it is not uncommon to have a set of tasks that fails the sufficiency test, but is still schedulable using RMS technique. If the sufficiency condition is satisfied, the task set is definitely schedulable under RMS policy.

3. *Another sufficiency test*: A more elaborate sufficiency check can be made using *Lehoczky test*. The test can be stated as follows.

   A set of periodic real-time tasks are schedulable using RMS technique under any task phasing if all the tasks meet their respective first deadlines under zero phasing.

   When a task arrives to the system, it needs to wait as long as there are higher priority tasks running/waiting. Thus, a ready task waits for the longest period of time if all other higher priority tasks are also ready at that point. It should also be noted that multiple instances of higher priority tasks may arrive during the periodicity of the lower priority task. The worst situation occurs when all these tasks are in-phase with each other, rather than being out of phase. Thus, if a set of tasks meet their deadlines with zero phasing, the tasks will meet all deadlines with non-zero phasings also.

   Consider a set of tasks $P_1, P_2 \ldots P_n$ with their corresponding execution times $e_1, e_2 \ldots e_n$, and periodicity values $p_1, p_2, \ldots p_n$. Without any loss of generality, it can be assumed that the tasks are ordered in decreasing order of priority, P_1 having the highest priority and P_n the lowest priority. The task P_i will meet its first deadline, provided,

$$e_i + \sum_{k=1}^{i-1} \left(\frac{p_i}{p_k}\right) \times e_k \le p_i$$

   Within the period p_i of task P_i, a higher priority task P_k can appear (p_i/p_k) times. All these instances of P_k must be completed before the task instance of P_i gets scheduled. Checking in this way, if all tasks meet their first deadlines, the task set is definitely schedulable under RMS policy. For the task set mentioned in Example 4.1, let us check the zero-phase schedulability of all tasks.

   - For task P_1, $e_1 = 1 \le p_1 = 3$.
   - For task P_2, $e_2 + (p_2/p_1) \times e_1 = 2 + (5/3) \times 1 = 2.6 \le p_2 = 5$.
   - For task P_3, $e_3 + (p_3/p_1) \times e_1 + (p_3/p_2) \times e_2 = 3 + (15/3) \times 1 + (15/5) \times 2 = 14 \le p_3 = 15$.

   As all tasks pass the test, the task set is schedulable using RMS technique.

   It may be noted that even if a set of tasks do not satisfy the Lehoczky's test, the tasks may still be schedulable using RMS policy. The test checks for the schedulability of the tasks under zero phasings. This is a bit stringent for a system, as the individual tasks may have non-zero phasings, thus allowing more time to schedule the instances satisfying the deadlines.

4.5.2 Advantages and Disadvantages of RMS

The RMS policy is very simple in nature. A naive implementation of the scheduler may be based on interrupts from the timer. At each invocation of the scheduler, the scheduler may scan through the list of ready tasks and schedule the highest priority ready task. A more complex implementation may monitor task arrival and completion instants and invoke the scheduler accordingly. The priorities being static in nature, the ready tasks can be kept in a simple array data structure. Most of the commercial real-time operating systems support the RMS policy. Another advantage of RMS is in handling *transient overloads* efficiently. Transient overload situation occurs when the execution time of a lower priority task instance gets extended with the possibility of delaying the scheduling of a higher priority task with a potential to miss its deadline. In RMS, such situation cannot occur. Even if the lower priority task overshoots its execution time, arrival of higher priority task will definitely preempt it. Thus, the higher priority task cannot miss its deadline.

The disadvantages of RMS policy are as follows.

1. Aperiodic and sporadic task handling becomes an issue. Since these tasks do not have any periodicity metric attached, no priority can be assigned to them.
2. Optimality is not guaranteed if deadlines of tasks differ from their periodicity values. For such situations, another strategy, known as *Deadline Monotonic Algorithm* (*DMA*) can be used, in which, priorities are assigned to the tasks based on their deadlines. Tasks with shorter deadlines are assigned higher priorities. There can be task set examples on which RMS fails and DMA succeeds. However, for a task set, if DMA fail, RMS will definitely fail.
3. *Context Switching Overhead* has been ignored in the rate monotonic analysis theorem. However, this needs to be considered particularly for large task sets, as the number of context switching may be large enough to create considerable wastage of CPU time. To accommodate this, the context switching times need to be added to the RMS pert chart. For the set of tasks in Example 4.1, the total number of context switches is 13. Assuming each context switch takes 0.1 time unit, an additional 1.3 time unit has to be accommodated within the LCM of 15 time units. However, for the task set, adding this 1.3 time unit makes the schedule infeasible as the total time becomes 15.3, a value more than the LCM 15.

4. *Critical tasks with long periods* pose another challenge. The tasks being critical, need to be scheduled early, so that their deadlines are not missed. However, due to large periodicity, the priority of such a task may be low enough to force it to wait till many other relatively noncritical tasks finish their execution. For such situation, the DMA policy may be followed. Another solution may be to virtually divide the critical task into *k* subtasks. Periodicity of each subtask is reduced by a factor *k*. This reduction in periodicity value should be sufficient to ensure that when the critical task arrives, it can preempt any of the running tasks. The virtual division does not affect the monolithic nature of the critical task. The virtually divided critical task is executed as one single task only. It may be noted that each virtual task now has execution time e_i/k and periodicity p_i/k. Thus, for the overall critical task, the CPU utilization becomes $k(e_i/k)(p_i/k) = k(e_i/p_i)$, though the actual utilization is e_i/p_i. This may wrongly indicate he task set to be not schedulable under RMS.
5. *Limited priority levels* may only be available in the underlying hardware and operating system. Thus, for a task set with a large number of tasks, several tasks may need to be grouped into the same physical priority level.

4.5.3 Aperiodic Server

An *Aperiodic Server* is a periodic task that picks up waiting aperiodic and sporadic tasks for execution. Based on the periodicity, the server task is assigned a priority, similar to other periodic tasks in the system. The server gets scheduled accordingly. There can be one or more aperiodic servers in a system. An aperiodic server is allocated a certain fixed budget by the system designer. Similarly, each aperiodic/sporadic task has an assigned cost. The server can pick up an aperiodic task for execution provided it has with it enough budget to spend to cater to the cost of the task. For more critical aperiodic tasks, the system designer may assign relatively lower costs than the non-critical ones, so that the critical tasks can always be picked up for execution by the server.

There are two types of aperiodic servers – *deferrable server* and *sporadic server*. The two servers differ in the policy of budget replenishment. For a deferrable server, budget is replenished to its full value at regular intervals of time (periodicity of the server). Consider the situation in which an aperiodic task arrives and gets scheduled through the server. The execution time of the aperiodic task is assumed to be matching with the periodicity of the server. As per the budget replenishment policy, at the end of the aperiodic task, the server again gets its budget credited. Thus, if another instance of the aperiodic task arrives, that also will get scheduled. Continuing like this, a large number of aperiodic tasks will get scheduled in a burst. It makes the normal periodic tasks to wait for long time, possibly missing their deadlines. *Sporadic servers* solve this problem by replenishing the budget only after a fixed time interval from the completion of previous aperiodic task. A timer is started on utilization of budget by the server. Budget is replenished only after the expiry of the timer. This guarantees a minimum separation between the scheduling of two aperiodic task instances.

4.5.4 Handling Limited Priority Levels

In RMS, based on their periodicities, the tasks are assigned unique priorities. However, the underlying operating system may not have sufficient number of priority levels available with it to be assigned to the individual tasks in task set. Hence, for implementation, tasks with different priorities may need to be grouped into the same priority level. This grouping can be done following any of the policies noted next.

- *Uniform*. Equal number of tasks are assigned to all the levels. If it is not possible to do a uniform distribution, the lower priority levels are assigned more tasks, so that, there are will be less contention for resources among the higher priority tasks. For example, consider 11 tasks to be assigned to 4 priority levels. The highest level is assigned two tasks. Now, there are three levels to contain the remaining 9 tasks, for which a uniform distribution of three tasks per level is followed.

- *Arithmetic*. In this scheme, an arithmetic series is followed to assign tasks to the levels. For example, if there are 15 tasks and 5 priority levels, the tasks assigned to successive levels (from the highest to the lowest level) may be 1, 2, 3, 4 and 5.

- *Geometric*. In this case, number of tasks assigned to the successive priority levels form a geometric progression. For the case of 15 tasks, to be assigned to 4 priority levels, the number of tasks put into different levels (from the highest to the lowest level) may be 1, 2, 4 and 8 respectively.

- *Logarithmic*. In this policy, the range of task periods assigned to successive levels form logarithmic intervals. Assuming that the smallest period of any task in the set is p_{min}, the highest period p_{max} and the number of priority levels is n, first a factor r is calculated as $r = (p_{max}/p_{min})^{1/n}$. Now, the tasks with periods less than $p_{min} \times r$ is assigned to the highest priority level. The tasks with periods between $p_{min} \times r$ and $p_{min} \times r^2$ are assigned to the next lower level, and so on. Consider a set of 11 tasks with periods 5, 6, 7, 8, 9, 10, 11, 12, 13, 14, 15. Let the number of priority levels be 4. Thus, $p_{min} = 5$, $p_{max} = 15$ and $n = 4$.

$$p_{min} \times r = 6.58$$

$$p_{min} \times r^2 = 8.66$$

$$p_{min} \times r^3 = 11.79$$

$$p_{min} \times r^4 = 15.0$$

The highest priority level will get tasks with periods 5 and 6 time units. The next level will hold the tasks with periods 7 and 8, the third level will have tasks with periods 9, 10, 11, finally the fourth level will have tasks with periods 12, 13, 14, 15.

4.6 Earliest Deadline First Scheduling

Earliest Deadline First (*EDF*) is a scheduling algorithm supporting dynamic task priorities. In this policy, priority of a task can vary across its instances. Each instance of a task is assigned priority based on its deadline. This is a marked deviation from the RMS policy in which the priority assigned (based on periodicity) is static in nature. At any scheduling point, the decision to select the next task for execution is guided by the deadlines of the ready task instances at that point. The task with the earliest deadline gets scheduled for execution. This justifies the name earliest deadline first. Due to the importance attached to the urgency of task instances based on their deadlines, it often becomes possible to schedule a set of tasks under EDF policy, which otherwise fails under any static priority scheme. To illustrate the fact, consider the task set shown in Table 4.2, containing three tasks P1, P2 and P3. Fig 4.7 shows the situation when the tasks have been scheduled using the RMS policy. It may be seen that the instance of task P3 that arrived at time instant 0 finishes it execution at time instant 9, though its deadline has been 8. Hence, the task misses its deadline. Fig 4.8 shows the situation where the tasks have been scheduled using the EDF policy. Here, all task instances could be scheduled within their deadlines.

Table 4.2: Example tasks

Task	Execution time	Period
P1	1	4
P2	2	6
P3	3	8

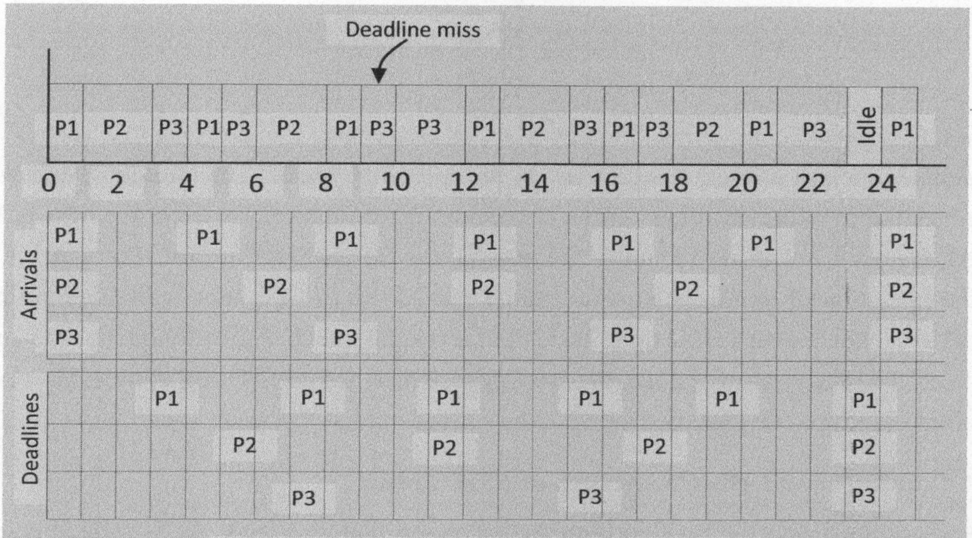

Fig 4.7: RMS schedule of tasks in Table 4.2

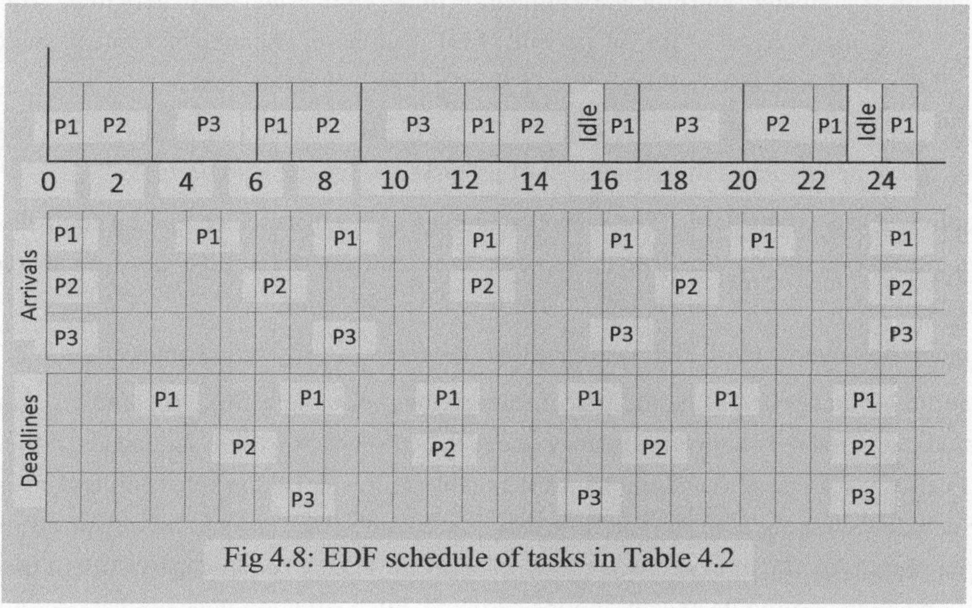

Fig 4.8: EDF schedule of tasks in Table 4.2

Condition for EDF schedulability:

A set of tasks is schedulable under the EDF policy if and only if the total utilization is less than or equal to unity. Thus, if there are n tasks in a task set with the ith task having execution time e_i and periodicity p_i, utilization,

$$U = \sum_{i=1}^{n} \frac{e_i}{p_i} \leq 1.$$

In the simplest possible implementation of EDF, all ready tasks can be put into a queue. When a new instance of a task arrives, it is attached at the end of the queue. The individual entries in the queue notes the absolute deadlines of the corresponding instances. To select the next task to be executed, the list is scanned to identify the task having the earliest deadline. For a queue with *n* tasks, the operation of joining the queue can be carried out in O(1) time while determining the next task to schedule needs O(*n*) time. Instead of a normal queue, a priority queue data structure can be used. To join a priority queue, the arriving task instance takes O(log *n*) time. However, the selection of the task to be executed next can be carried out in O(1) time.

4.6.1 Advantages and Disadvantages of EDF Policy

EDF is an optimal scheduling algorithm in the sense that if a task set is schedulable under any policy, it is schedulable under EDF as well. The phases of tasks do not have any effect on the schedulability parameter. The processor utilization under EDF is generally very high, reaching close to 100% in many cases. Also, in general, EDF has lesser number of context switches. However, EDF scheduling also has a number of shortcomings as noted next.

1. It is difficult to predict the response time for a particular instance of a task. Response time depends upon the deadlines of instances of other tasks, which are also variable.
2. EDF policy is less controllable. The response time of a task instance cannot be controlled. In a fixed priority system (like RMS), response time and controllability can be ensured by assigning suitable priorities to the tasks. This is not possible with EDF.
3. Implementation overhead of EDF is higher than the fixed priority based approaches.
4. *Transient overload problem*. Some task instances may take more time to complete than the estimated one. This may happen primarily due to exceptional execution sequences of the task. This is called transient as the additional time requirement is not same across all instances of a task. Such overshooting in execution time may cause some other tasks to miss their deadlines. In the extreme case, the most critical task of an application may become the victim of the least critical one overshooting its execution time estimate. Such situation does not happen in RMS as the higher priority tasks will always pre-empt the lower priority ones. The highest priority task will never miss its deadline.
5. *Domino effect*. This is a situation in which all tasks in the system start missing deadlines of their instances. It occurs when the utilization of a set of tasks becomes greater than 1. Since utilization cannot be more than 100%, some tasks are bound to miss their deadlines. However,

in *domino effect*, all tasks in the application miss their deadlines, one after the other like a set of dominos – falling of one domino initiates the falling of other dominos in sequence. In Table 4.3, four such tasks P1, P2, P3 and P4 have been taken with different execution times and periods. Utilization corresponding to these four tasks is 2/5 + 2/6 + 2/7 + 2/8 = 1.27. Fig 4.9 shows the situation when the tasks are scheduled following EDF policy. As shown in the figure, all the tasks miss their deadlines. Here, the task P1 misses its deadline at time instant 15. Successively, the instances of tasks P4, P2 and P3 also miss their deadlines. It may be noted that domino effect does not occur in RMS since the highest priority task will never miss its deadline, the next lower priority task may miss some of its deadlines. In the worst case, some low priority tasks may miss all their deadlines.

Table 4.3: Example tasks

Task	Execution time	Period
P1	2	5
P2	2	6
P3	2	7
P4	2	8

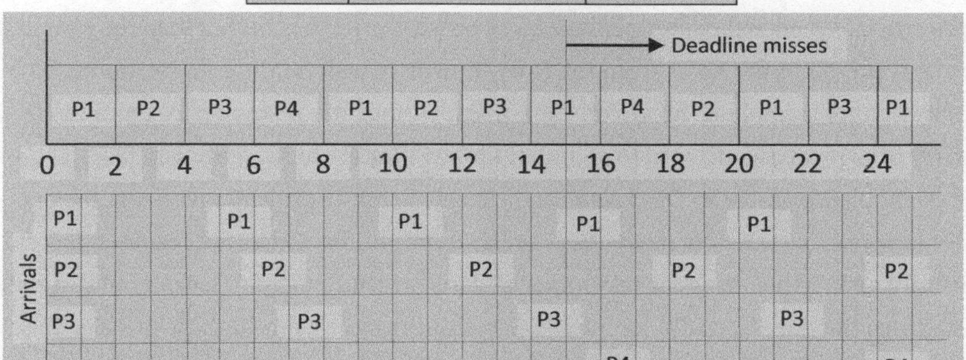

Fig 4.9: Domino effect with EDF scheduling

4.7 Resource Sharing

An embedded system may contain a number of resources. Some examples are CPU, shared memory variables, synchronization primitives, peripheral devices like monitor, printer, sensors and actuators. The tasks in an embedded system are targeted towards one or few dedicated jobs.

Thus, the tasks need to coordinate between themselves. The system resources are to be shared between the set of tasks. The resources in an embedded can be broadly divided into two categories – *pre-emptible resources* and *non-pre-emptible resources*. A *pre-emptible* resource can be taken back from the task currently using it. The typical example is the processor. On arrival of a higher priority task, the processor can be taken from any currently executing lower priority task and allotted to the higher priority one. The low priority task can be resumed later when the resource is available in future and is allotted to the process. In the contrary, *non-pre-emptible* resources cannot be taken prematurely from any task to which the resource has been allotted currently. A typical example is the printer device. The printer may be allotted to a task currently carrying out a printing operation. If it is taken back from the task in between and allotted to another task, the print output may become meaningless as the outputs of two tasks get mixed up. In general, this leads to an inconsistent state of the resource. As a result, if a low priority task has been allotted a non-pre-emptible resource, a higher priority task will need to wait for the lower priority task to finish its execution and release the resource. In this situation, a higher priority task has to wait while the relatively lower priority task continues executing. The situation is known as *priority inversion*. To make the definition more precise, it is also known as *simple priority inversion*. The situation becomes more complex with the arrival of some *intermediate priority* tasks. These intermediary priority tasks may not be willing to use the shared resource currently under use by the low priority task. Since the intermediary tasks possess priorities higher than the lowest priority task, they will pre-empt the CPU from the lowest priority task holding the resource. The lowest priority task cannot complete, however, continues to hold the resource. A continuous flow of intermediary priority tasks will lead to an indefinite wait for the highest priority task. The situation is known as *unbounded priority inversion*. In the case of simple priority inversion, the delay faced by the highest priority task is at most equal to the duration for which the resource is held by the lowest priority task. If the designer takes special care to ensure that the tasks hold resources only for the duration they are actually needed, the waiting time of the highest priority task can be minimized to a large extent. The possibility of deadline miss may be low. With the presence of intermediary priority tasks, unbounded priority inversion may get initiated, creating higher chance for a deadline miss for the highest priority task.

4.7.1 Priority Inheritance Protocol

Priority Inheritance Protocol (*PIP*) is the basic mechanism to solve the unbounded priority inversion problem. Under this protocol, whenever a task suffers priority inversion, the priority of the lower priority task holding the resource is raised to be equal to the highest priority waiting task. The lowest priority task thus *inherits* the priority of the highest priority task, while using the resource. With this priority inheritance mechanism, the priority of the lowest priority task gets sufficiently increased so that the intermediary tasks cannot pre-empt the lowest priority task now. The problem of unbounded priority inversion is thus resolved. As soon as the shared resource is released by the lowest priority task, its priority is reverted back to its original value. The highest priority task now pre-empts the lowest priority running task and gets scheduled along with the resource.

There are two serious issues with the priority inheritance protocol, as noted in the following.

1. *Deadlock.* The priority inheritance policy may lead to potential deadlock situation in which none of the tasks can progress. Consider the two tasks T1 and T2 using the non-pre-emptible shared resources R1 and R2. It is further assumed that T1 has priority higher than T2, however, when an instance of T1 arrives, an instance of T2 is already running and has acquired the resource R2. Since T1 is of higher priority, it pre-empts T2 and starts executing. T1 acquires R1 and then attempts to acquire R2 held by T2. T1 sees a priority inversion and gets blocked, T2 acquires the priority of T1 via the priority inheritance protocol. T2 now tries to grab R1, however, gets blocked due to non-availability of R1. Both the tasks T1 and T2 are now blocked, leading to a deadlock situation.

T1:	Acquire R1	T2:	Acquire R2
	Acquire R2		Acquire R1
	Use resources		Use resources
	Release R2		Release R1
	Release R1		Release R2

2. *Chain blocking.* The situation occurs when a task attempts to acquire multiple shared resources. In the worst case, a high priority task may need n such resources, all of which are held by different lower priority tasks. As a result, in an effort to acquire these n resources, the high priority task will see n priority inversions, creating n blockings for it. The situation may occur in conjunction with a single lower priority task as well. Let the high priority task T1 need shared resources R1, R2 … Rn, all of them currently held by the running low priority task T2. When T1 arrives, it pre-empts T2 and tries to acquire R1. A priority inversion occurs, T2 assumes the higher priority of T1 and resumes execution. Task T1 sees its first blocking. As

soon as T2 releases R1, its priority gets restored to the original value. The task T1 resumes, acquires R1 and then attempts to acquire R2 (held by T2). The task T1 gets blocked again and priority inheritance occurs. This way, the task T1 may see inversions for each of the n resources and face n blockings in a chained manner.

In order to take care of the problems mentioned here, the following two protocols have been proposed – *Highest Locker Protocol* (*HLP*) and *Priority Ceiling Protocol* (*PCP*).

1. *Highest Locker Protocol* (*HLP*). In this protocol, a *ceiling priority* is assigned to every non-pre-emptible, shared resource (also called a *critical* resource). The ceiling priority of a resource is set to be equal to the maximum priority of a task amongst the tasks that may request for the resource. Whenever a task acquires a critical resource, its priority is set to be equal to the ceiling priority of the resource. For a task holding multiple critical resources, the priority is set to be equal to the highest ceiling priority of all the held resources.

   It can be shown analytically that HLP can be used to resolve the problems of unbounded priority inversion, deadlock and chain blocking. On the flip side, it introduces an *inheritance related inversion*. As per the protocol, whenever a low priority task acquires a critical resource, its priority is increased to the ceiling priority of the resource, irrespective of whether any higher priority task has arrived and made to wait for the resource. There may be a number of tasks with intermediary priorities that arrive now which do not need this critical resource for their execution. All these tasks are now made to wait for the low priority task to complete its usage of the critical resource and revert to its original low priority. Only after that the intermediate priority tasks can be taken up for execution.

2. *Priority Ceiling Protocol* (*PCP*). This protocol has the potential to solve the problems of unbounded priority inversion, chain blocking and deadlock. It can also reduce the probability of occurrence of inheritance related inversions. Here, when a task requests for a critical resource, it may or may not be allotted to the task, even if the resource is free. The allocation is guided by a *resource-grant* rule. Similar to HLP, each critical resource Ri has an associated *ceiling priority* CRi. Apart from that, a *current system ceiling* (CSC) is maintained keeping track of the maximum ceiling value of all critical resources active at this point of time. The CSC is initialized to a very low value – lower than the priority of the lowest priority task for the application. Resource grant and release are handled by the corresponding rules noted next.

   - *Resource grant rule*. The rule is applied to decide upon the allocation when a task Ti requests for a critical resource. It consists of two clauses – *Request* clause and *Inheritance* clause.

- o *Request clause*. The resource is allocated to the task Ti if it is already holding another resource with ceiling priority equal to the current CSC or if the task priority is higher than the current CSC value. The CSC value is updated to reflect the maximum ceiling value of all active critical resources.
- o *Inheritance clause*. If a task asks for a critical resource but cannot be allocated failing the request clause, the task gets blocked and the task holding the resource inherits the priority of this blocked task, provided the holding task has lower priority than the blocked task.

- *Resource release rule*. On releasing a critical resource by a task, the current CSC value is updated to reflect the maximum ceiling priority of the active critical resources. The task priority is set to the maximum of its original priority and the highest priority of all tasks waiting for any resource still held by this task.

Compared to HLP, in PCP the priority of a task is not upgraded just because it has grabbed a critical resource – only the CSC value gets updated. A low priority task holding a resource inherits the priority of a higher priority task only if the higher priority task asks for the resource. This reduces the possibility of inheritance related inversions significantly.

4.8 Other RTOS Features

In the last few sections we have seen that the real-time operating systems provide support for scheduling policies like RMS, EDF etc. targeting real-time tasks. These policies are not available in the generic operating systems, such as Windows and Linux. Apart from the scheduling policies, there are some other features that need to be discussed in the context of RTOS.

1. *Timers*. Most of the real-time embedded systems would need high-precision timers, may be more than one. The resolution of these timers are often much higher than those supported by the ordinary operating systems. The timers available in RTOS can be classified into the following categories.
    a. *Periodic Timers*. These timers are primarily used by the periodic tasks to support sampling at regular time intervals.
    b. *Aperiodic/Watchdog Timers*. These are one-time timers, mainly used for detecting deadline misses of tasks. Once a critical function of the system has started, it must finish within its deadline. To detect a deadline miss, when the function is started, a watchdog timer is also started with its time out period set to be equal to the deadline of the task. If the task finishes

within deadline, the timer is reset as the last operation of the task. On the other hand, if the task does not complete within its deadline, time out occurs, a timer interrupt is sent to the processor to initiate appropriate action. Thus, the timer used to keep watch on occurrence of deadline miss of some critical task.

2. *Task Priorities*. In general operating systems, depending upon the resource usage pattern of the task, its priority may increase or decrease over the lifetime. In contrast, in RTOS, priority of a task instance cannot change over its lifetime for reasons other than priority inheritance. It may be noted that in general operating systems, task priorities are modified to improve system throughput. In real-time systems, goal is to meet the deadlines, not throughput optimizations.
3. *Context Switching Time*. Whenever the operating system changes the task, currently being executed by it, with a new task, enough information needs to be saved for resuming the exiting task later. Also, the environment (in terms of CPU register contents) for the new task has to be set up. This process is known as context switching. As this is an overhead for the processor, the context switching time must be reduced for critical tasks in a real-time system. In traditional operating systems, *kernel* (holding major OS routines and data structures) is designed to be non-pre-emptive so that the system calls can be executed atomically without any pre-emption. This has the potential to cause deadline miss for the critical tasks. In real-time operating systems, the kernel is designed to be pre-emptive in nature, so that context switching can be much faster, of the order of a few microseconds only.
4. *Interrupt Latency*. *Latency* for an interrupt is defined to be the time needed to invoke the corresponding *interrupt service routine* (*ISR*) after the occurrence of the interrupt. For real-time systems, the upper bound of the latency value is expected to be small, of the order of microseconds. A policy, known as *deferred procedure call* (*DPC*) is often used to reduce the interrupt processing time. Bulk of the ISR activity is transferred to this deferred procedure. The ISR performs the most important part of the service, rest are taken care of by the DPC. For example, in a real-time temperature monitoring system, the ISR may just read the temperature sensor data. The DPC may perform other activities to generate the statistics from the temperature data. The DPC executes at a much lower priority, compared to the ISR. Thus, the latency to response to the interrupts and events reduce significantly.
5. *Memory Management*. Efficient utilization of the memory resources is an important responsibility of the operating system. General purpose operating systems support the virtual memory and memory protection features. Virtual memory uses a part of hard disk to hold the task with only a few pages loaded into the main memory that interacts with the processor. In

case the processor generates an address beyond the pages available in the main memory, a *page fault* occurs. The task is put into a blocked state till the referred page is loaded into the main memory. Thus, virtual memory allows the task size to be practically infinite, the execution time becomes unpredictable. Hence, in real-time systems virtual memory is either fully avoided or is used only for non-real-time tasks. *Memory locking* is a policy that prevents a page being swapped out of the memory. This makes the execution time of tasks more predictable and thus useful for real-time tasks.

4.9 Some Commercial RTOS

In the following we shall look into some of the commonly available real-time operating systems. A set of compliance criteria regarding the services to be provided by any RTOS has been standardized in the IEEE Portable Operating System Interface for Computer Environments, POSIX 1003.1b. Some of the important requirements are as follows.

- Asynchronous input-output
- Synchronous input-output
- Memory locking
- Semaphores
- Shared memory
- Execution scheduling
- Timers
- Interprocess communication primitives
- Real-time files
- Real-time threads

The commercially available real-time operating systems can be grouped into two major categories. The first one includes the general purpose operating systems that possess real-time extensions. The most important examples in this category are Windows NT and Unix. The other category contains the tailor-made real-time operating systems. Some important examples in this category are Windows CE, LynxOS and VxWorks.

4.9.1 Real-Time Extensions

Some of the popular general-purpose operating systems possess extensions to handle real-time tasks. Two most common examples are Windows NT and Unix. Table 4.4 summarizes the important real-time extension features of these two operating systems. It may be noted that though the kernel of Windows NT is non-pre-emptible, at certain points, pre-emption is permitted. Real-time Unix also provides pre-emption points within a system call. DPCs are supported in Windows NT but not in Unix. Both the operating systems manipulate priorities for better system throughput. However, in Windows NT, there is a band of interrupt priorities that cannot be modified. This band is useful for real-time tasks. The band supports 16 priority levels, however, each task is restricted to a range of ±2 levels with reference to its initial priority. Through DPCs, Windows NT provides fast response to tasks, though it is not a hard real-time system. Priority inheritance not supported in Windows NT, hence may lead to deadlock situation.

Table 4.4: Extensions in Windows NT and Unix

Real-time feature	*Windows NT*	*Unix*
Pre-emptive, priority-based multitasking	Yes	Yes
DPC	Yes	No
Non-degrading priorities	Yes	No
Memory locks	Yes	Yes

4.9.2 Windows CE

Windows CE is made for 32-bit mobile devices with limited memory capacity. The CPU time is divided into slices. The time slices are assigned to individual tasks for execution. There are 256 priority levels available in this RTOS. The tasks are run in kernel mode – eliminating the need of switching for the system calls. This enhances the performance of the system. To protect the device dependent routines, an *equipment adaptation layer* has been defined that isolates the routines from general tasks. Trusted modules and tasks can be defined allowing access to the system APIs (*Application Programming Interfaces*). The non-pre-emptible portion of the kernel routines are broken down into small sections, called *Kcalls*. This reduces the durations of non-pre-emptible codes. Virtual memory is used with the provision of memory locks for the kernel data during the execution of non-pre-emptive kernel codes.

4.9.3 LynxOS

LynxOS is a multithreaded operating system targeting complex real-time applications that require fast, deterministic response. It can cater to a wide range of platforms – from very small embedded products to very large ones. Services like TCP/IP, I/O and file handling, sockets etc. are supported. To serve interrupts, kernel threads (tasks) are created that can be assigned priorities and scheduled as other threads. Response time is always predictable. Memory protection is supported though virtual memory and is also available. Scheduling policies, such as, Prioritized First-In-First-Out,

Dynamic DMS, Time-slicing are supported. There are 512 priority levels available with the possibility of remote operation.

4.9.4 VxWorks

VxWorks is a widely adopted RTOS supporting a visual development environment. It is available on most of the popular processor platforms. The OS contains more than 1800 APIs. There are 256 priority levels supported by the microkernel, along with multitasking, dynamic context switching. Pre-emptive and round robin scheduling policies are available coupled with priority inheritance. It offers facilities like network support, file system and I/O management.

4.9.5 Jbed

The RTOS Jbed supports applications and device drivers in Java. The byte-code, instead of being interpreted, is translated into machine code before class loading. Features like real-time memory allocation, exception handling etc. are supported. Specific class libraries have been introduced for the hard real-time tasks. The number of priority levels supported is ten. The EDF policy is available for task scheduling.

4.9.6 pSOS

This is an object-oriented operating system with the facilities for tasks, memory regions, message queue and synchronization primitives. The scheduling policies supported include pre-emptive, priority-driven and EDF. For priority inversion, both *priority inheritance* and *priority ceiling* protocols are available.

UNIT SUMMARY

Many of the embedded applications are real-time in nature, requiring the intended tasks to be completed in a time-bound manner within their deadlines. Moreover, for a relatively complex embedded system, it may be designed as multiple processes, each accomplishing a specific task. The tasks need to be initiated at proper times and the resources need to be made available to them. For this, the systems often use a Real-Time Operating System (RTOS) to handle the task scheduling and priority concerns. All tasks may not be equally sensitive to the deadlines. Accordingly, tasks can be grouped into hard-, firm- and soft real-time categories. Depending upon the frequency of occurrence of a task, it may be a periodic task, aperiodic task or sporadic task. Scheduling algorithms have been developed to cater primarily to the periodic tasks. This unit has discussed about the popular event-driven scheduling algorithms – RMS and EDF along with their shortcomings and the avenues to come over them. Priority of tasks are handled using several protocols that ensures the avoidance of deadlock and the maximum availability of shared resources. Finally, the unit has looked into the most important features of many of the popular real-time operating systems.

EXERCISES

Multiple Choice Questions

MQ1. Which of the following is not a class of real-time tasks

(A) Hard (B) Firm

(C) Soft (D) Permanent

MQ2. Deadline miss for a hard real-time task in a system means failure of the

(A) Task (B) System (C) RTOS (D) None of the other options

MQ3. After the deadline, utility of the output of a firm real-time task is

(A) 100% (B) 50% (C) 10% (D) 0%

MQ4. Which of the following is not a feature of periodic tasks?

(A) Deadline (B) Periodicity (C) Phase (D) None of the other options

MQ5. A minimum separation between two instances is ensured for task type

(A) Aperiodic (B) Sporadic

(C) Both aperiodic and sporadic (D) None of the other options

MQ6. All deadlines are met by a schedule that is

(A) Valid (B) Feasible (C) Conservative (D) None of the other options

MQ7. The RMS policy assigns priorities to the tasks in manner

(A) Static (B) Dynamic (C) Static or dynamic (D) None of the other options

MQ8. Aperiodic server task is

(A) Periodic (B) Aperiodic (C) Sporadic (D) None of the other options

MQ9. EDF policy assigns task priority that is

(A) Static (B) Dynamic

(C) Either static or dynamic (D) None of the other options

MQ10. Processor utilization in EDF is

(A) Close 60% (B) Close to 100%

(C) More than 100% (D) None of the other options

MQ11. Between RMS and EDF, the more controllable scheduling policy is

(A) RMS (B) EDF (C) Both (D) None of the other options

MQ12. Transient overflow problem occurs in

(A) RMS (B) EDF

(C) Both RMS and EDF (D) None of the other options

MQ13. Domino effect occurs in

(A) RMS (B) EDF

(C) Both RMS and EDF (D) None of the other options

MQ14. Priority inversion occurs with

(A) Shared resources (B) Non-shared resources

(C) All resources (D) None of the other options

MQ15. Unbounded priority inversion can be solved using

(A) Priority assignment (B) Priority inheritance

(C) Priority reduction (D) None of the other options

MQ16. Inheritance related inversion is introduced by

(A) HLP (B) PCP

(C) Both HLP and PCP (D) None of the other options

MQ17. Ceiling priority is used in

(A) HLP (B) PCP

(C) Both HLP and PCP (D) None of the other options

MQ18. Watchdog timers are

(A) Periodic (B) One time

(C) Repeatable (D) Sporadic

MQ19. Between generic and real-time operating systems, priority levels are more in

(A) Generic (B) RTOS

(C) Either generic or RTOS (D) None of the other options

MQ20. Interrupt latency is reduced via

(A) DMA (B) DPC (C) Context (D) None of the other options

MQ21. Virtual memory is suitable for

(A) Real-time tasks (B) Non-real-time tasks

(C) All tasks (D) None of the other options

MQ22. Memory locking is suitable for

(A) Real-time tasks (B) Non-real-time tasks

(C) All tasks (D) None of the other options

MQ23. Number of priority levels in Windows CE is

(A) 32 (B) 64 (C) 128 (D) 256

MQ24. In LynxOS, response time is

(A) Predictable (B) Unpredictable

(C) Variable (D) None of the other options

MQ25. DPC is supported in

(A) Windows NT (B) Unix

(C) Windows NT and Unix (D) None of the other options

Answers of Multiple Choice Questions

1:D, 2:B, 3:D, 4:D, 5:B, 6:B, 7:A, 8:A, 9:B, 10:B, 11:A, 12:B, 13:B, 14:A, 15:B, 16:A, 17:C, 18:B, 19:B, 20:B, 21:B, 22:A, 23: D, 24: A, 25: A

Short Answer Type Questions

SQ1. How does a real-time operating system differ from a generic operating system?

SQ2. Enumerate the classification of real-time tasks based on their periodicity.

SQ3. Distinguish between a valid schedule and a feasible schedule.

SQ4. Identify the scheduling points in clock-driven and event-driven schedulers.

SQ5. Why is RMS called static and EDF dynamic?

SQ6. Explain the transient overload problem. Why is RMS not affected by the same?

SQ7. Explain the Domino effect in EDF. Why does it not occur in RMS?

SQ8. Explain priority inversion.

SQ9. Enumerate the priority inheritance protocol and the inheritance related inversion.

SQ10. State the working principle of HLP.

SQ11. How does PCP work?

SQ12. Why is virtual memory not recommended for hard real-time tasks?

Long Answer Type Questions

LQ1. Why most of the tasks in an embedded application are periodic? Identify the parameters of periodic tasks.

LQ2. For the following task set, show a pert chart for RMS scheduling.

Task	*Execution time*	*Periodicity*
T1	1	5
T2	2	10
T3	4	15
T4	3	15

LQ3. For the task set shown in LQ2, draw the pert chart for EDF scheduling.

LQ4. Show the results of RMS schedulability tests on the task set of LQ2.

LQ5. How are critical tasks with large periodicity handled in RMS? Why does it not need any special treatment in EDF?

LQ6. How are aperiodic and sporadic tasks handled in RMS?

LQ7. Assume there are 100 periodic tasks with the ith task having priority i. If there are 10 priority levels available with the RTOS, show the grouping of tasks for uniform, arithmetic, geometric and logarithmic distributions.

LQ8. Why are watchdog timers useful for real-time systems?

LQ9. Explain the difference between simple and unbounded priority inversions with suitable examples.

LQ10. Compare the commercial RTOSs in terms of features.

KNOW MORE

Process control systems in industrial applications are few major users of real-time operating systems. Tasks in such applications help in maintaining the quality and improve performance and collecting relevant data. This data may be returned to the console for monitoring and troubleshooting. For example, in the oil and gas sector, adoption of these techniques may facilitate less downtime and fewer losses. Machine vision is another area having usage of real-time systems. The tasks may help the systems to process data at near real-time. *Robot Operating Systems* are the valuable parts of robotics technology targeting real-time computing and processing. Manufacturers can use real-time tasks to maximize productivity and improve product quality. It can also ensure enhanced safety on the factory floor. In the domain of healthcare, real-time systems can play very important role to ensure that the data from patient monitoring systems can reach the doctors at real-time to keep the patient safe and healthy.

REFERENCES AND SUGGESTED READINGS

[1] S. Chattopadhyay, "Embedded System Design", PHI Learning, 2023.

[2] R. Mall, "Real-Time Systems Theory and Practice", Pearson, 2006.

[3] X. Fan, "Real-Time Embedded Systems Design Principles and Engineering Practices", Elsevier, 2015.

Dynamic QR Code for Further Reading

1. R. Mall, "Real-Time Systems Theory and Practice".
2. X. Fan, "Real-Time Embedded Systems Design Principles and Engineering Practices".

5 Embedded Programming

UNIT SPECIFICS

Through this unit we have discussed the following aspects:

- *Popular programming languages for embedded software development;*
- *Features of embedded programming languages;*
- *Criteria to choose language for embedded system design;*
- *Additional data types available in embedded C, over the conventional C language;*
- *Programming with embedded C for 8051;*
- *Programming with embedded C for ARM7 processor;*
- *Interface I/O devices with microcontrollers using embedded C;*

The discussion in this unit gives an overview of embedded software development targeting microcontroller based system design. It is assumed that the reader has a basic understanding of generic microcontrollers, programming and the C/C++ language.

A large number of multiple choice questions have been provided with their answers. Apart from that, subjective questions of short and long answer type have been included. A list of references and suggested readings have been given, so that, one can go through them for more details. The section "Know More" has been carefully designed so that the supplementary information provided in this part becomes beneficial for the users of the book. This section mainly highlights the latest developments in embedded programming techniques.

RATIONALE

This unit on embedded programming introduces the readers to the techniques followed and languages used to develop embedded software. A program for an embedded application may have a complex algorithm to be implemented and also have direct interactions with the system hardware resources. The resources may be CPU registers, memory locations, I/O ports and so on. An *embedded system programmer must have the facility to perform read/write operations onto them. This can naturally be done by writing programs in the assembly language of the processor. However, the absence of structured programming primitives like if-then-else, switch-case and loop in the assembly language may make the programming untidy, particularly for algorithms with complex computational requirements. Thus, embedded programming languages should have the features of high-level languages commonly used in software system development and also low-level features like direct hardware resource access. Keeping these two objectives in view, many of the conventional structured programming languages have been augmented to evolve their embedded variants. Amongst them, the languages C/C++ have been the front-runners and their embedded variants have been used extensively by the embedded system design community. The major augmentations in the these languages have come in terms of the new data types like signed/unsigned character/integer, bit, and special function register usage. With these, an embedded program can directly control the I/O ports, timers, counters and communication facilities (like SPI, I^2C, UART and Bluetooth) available in the platform designated for software execution. It is to be noted that even if two hardware platforms use the same processor, the other system resources may differ significantly. This implies that an embedded program developed for one of the platforms may not be directly portable onto the other, even if we consider the programs at their source code level. Each platform will have its own development environment that can translate the high-level program into machine code suitable for that platform. This unit enumerates all these aspects of embedded programming and presents a large number of example programs and device interfaces using the embedded C language. The designer of an embedded application may choose the most appropriate language alternative for the desired system and develop the software code accordingly. However, unlike normal software developers, an embedded software developer needs to consult the design environment and specific hardware resources available with the target platform in order to have an efficient system realization.*

PRE-REQUISITES

Programming, C/C++ language, Microcontrollers

UNIT OUTCOMES

List of outcomes of this unit is as follows:

U5-O1: List commonly used embedded programming languages

U5-O2: Choose suitable language for programming in developing embedded application

U5-O3: Enumerate the data types available in embedded C language

U5-O4: Write code for embedded software development in C

U5-O5: Access internal hardware resources of microcontrollers via embedded C

U5-O6: Interface input/output devices with 8051 microcontroller using embedded C

U5-O7: Interface I/O devices with LPC214x microcontrollers using embedded C

Unit-5 Outcomes	***EXPECTED MAPPING WITH COURSE OUTCOMES*** *(1- Weak Correlation; 2- Medium correlation; 3- Strong Correlation)*			
	CO-1	***CO-2***	***CO-3***	***CO-4***
U5-O1	1	3	3	-
U5-O2	1	3	3	-
U5-O3	-	3	2	-
U5-O4	1	3	2	-
U5-O5	2	3	3	-
U5-O6	1	3	2	-
U5-O7	1	3	2	-

5.1 Introduction

Embedded programming refers to the task of developing the software to be executed by a target processor, in order to realize an embedded application. The programming techniques should have capabilities to access hardware resources like CPU registers, memory locations and other device internals (like sensors and actuators) interfaced to the system. Development of such software is constrained by allowed execution time and memory requirements. Most of the electronic devices now contain one or more embedded processor(s) along with software. The software can be very simple, such as, controlling a few lights via processor controlled switches. It can also be at the complexity levels of routers, missiles and other process control systems. Embedded software interacts with the underlying hardware and is definitely different from the firmware in general computing systems. Unlike firmware, embedded software is generally written in high-level languages like *C*, *C++*, *Java*, *Python* and so on. It is more sophisticated in the sense that an embedded software performs interactions with devices, along with high-level data processing tasks.

Myriads of programming languages have been developed over the years to design software systems. Each such language is generic in nature, in the sense that a corresponding compiler generates the code for a specific processor. As a programmer, the user is not bothered about the internal architecture of the CPU executing the program. The optimizing compiler takes care of the task of efficient execution of programs by the target processor. Many-a-times, the user may not be aware of the computation, communication and interfacing features of the underlying processor. Embedded system programs are a marked deviation from this high-level view of the target processor. The programs will rather like to manipulate the hardware resources (like CPU registers, memory locations, I/O ports) via control exercised by them. This is commonly done by assembly language programming. However, an assembly language program may be tedious and complicated to be developed manually. Unavailability of high-level language constructs (like *if-then-else*, *switch-case* and *loop*) in an assembly language is a serious constraint in structured program development. Due to their complex nature, embedded programs need to be developed in languages similar to the conventional high-level ones. Additionally, there should be facilities to interact with the hardware. This makes the language more specific towards the target platform. It may be noted that, even if two/more platforms use the same processor, the hardware modules interfaced with them may be different. The software for different boards (even with same processor) may need to utilize different sets of registers built-in with the processor, to access interfaced devices. For example, two boards may both utilize the ARM7 processor but one of them may contain only SPI while the other one may have SPI, I^2C and Bluetooth interfaces. Thus, the program developed for one board is not compatible with the other, even if both of them utilize the same high-level language (such as, *C*).

5.2 Embedded Programming Languages

These are the programming languages used for developing embedded software. Following are some of the popular languages belonging to this category.

1. *C*: This is an efficient and very widely used programming language, developed way back in 1970s. *C* is a compiled language and is very structured in nature, supporting bit and register-level access of the variables. About 80% of the industrial embedded systems use *C* as the programming language. However, coding style may be complicated and difficult to understand for maintenance purpose.

2. *C++*: This is a superset of *C* language with object-oriented features. Usage of libraries can save the time in writing code. The language is of course difficult to learn and only a subset of features can be used by embedded developers.
3. *Python*: Developed in 1980s, the language is highly suitable for machine learning, artificial intelligence and data analytics. The language is easy to learn, read and write. However, the language is non-deterministic and hence not suitable for real-time applications. Thus, the language can be used for non-real-time embedded system development.
4. *MicroPython*: This is a version optimized for microcontrollers. Similar to Python, it is open-source, easy to use. However, the code written is not generally as fast as *C*/*C++* and possibly end up using more memory.
5. *Java*: This is one of the efficient, general-purpose languages, widely used for internet based applications. *Java* is the most suited language for embedded systems, developed over the *Android* operating system. The code is portable across devices and operating systems. It is quite reliable as well. However, it cannot be used for real-time systems. Particularly, systems with *graphical user interfaces* (*GUIs*) may have performance issues.
6. *JavaScript*: It is a text-based programming language used by some of the embedded system developers. It may be useful for systems with good amount of networking and graphics. However, it may show poor runtime performance.
7. *Ada*: The language was developed in 1970s as a U.S. Department of Defense project for usage in its own embedded system designs. The language is efficient and reliable, however, it is difficult to run and is also not used widely.
8. *Assembly*: This is the language closest to the processor, directly interacting with the underlying computer hardware. It has the potential to result into memory efficient, fast code. However, the language is highly processor specific, difficult to read and maintain.

5.3 Choice of Language

In the development of an embedded system, selecting a proper programming language has a crucial role to play in the quality of the designed system. Following are some of the guidelines in the selection process.

- *Compatibility with chosen processor*. The language should have hardware compatibility with the selected microprocessor/microcontroller architecture. Popular languages like *C* and *C++* are very versatile. Due to their existence over a long time, a broad range of hardware support is also available for them. This makes these two languages highly suitable for embedded system development platforms.

- *Real-time requirements*. Many embedded systems need to respond to the events in its environment in a time-bound manner. Choice of programming language for such systems will be guided by factors like, how well it can handle real-time operations, interrupts, scheduling of tasks and event-driven programming. Languages like *C* and *Ada* have such real-time capabilities and control over hardware resources.
- *Memory efficiency*. Embedded systems generally possess limited RAM and flash storage. Thus, judicious memory allocation is an important aspect. Languages like *C* and *C++* allow manual memory management for optimization by the embedded system developers.
- *Development tools*. Availability of development tools, libraries and other support often decide the language selection. Compilers, debuggers and *integrated development environments* (*IDEs*) are some such important tools. Well-established languages like *C* and *C++* have tool-chains, large number of libraries and large open-source community supporting system developments.
- *Available expertise*. The expertise and language familiarity of the development tool influence the choice significantly. For relatively less complex projects or the development team being more familiar with high-level languages, *Python* or *JavaScript* may be good option targeting rapid development. On the other hand, for complex, performance-critical applications, *C* and *C++* may provide better control and optimization.
- *C vs. C++*. The choice between *C* and *C++* is more of a personal choice of the designer. This is because the language *C++* is a superset of *C* with additional features and introduction of *class* concept. *C* is a more traditional language and it is likely that many designers are more comfortable with it. For many designers, *C++* coding can make the code cumbersome to understand and modify. However, there is no solid logic in favour of using *C* instead of *C++* for embedded system design, excepting availability of large number of development platforms of *C*. Since our objective is to understand the basic features of embedded programming languages, we shall look into the *embedded C* language, for the sake of simplicity.

5.4 Embedded *C*

The programming language *C* was introduced by *Dennis Ritchie*, in the year 1969. This is one of the most structured programming languages. A program in *C* language is a collection of one or more functions. Every *C* program should have a unique function, called *main*(), which may in turn call other functions defined in the program. The language is sometimes referred to as middle-level programming language, as it enables the programmers to write at a very high-level of abstraction and also at a level close to the assembly language programming, accessing the bare hardware.

The variants of *C* used for embedded software development form the class of embedded *C* languages. This is not a single, unique language as the hardware resources (like I/O ports, timers, memory location addresses) vary across the microprocessors/microcontrollers. As a result, program developed targeting one processor may not be fully compatible with another, even at the source code level. For example, the names of the I/O ports and their sizes are not uniform across all the microcontrollers. Each processor vendor provides processor-specific *C* compiler for the purpose, In our discussion, we shall be looking into two such variants of embedded *C* – one for 8051 and the other for ARM processor.

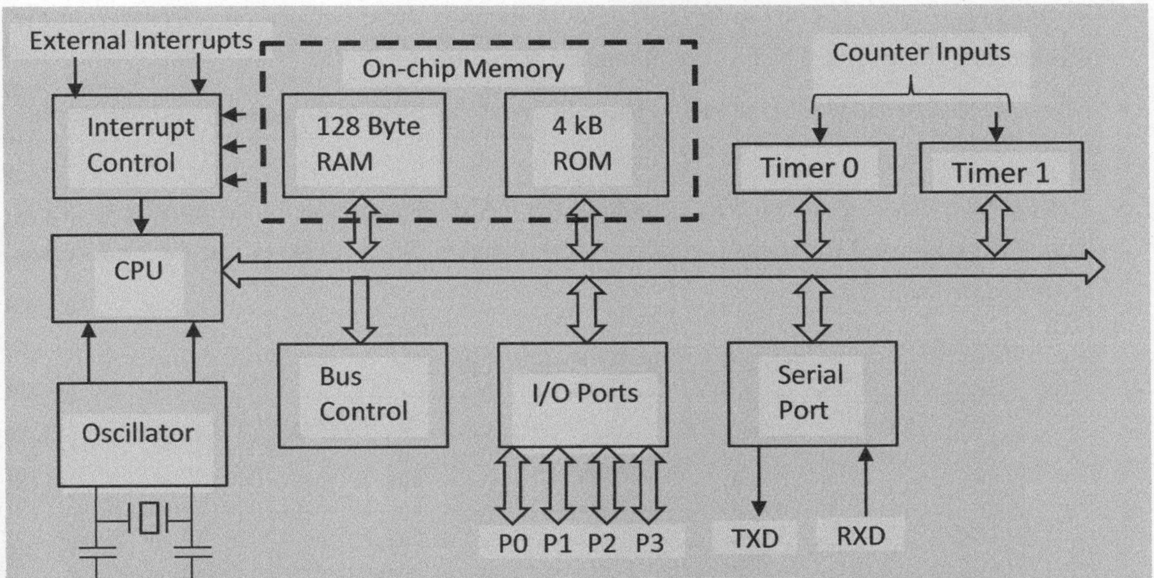

Fig 5.1: Internal Block Diagram of the 8051

5.5 Embedded *C* for 8051

In this section, we shall elaborate the structure of embedded *C* programs, targeting the microcontroller 8051. However, before we delve into the language features, it is imperative to understand the basic architecture of 8051 microcontroller. Fig 5.1 shows the internal block diagram of the processor. The major components in the microcontroller are as follows.

1. *CPU.* As in any other processor, CPU constitutes the main part of it, having components like *Arithmetic Logic Unit* (*ALU*), *Instruction Decoder and Control* and a number of *registers*, such as, *Program Counter* (*PC*) and *Instruction Register* (*IR*). The supported arithmetic and logic operations are on 8-bit data. A number of general-purpose registers are part of the CPU, but are mapped as RAM locations.
2. *Memory.* The 8051 chip contains 4kB program memory realized using EPROM/flash technology. Apart from that, the chip contains 128 byte data memory realized using RAM with addresses ranging over 00H to 7FH. The RAM area has the following parts in it.
   - *Register Banks* (00H to 1FH). These are the lowest 32 bytes of RAM divided into four register banks with 8 registers in each bank. The registers are named as R0 through R7. Only one bank is active at a time.
   - *Bit Addressable RAM* (20H to 2FH). These 16 memory locations can be referred to at the level of individual bits. The bits are numbered from 00H to 7FH.
   - *General Purpose RAM* (30H to 7FH). These 80 bytes can be used for general purpose storage bytes.
   - *Special Function Registers* (*SFRs*). Some of the RAM addresses in the range 80H to 0FFH have been dedicated for some special-purpose registers. Such registers and their addresses are noted in Table 5.1.

Table 5.1: Special Function registers

Group	*Name*	*Address*	*Bit-addressable*
	A	E0H	Yes
	B	F0H	Yes
	PSW	D0H	Yes
	SP	81H	No
	DPTR	83H-82H	No
	DPH	83H	No
	DPL	82H	No

Interrupt related	IE	A8H	Yes
	IP	B8H	Yes
Timer related	TL0	8AH	No
	TH0	8CH	No
	TL1	8BH	No
	TH1	8DH	No
	TCON	88H	Yes
	TMOD	89H	No
Serial communication	SCON	98H	No
	SBUF	99H	No
Power	PCON	87H	No

3. *Digital I/O Ports*. There are four 8-bit I/O ports – P0, P1, P2 and P3. The port bits can be programmed individually to act as either input or output. The port bits are also used for some other functions (details could be found in the 8051 manual).
4. *Timers*. There are two timers – *Timer-0* and *Timer-1*, each configurable as 8-, 13- or 16-bit modules. The timers can also act as counters for the external events occurring on *T0* and *T1* pins.

5.5.1 Embedded *C* Data Types and Programming

There are certain data types in standard *C* that are used extensively in embedded programming. In the following, we shall be looking into those data types, along with some new data types used exclusively in *Embedded C*. Sizes of data types are very important. For example, a variable of certain type of size 8-bits can easily be used in an I/O operation via 8-bit ports. The same operation becomes difficult and need multiple steps if the data is of size 16 bits. The programmer must be very careful about such decisions. In normal *C* language program, this may not be an issue. In those programs, if a variable is declared as 16-bit type instead of 8-bit, it simply occupies one extra memory byte, however the I/O operations are not affected. For an embedded *C* program, this data type mismatch cannot be ignored as it may affect other hardware resources.

1. **Unsigned char:** This is an 8-bit data type supporting values in the range 0 to 255. It is one of the most used data types for embedded *C* programming on 8051. The program noted in Example 5.1 uses a variable of this type.

Example 5.1: The following *C* language program outputs the values 00-7FH sequentially to the port P1 of 8051.

```
#include <reg51.h>
void main (void)
{
    unsigned char x;
    for (x = 0; x < 0x80; x++)
        P1 = x;
}
```

2. **Signed char:** This is also an 8-bit data type that can be used to store signed characters with values in the range –128 to +127. *Signed char* is the default data type in embedded *C*. It may be noted that *unsigned char* can store values in the range 0 to 255, requiring specific declarations in the program. The program shown in Example 5.2 uses both *signed* and *unsigned char* data types.

Example 5.2: The following *C* language program adds 10 signed characters stored in an array a. The result is put in the variable sum.

```
#include <reg51.h>
void main (void)
{
    signed char a[] = { -2, 5, 10, 20, -3, 17, -1, 45, 25, -6 };
    signed char sum = 0;
    unsigned  char j;
    for (j = 0; j < 10; j++)
        sum += a[ j ];
}
```

3. **Unsigned int:** This is a 16-bit data type that can represent numbers in the range 0 to 65535 (FFFFH). It may be noted that in 8051, 16-bit numbers are used for some specific purposes only, such as, memory address, counter values etc. All arithmetic and logic operations are performed on 8-bit data. The memory locations are also 8-bit wide, hence, an unsigned integer variable will occupy two bytes. Accessing these two-byte memory locations is also more complex than a byte access. As a result, the machine code generated by the compiler may be much larger than the same program using unsigned character variables only. The program noted in Example 5.3 shows some uses of *unsigned int* data type variables.

Example 5.3: The following *C* language program uses an unsigned integer variable to introduce some delay in the execution so that the bits of the port P2 are flipped continually.

```
#include <reg51.h>
void main (void)
{
    unsigned int m;
    for (; ;) {
        P2 = 0x55;
        for (m = 0; m < 65530; m++);
        P2 = 0xAA;
        for (m = 0; m < 65530; m++);
    }
}
```

4. **Signed int:** This is the 16-bit data type variant allowing representation of signed integers. Variables of this type can hold values in the range –32768 to +32767. This is the default integer data type used by the embedded *C* compilers.
5. **Single bit:** Bit operands are special for embedded *C* programming. In this direction, there are two bit data types supported by the compilers of 8051. One of them, *bit* can be used to refer to the bits in the bit-addressable RAM locations 20H-2FH. The other type *sbit* can be used to refer to the individual bits of *special function registers*. The program noted in Example 5.4 shows the usage of *bit* and *sbit* data types.

Example 5.4: The following *C* language program flips the bit-4 of port P1 continually.

```
#include <reg51.h>
sbit BIT4 = P1^4;                    // Bit-4 of Port P1
void main (void)
{
    unsigned char m;
    for (; ;) {
        BIT4 = 0;
        for (m = 0; m < 65530; m++);
        BIT4 = 1;
        for (m = 0; m < 65530; m++);
    }
}
```

6. **Special function register:** This is a byte type data, written as *sfr*, corresponding to the special function registers of the 8051. Compared to *sbit*, *sfr* data type corresponds to the byte-size special function registers. The program noted in Example 5.5 shows the usage of *sfr* data type.

Example 5.5: The following *C* language program flips the bits of the port P2 continually using sfr data type.

```
#include <reg51.h>
sfr P2 = 0xA0;
void main (void)
{
    unsigned char m;
    for (; ;) {
        P2 = 0x55;
        for (m = 0; m < 65530; m++);
        P2 = 0xAA;
        for (m = 0; m < 65530; m++);
    }
}
```

Next, we shall be looking into two embedded *C* programs for 8051 that use mix of data types discussed so far. The programs mainly read some port bits, perform some operation on input data and outputs the result on some port. The first program noted in Example 5.6 works with ports at 8-bit *unsigned char* level. The second program noted in Example 5.7 works at bit level.

Example 5.6: The following program reads the ports P0 and P1 continually, computes AND of the values read and outputs to the port P2.

```
#include <reg51.h>
unsigned char data1;
unsigned char data2;
unsigned char result;
void main (void)
{
    while (1) {
        data1 = P1;
        data2 = P0;
        result = data1 & data2;
        P2 = result;
    }
}
```

Example 5.7: The following program reads the port bits P0.0 and P1.4 continually, computes AND of the values read and outputs to the port P2.1.

```
#include <reg51.h>
bit data1 = P0.0;
bit data2 = P1.4;
bit result = P2.1;
void main (void)
{
    while (1) {
        result = data1 & data2;
    }
}
```

The following program in Example 5.8 illustrates how the internal registers corresponding to the timer operation in 8051, can be utilized in a high-level embedded *C* program. It uses Timer-0 for producing delays.

Example 5.8: Consider the problem of generating a square wave with 50% duty cycle and ON/OFF periods of 10 mS. The time delay of 10 mS will be generated using the Timer 0 in mode 1. The square wave is generated at bit 5 of port P2.

```
#include <reg51.h>
void Delay_Rtn (void);
sbit p2_5 = P2^5;
void main (void)
{
    while (1) {
        p2_5 = ~p2_5;              // Toggle P2.5
        Delay_Rtn();               // Call delay
    }
}
void Delay_Rtn (void)
{   // Refer to 8051 manual for the settings needed for timer operation
    TMOD = 0x01;                   // Timer 0, Mode 1
    TL0 = 0xFF;  TH0 = 0xDB;       // Load TL0 and TH0
    TR0 = 1;                       // Start timer
    while (TF0 == 0);              // Wait for TF0 rollover
    TR0 = 0;  TF0 = 0;             // Turn off timer and clear TR0
}
```

5.5.2 Interfacing using Embedded *C*

In this section, we shall look into the usage of embedded *C* programming for interfacing certain input-output devices with the 8051. The devices are driven by the port bits of 8051. The control programs are developed in embedded *C*. The devices interfaced are as follows.

- Eight DIP switches and LEDs

- Four multiplexed 7-segment displays
- Analog-to-Digital converter ADC0808/09
- Digital-to-Analog converter DAC0808

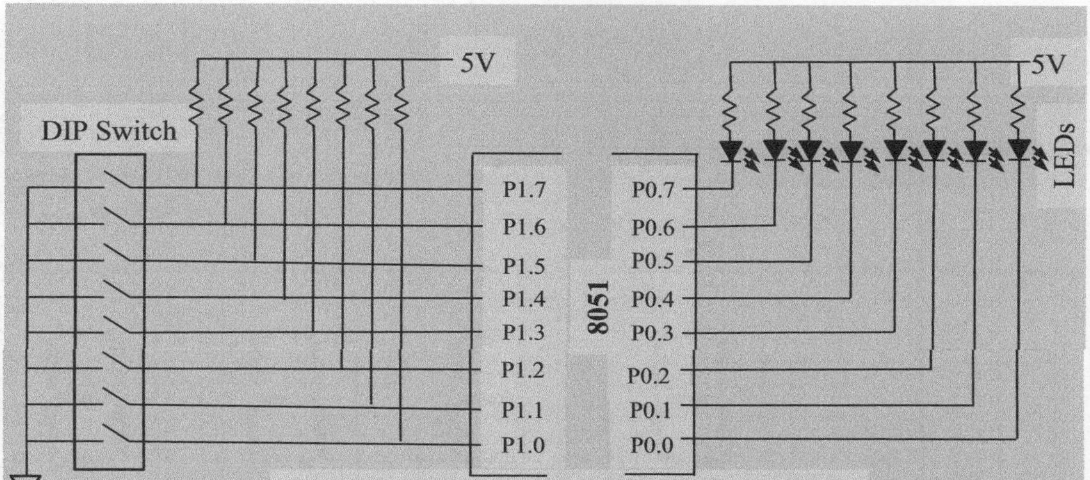

Fig 5.2: Interfacing 8 DIP switches and 8 LEDs

1. *Interfacing eight DIP switches and LEDs*. Fig 5.2 shows the hardware connection for interfacing of eight switches and LEDs to the ports of 8051. The switches are connected to Port 1, while the LEDs are connected to Port 0. The *C* language program for the task has been noted next. The program reads the settings of the switches through Port 1. If a switch is pressed, the corresponding port bit will be read as a 0. The pattern read is output to Port 0. Thus, the corresponding LED will turn ON.

```
#include <reg51.h>
    void main (void)
    {
        while (1)  PO = P1;
    }
```

2. *Interfacing four multiplexed 7-segment LED displays*. This example illustrates the hardware connection and the software program needed to glow the specific segments in a multiplexed display to output the desired pattern for display. Fig 5.3 shows the hardware connection. To display a particular digit on a 7-segment module, first the module has to be selected. This has been accomplished via the four least significant bits of port P2. Then, the specific bit pattern to

glow the required segments (out of {a, b, c, d, e, f, g, dp}) are sent via the bits of port P1, to all the display modules. However, the segments get activated only for the module selected via P2. This is repeated across the display modules at a sufficiently high speed to produce a flicker-free display for the human eyes.

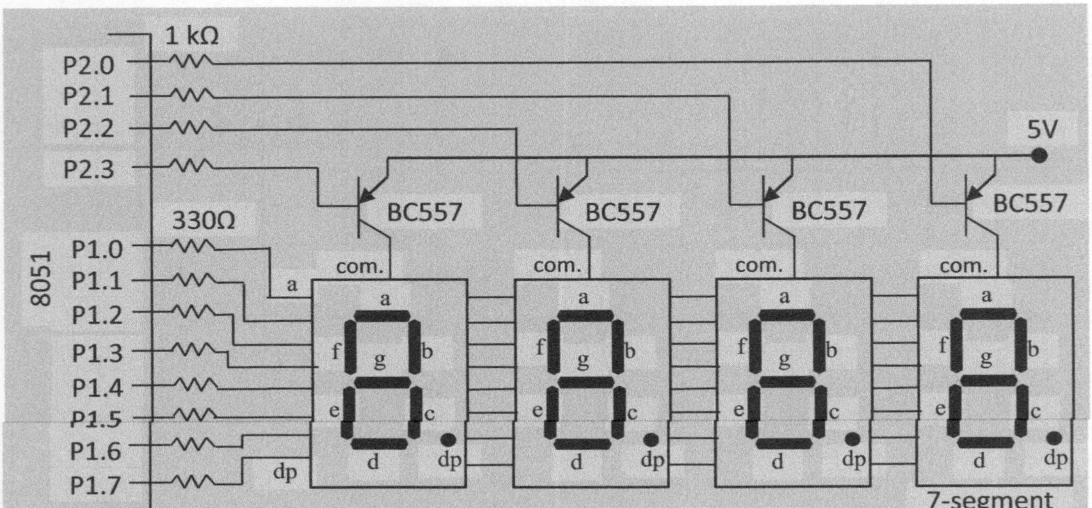

Fig 5.3: Four multiplexed 7-segment displays

Let us assume that the pattern to be displayed is "1947", stored in array STRING. The array DGT_PATT stores the bit pattern to be output to a module to glow the required segments for a digit. For details about the determination of the contents of DGT_PATT, the datasheet for the display modules may be consulted. The corresponding *C* language can be as follows.

```
# include <reg51.h>
void delay_rtn( unsigned int del_val );
unsigned char DGT_PATT[10] = { 0xC0, 0xCF, 0xA4, 0xB0, 0x99,
                               0x92, 0x82, 0xF8, 0x80, 0x90 };
unsigned char STRING[] = "1947";
void main()
{         while (1) do {
            P1 = DGT_PATT[ STRING[ 0 ] – '0']; P2 = 0xF7; delay_rtn( 20 );
            P1 = DGT_PATT[ STRING[ 1 ] – '0']; P2 = 0xFB; delay_rtn( 20 );
```

```
            P1 = DGT_PATT[ STRING[ 2 ] – '0']; P2 = 0xFD; delay_rtn( 20 );
            P1 = DGT_PATT[ STRING[ 3 ] – '0']; P2 = 0xFE; delay_rtn( 20 );
        }
    }
    void delay_rtn( unsigned int del_val )
    {       unsigned int x, y;
            for (x = 0; x < 1000; x++)
                    for (y = 0; y < del_val; y++);
    }
```

3. *Interfacing ADC0808/0809*. Next we look into the usage of embedded *C* programming for interfacing an analog-to-digital converter with 8051 ports. Fig 5.4 shows the connection for interfacing ADC0808/0809 to the 8051. Out of eight available analog channels, in this interface a single channel (Channel 1) has been used. As this is an 8-bit ADC, the port P1 of the 8051 has been used to read-in the converted digital value. Port P2 has been used to connect to other signal lines of the ADC. Bits 0, 1 and 2 of port P2 have been used to provide proper select values needed for the input channel 1.The Vref(+) has been set to 2.56V and Vref(-) to 0 to ensure

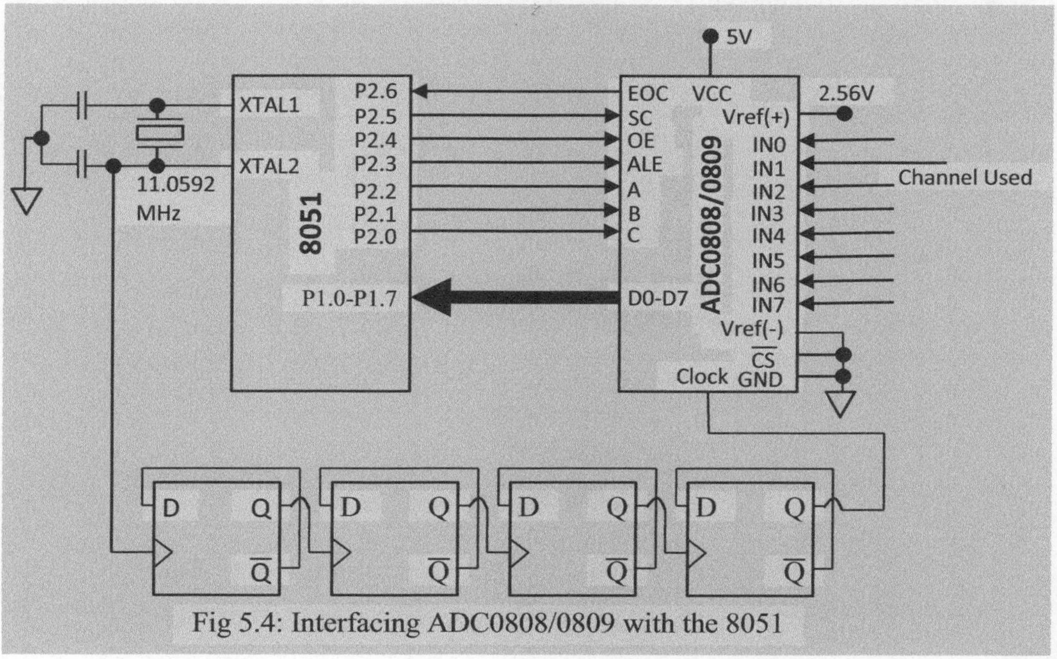

Fig 5.4: Interfacing ADC0808/0809 with the 8051

10mV step size. Bit P2.3 controls ALE for the ADC. Bits P2.4 and P2.5 provide the output enable (OE) and start conversion (SC) for the ADC. The end-of-conversion (EOC) pin of the ADC has been connected to the port bit P2.6. The clock input for the ADC has been drawn from the crystal connected to the 8051. Since the crystal frequency is high, it is passed through four D flip-flops (with $\overline{Q}$ connected to D) to reduce it. Each such flip-flop divides the frequency by two. The VCC is connected to 5V, GND to 0 and chip select (CS) also put at zero to select the ADC chip. The *C* language program for the ADC interface can be as follows.

```
#include <reg51.h>
sbit SEL_C = P2^0;
sbit SEL_B = P2^1;
sbit SEL_A = P2^2;
sbit ALE = P2^3;
sbit OE = P2^4;
sbit SC = P2^5;
sbit EOC = P2^6;
sfr DIG_VAL = P1;
void delay_rtn( unsigned int del_val );
void main()
{
        DIG_VAL = 0xFF;             // Configure P1 as input
        EOC = 1;                    // Configure EOC line as input
        ALE = 0;                    // Clear ALE
        SC = 0;                     // Clear SC
        OE = 0;                     // Clear OE
        while (1) {
                SEL_C = 0; SEL_B = 0; SEL_A = 1;  // Choose channel 1
                delay_rtn(1);
                ALE = 1;
                delay_rtn(1);
                SC = 1;
                delay_rtn(1);
```

```
            ALE = 0;
            SC = 0;                // Start conversion
            while (EOC == 1);  // Wait for conversion to complete
            while (EOC == 0);
            OE = 1;                // Enable output to be read
            delay_rtn(1);
            A = DIG_VAL;
            OE = 0;
        }
}
void delay_rtn( unsigned int del_val )
{
        unsigned int x, y;
        for (x = 0; x < 1000; x++)
            for (y = 0; y < del_val; y++);
}
```

4. *Interfacing DAC0808*. Fig 5.5 shows an interface of DAC0808 with the 8051. Port P1 of the 8051 has been used to provide the digital input to be converted to analog current/voltage. VEE has been given -15V while VCC has got +5V. VREF+ has been connected to 10V, VREF– to zero and the resistance as 5kΩ. This ensures the reference current I_{ref} to be 10mA. An operational amplifier (such as, 741), can be used with feedback resistance 5kΩ to convert the output current to analog voltage.

The interface shown in Fig 5.5 can be used to generate different types of analog waveforms. The following program shows how to generate a triangular wave through the DAC interface. For this, the values 0 to 255 can be output to port P1 followed by decrementing upto 0. The digital values, when converted by the DAC will provide an analog triangular waveform as output. After output of a digital value, a small delay has been introduced to allow time to the DAC to convert the pattern. It may be noted that increasing the delay value will convert the waveform to be more of staircase in shape. The waveform can be viewed on an oscilloscope to see the shape and adjust the delay value accordingly.

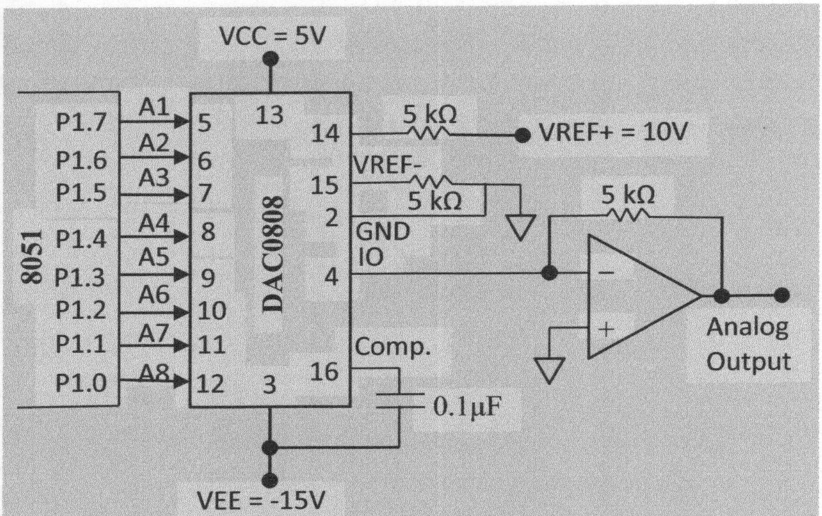

Fig 5.5: Interfacing DAC0808 with 8051

```
#include <reg51.h>
void main (void)
{
        unsigned char i;
        while (1) {
            for (i = 0; i < 255; i++) { P1 = i; delay_rtn(2);
        }
            for (i = 255; i > 0; i --) { P1 = i; delay_rtn(2); }
         }
}
void delay_rtn( unsigned int del_val )
{         unsigned int x, y;
          for (x = 0; x < 1000; x++)
          for (y = 0; y < del_val; y++);
}
```

5.6 Embedded *C* for ARM

In the last section, we have seen how the *C* language has been extended to have a variant that can be used to describe the software of an embedded application to be realized using the 8051 microcontroller. In particular, the language has been augmented to include the hardware resources in 8051, such as, ports, timers and configuration registers. These augmentations do not have any meaning when a different processor is targeted. To illustrate the issue further, in the following, we shall look into another embedded *C* variant that is used to describe the software to be executed by ARM7 processor based systems. It may be noted, there are several manufacturers for the microcontrollers based on ARM7 architecture. The hardware resources across them are again not uniform. Thus, the embedded *C* language for each of them is different from the others. The programmer needs to refer to the manual of the specific manufacturer to know the exact set of available resources and their access mechanism. In the following we shall look into one such series of microcontrollers developed around the ARM7 architecture.

5.6.1 LPC214x – An ARM7 Implementation

In this section, a typical implementation of ARM7 architecture, LPC214x has been discussed. This is one of the most popular series of microcontrollers, due to their tiny size and low power consumption. Devices are pretty small targeting miniaturisation of the full system. There are five different microcontrollers in the series – LPC2141/42/44/46/48. Table 5.2 shows a comparison between the devices. The quad-flat package can contain 8-40kB of SRAM and 32-512kB flash memory. For communication, USB 2.0 is supported. One/two on-chip 10-bit ADCs are available that can provide a total of 6-14 analog channels. Some variants have on-chip 10-bit DAC as well. Two 32-bit timers/counters are there, along with four capture and four compare channels. A 6-channel pulse width modulation module and a watchdog timer are also included. Apart from USB, interfaces like SPI, SSP, I^2C, USART are available for communication. A real-time clock module with independent power supply has been provided in it. The number of external interrupt pins is upto 21. Fig 5.6 shows the block diagram of a generic LPC214x microcontroller.

Table 5.2: Comparison across LPC214x devices

Device	*SRAM (kB)*	*Flash (kB)*	*No. of ADC channels*	*No. of DAC channels*
LPC2141	8	32	6	-
LPC2142	16	64	6	1
LPC2144	16	128	14	1
LPC2146	40	256	14	1
LPC2148	40	512	14	1

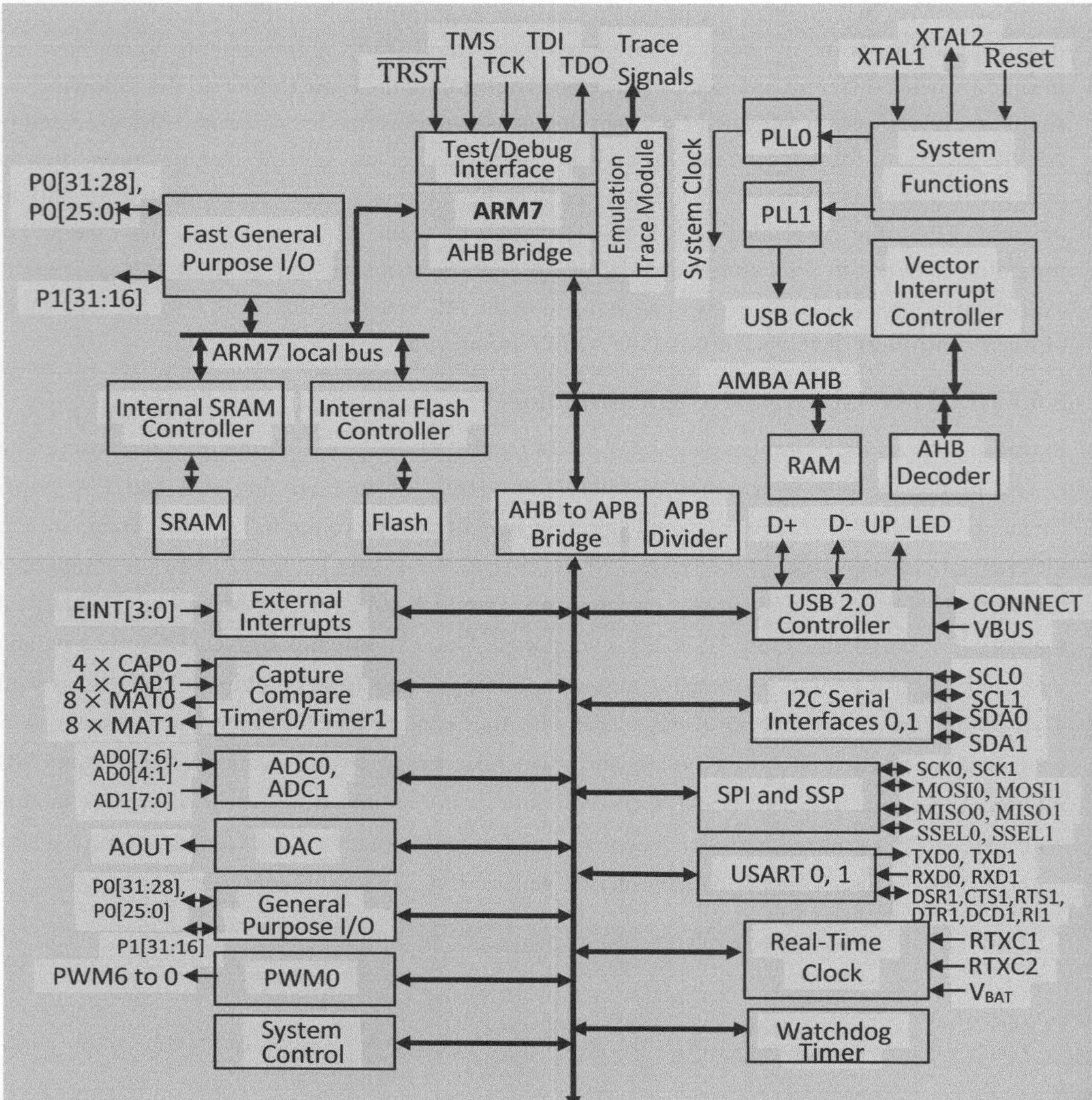

Fig 5.6: Block Diagram of LPC214x

5.6.2 I/O Port Programming for LPC2148

LPC2148 has got two General Purpose I/O (GPIO) ports, namely, Port 0 (P0) and Port 1 (P1). Both the ports are 32-bit wide, however, for P1, the bits 16 to 31 are only available for input/output. All bits of P0 are available for I/O, however, these pins also have several functions multiplexed to them. As a result, the actual number of I/O pins available, depends upon the application in hand which may use other modules of the chip as well. For example, pin P0.21 also acts as PWM5 (Pulse Width Modulation), AD1.6 (ADC), CAP1.3 (Capture input for Timer1, Channel 3). For Port 0, 28 out of 32 pins can be configured as bidirectional. P0.24, P0.26 and P0.27 are unavailable. P0.30 can be used as output pin only.

Table 5.3 shows the important registers and their settings for GPIO operations. The registers need to be programmed properly to get the I/O operations done. The registers control the functionality of the pins, I/O directions, setting and resetting of bits. Individual bits can be programmed separately. In particular, for I/O operation, first the direction of the port bit be set. For example, the setting "IO0DIR = 0x04" will configure the Pin 2 of Port 0 (P0.2) as output and other bits as input. For an input operation, the IO*x*PIN register can be read. However, for output operation, to write a 1, corresponding bit of IO*x*SET register should be set to 1. To output a 0, the bit in IO*x*CLR be set to 1. After a port pin has been written with some value, the value can be read from the IO*x*PIN register bit.

Table 5.3: Registers for I/O Port Programming

Register (x = 0, 1)	*Functionality*
IO*x*PIN	Register can be read to get the current state of the GPIO pins.
IO*x*DIR	Controls direction of port bits. Setting a bit to 0 makes port pin to act as input, 1 makes the pin output.
IO*x*CLR	Drives the corresponding pin to 0.
IO*x*SET	Drives the corresponding pin to 1.

Example 5.9: Consider the problem of setting P0.14 pin to high first and then low. The *C* code fragment for it is as follows.

```
IO0DIR |= (1 << 14);        // P0.14 set as output pin
IO0SET |= (1 << 14);        // Output high to P0.14
IO0CLR |= (1 << 14);        // Output low to P0.14
```

Next, we shall look into two more examples of GPIO operations. The first example assumes two LEDs connected to Port 0 pins 0 and 1. When the program is executed, the LEDs will blink. In the second example, a switch and an LED are connected to port pins 0 and 1 respectively. When the switch is closed, the LED will glow.

Example 5.10: Two LEDs are connected to port pins P0.0 and P0.1. The LEDs should blink continually. The complete *C* program for the purpose is shown next.

```
# include <lpc214x.h>
void Delay_rtn(void);
int main(void)
{
    IO0DIR = 0x3;        // Configure P0.0 and P0.1 as output
    while (1)
    {
        IO0SET = 0x3;     // Turn LEDs on
        Delay_rtn();
        IO0CLR = 0x03;  // Turn LEDs off
        Delay_rtn();
    }
}
void Delay_rtn(void)
{
        int a, b;
        b = 0;
        for (a = 0; a < 2000000; a++) b++; // Do something, else compiler may
                                            // remove the loop
}
```

Example 5.11: A switch is connected to P0.0, an LED to P0.1. The LED should glow whenever the switch is closed. The corresponding C program is shown next.

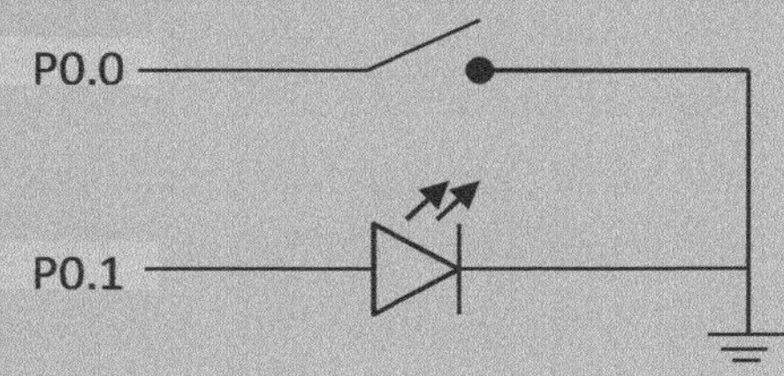


```
# include <lpc214x.h>
int main(void)
{
    IO0DIR &= ~(1); // Make P0.0 input
    IO0DIR |= (1<<1); // Configure P0.1 as output
    while (1) {
        if (!(IO0PIN & (1))   // Becomes true if P0.0 = 0
            IO0SET |= (1 << 1); // Drive P0.1 high
        else
            IO0CLR |= (1 << 1); // Make P0.1 low
    }
}
```

UNIT SUMMARY

A large number of programming languages have been developed over the years for software systems. Most of these languages do not directly interact with the underlying hardware, in the sense that the resources like registers, I/O ports and memory locations are not directly mentioned in the high-level language programs. The compilers map the storage and I/O operations of the program to the system resources aiming an efficient realization of it. Embedded programs, on the other hand, interact directly with such system resources. Many of the conventional structured programming languages have got augmented to support embedded programming as well. The most popular amongst them are embedded *C/C++*. The embedded variants have new data types supporting character and integer variables of both unsigned and signed types. Bit-level data types are also supported. These languages allow access to the system registers of the underlying microcontrollers. As a variant is targeted to one platform with specific hardware resources, each platform needs a separate variant of the same embedded language. The unit has seen a large number of embedded programs targeting the 8051 microcontroller. A good number of device interfacing examples have been included. The same embedded language changes significantly when it is targeting a different platform, such as, a particular ARM7 based implementation. The set of registers that the programmer can access in the high-level language program becomes different. For the same I/O operations, the programming technique goes through significant modifications. Thus, in order to design program for any target platform, the user needs to use the development environment provided by the platform vendor and look into the manual to identify the resources and their access mechanism.

EXERCISES

Multiple Choice Questions

MQ1. An embedded software is targeted to

(A) Single processor (B) Dual processor

(C) Multiple processors (D) None of the other options

MQ2. Embedded software and firmware are

(A) Equivalent (B) Structurally same

(C) Nonequivalent (D) None of the other options

MQ3. For generic programming languages, optimization is done by

(A) Compiler (B) Operating System

(C) Linker (D) None of the other options

MQ4. The construct "if-then-else" is generally available in

(A) High-level languages (B) Assembly languages

(C) Both high-level and assembly languages (D) None of the other options

MQ5. Object-oriented features are available in

(A) *C* (B) *C++*

(C) Both *C* and *C++* (D) None of the other options

MQ6. Python is not suitable for real-time applications due to

(A) Complexity (B) Non-determinism

(C) Simplicity (D) None of the other options

MQ7. Manual memory management is available in

(A) *C* (B) *C++*

(C) Both *C* and *C++* (D) None of the other options

MQ8. The function unique in *C* programs is

(A) main() (B) include()

(C) printf() (D) None of the other options

MQ9. Program memory size in 8051 is

(A) 4 kB (B) 2 kB

(C) 16 kB (D) None of the other options

MQ10. Number of register banks in 8051 is

(A) 1 (B) 2

(C) 3 (D) 4

MQ11. Number of I/O ports in 8051 is

(A) 2 (B) 4

(C) 8 (D) None of the other options

MQ12. Maximum value represented by "Unsigned char" is

(A) 127 (B) 255

(C) 1023 (D) None of the other options

MQ13. Minimum value in "Signed char" type is

(A) -128 (B) -256

(C) 0 (D) None of the other options

MQ14. Default character type in embedded *C* is

(A) Signed (B) Unsigned

(C) Integer (D) None of the other options

MQ15. In 8051, bits of special function register are of type

(A) bit (B) sfr

(C) sbit (D) None of the other options

MQ16. Bit-width of "Unsigned int" is

(A) 8 (B) 16

(C) 32 (D) None of the other options

MQ17. Default of integer in embedded *C* is

(A) Unsigned (B) Signed

(C) Char (D) None of the other options

MQ18. Size in bits of sfr data type is

(A) 8 (B) 16

(C) 4 (D) None of the other options

MQ19. Number of GPIO ports in LPC2148 is

(A) 2 (B) 4

(C) 8 (D) None of the other options

MQ20. Bits of P1 available for I/O in LPC2148 is

(A) 0 to 15 (B) 8 to 24

(D) 0 to 31 (D) 16 to31

MQ21. In LPC2148, direction of I/O port bits is controlled by the register

(A) IOxPIN (B) IOxDIR

(C) IOxPTH (D) None of the other options

MQ22. In LPC2148, to make an I/O pin 0

(A) IOxCLR be set to 0 (B) IOxCLR be set to 1

(C) IOxSET be set to 0 (D) IOxSET be set to 1

MQ23. In LPC2148, current state of an I/O pin is available in

(A) IOxPIN (B) IOxDIR

(C) IOxSET (D) IOxSET

MQ24. In LPC2148, to make a port bit input

(A) IOxDIR set to 0 (B) IOxDIR set to 1

(C) IOxPIN set to 1 (D) None of the other options

MQ25. In LPC2148, to make a port bit output

(A) IOxDIR set to 0 (B) IOxDIR set to 1

(C) IOxPIN set to 1 (D) None of the other options

Answers of Multiple Choice Questions

1:A, 2:C, 3:A, 4:A, 5:B, 6:B, 7:C, 8:A, 9:A, 10:D, 11:B, 12:B, 13:A, 14:A, 15:C, 16:B, 17:B, 18:A, 19:A, 20:D, 21:B, 22:B, 23:A, 24:A, 25:B

Short Answer Type Questions

SQ1. How does embedded software differ from firmware?

SQ2. Enumerate the drawbacks of assembly language for structured programming.

SQ3. Why is Python not suitable for real-time embedded system design?

SQ4. Distinguish between signed and unsigned char data types.

SQ5. Compare the data types signed and unsigned int.

SQ6. Distinguish between bit and sbit data types in embedded C.

SQ7. Distinguish between sbit and sfr data types.

SQ8. In a multiplexed display, it is required to connect six 7-segment modules. Identify the number of I/O port bits needed.

SQ9. Enumerate the ADC control procedure through the I/O port bits of 8051.

SQ10. Compare between the LPC214x series of devices.

SQ11. Enumerate the role of IOxDIR register in I/O operation.

SQ12. How are the IOxCLR and IOxSET registers used for I/O operation in LPC2148?

Long Answer Type Questions

LQ1. Identify the features of popular embedded programming languages.

LQ2. Enumerate the criteria guiding the selection of embedded programming language.

LQ3. Why an IDE is must for embedded programming?

LQ4. Enumerate the data types of embedded C.

LQ5. Draw the circuit diagram and write the program code to display the pattern "123456" onto multiplexed 7-segment display.

LQ6. Draw the circuit diagram and write corresponding program to interface ADC with 8051.

LQ7. Draw the circuit diagram and write corresponding program to generate a saw tooth waveform via interfacing a DAC with 8051.

LQ8. Enumerate the main features of LPC2148.

LQ9. Explain how the I/O operations can be performed in LPC2148.

LQ10. Modify the program in in Example 5.10 so that the LEDs at P0.0 and P0.1 are turned ON alternately with only one of them glowing at a time.

KNOW MORE

The languages *C/C++* have been the most popular ones for embedded programming over the years. Embedded *C* has been used in industrial automotive applications (highway speed checkers, signal control, vehicle tracking software etc.), robotics (such as, line-following robots, obstacle avoidance robots, robotic arms etc.), personal medical devices (such as, glucometers, pulse oximeters) and many other microcontroller-based applications. However, in 2010 a modern multi-paradigm programming language, called *Rust*, has been created by Mozilla. This is a fast and robust system language that can be used in many applications including embedded devices and web development. It is a statically typed programming language that combines the performance of *C/C++* with memory safety and expressive syntax. It ensures memory safety without a garbage collector. The memory is managed efficiently at compile-time itself avoiding data races and memory leaks. Thus, the programmer can debug the program at compile-time. The syntax of *Rust* is inspired by *C/C++*, enabling the developers to learn it quickly. The national security agency at White House, USA has referred to *Rust* as the most secure common programming language. The language provides fine-grained control over system resources. *Rust* has been used extensively in embedded automotive applications as it can be compiled into low-level code without additional runtime overhead. The built-in parallelism features of *Rust* can prevent many common problems faced by concurrent program developers. However, there is a need for creation of toolchain, standardization and development of available expertise, before *Rust* can possibly replace the languages like *C/C++* in embedded programming.

REFERENCES AND SUGGESTED READINGS

[1] K. Qian, D. Haring, L. Cao, "Embedded Software Development with C", 2009.

[2] M. Barr, "Programming Embedded Systems in C and C++", O'Reilly, 2004.

[3] S. Oualline, S. Oualline, "Bare Metal C Embedded Programming for the Real World", No Starch Press, 2022.

[4] M. Barr, A. Massa, "Programming Embedded Systems With C and GNU Development Tools", 2006.

[5] N.H. Tollervey, "Programming with MicroPython", O'Reilly, 2017.

[6] S. Klabnik, C. Nichols, "The Rust Programming Language", No Starch Press, 2023.

[7] "A Curated List of Awesome Embedded Programming", https://github.com, November, 2024.

Dynamic QR Code for Further Reading

1. Rust – A Language Empowering Everyone to Build Reliable and Efficient Software.

2. S. Oualline, S. Oualline, "Bare Metal C Embedded Programming for the Real World", No Starch Press.

6 Hardware-Software Codesign

UNIT SPECIFICS

Through this unit we have discussed the following aspects:

- *Design and usage of cosimulation for hardware-software codesign;*
- *Issues with hardware-software codesign;*
- *Integer Linear Programming formulation of the hardware-software partitioning problem;*
- *Extension of Kernighan-Lin graph bi-partitioning for hardware-software partitioning;*
- *Usage of metasearch techniques like GA and PSO for the partitioning problem;*
- *Power-aware hardware-software codesign;*
- *Functional partitioning technique to transform task-graph and partition;*

This unit includes a thorough discussion on the hardware-software codesign process. Techniques and algorithms designed for the problem have been elaborated. It is assumed that the reader has a basic understanding of computer hardware and software technologies.

A large number of multiple choice questions have been provided with their answers. Apart from that, subjective questions of short and long answer type have been included. A list of references and suggested readings have been given, so that, one can go through them for more details. The section "Know More" has been carefully designed so that the supplementary information provided in this part becomes beneficial for the users of the book.

RATIONALE

This unit on hardware-software codesign presents the strategies used for realizing embedded systems onto some target architecture. The target architecture may have some general purpose processors for software realization of tasks and ASIC/FPGA for hardware realization. Computationally intensive tasks may need hardware realization to meet the system deadlines. Other tasks may be mapped to either the software or the hardware component, based on issues like power consumption, system performance optimization etc. It becomes very crucial to take judicious decision about selection of tasks to be realized on target architecture component. The problem is computationally hard, with the brute force methods requiring exponential time. As a result, several heuristic and metasearch techniques have been developed to address the partitioning problem. Exact methods, such as integer linear programming formulation can be used to get optimal solution for small embedded designs. These techniques are not scalable with the increase in task-graph complexity, however, can act as yard-stick to judge other methods. Several heuristics have also evolved for the partitioning problem. An important one in this category is the Kernighan-Lin bi-partitioning technique, originally proposed for VLSI physical design. An extended version of the same can be used for the hardware-software partitioning problem as well. Due to the complex nature of the problem, researchers have explored metasearch techniques, such as, Genetic Algorithm and Particle Swarm Optimization for solving the partitioning problem. Apart from hardware area and delay, power consumption of the system is another important criteria to be optimized, particularly for reconfigurable platforms like FPGA. Algorithms have been developed targeting system architecture with general processor and FPGA. Transformations in the specification task graph may aid in the partitioning process. The strategy, known as functional partitioning, has been explored. This unit enumerates all these aspects of hardware-software codesign and presents an overview of different algorithms and policies available. The designer may choose the most appropriate alternative for the desired system and target architecture for system realization.

PRE-REQUISITES

Computer Hardware and Software

UNIT OUTCOMES

List of outcomes of this unit is as follows:

U6-O1: State the design of cosimulators

U6-O2: State the role of cosimulators in hardware-software codesign

U6-O3: Formulate hardware-software partitioning as an Integer Linear Programming problem

U6-O4: Extend Kernighan-Lin bi-partitioning for hardware-software partitioning

U6-O5: Formulate Genetic Algorithm based framework for hardware-software partitioning

U6-O6: Perform hardware-software partitioning using Particle Swarm Optimization

U6-O7: Partition task-graphs onto reconfigurable platform for power optimization

U6-O8: Restructure task-graphs via functional partitioning of specification

Unit-6 Outcomes	***EXPECTED MAPPING WITH COURSE OUTCOMES*** *(1- Weak Correlation; 2- Medium correlation; 3- Strong Correlation)*			
	CO-1	***CO-2***	***CO-3***	***CO-4***
U6-O1	1	3	-	3
U6-O2	1	3	-	3
U6-O3	-	3	-	3
U6-O4	-	2	-	3
U6-O5	-	2	-	3
U6-O6	-	2	-	3
U6-O7	1	2	-	3
U6-O8	1	3	-	3

6.1 Introduction

An embedded application typically consists of a number of tasks with deadlines, both at task-level and application-level. To meet the deadlines, it may be essential to realize at least a subset of tasks using hardware, while other tasks may not be that much critical and software realization of them may suffice. Realizing all tasks in software may not satisfy the performance requirements of the application. On the other hand, a complete hardware realization of the system may turn out to be too costly in terms of area and power consumption. An ideal solution to the problem is to have a mixed hardware-software realization for the tasks of the application. In such a system, while some tasks are realized in hardware, others are realized via software. This is called *hardware-software codesign* of the application. As an embedded system designer, one must be able to judge judicially the tasks that should go to hardware and those for software, so that the design constraints (as discussed in *Unit 1)* are met and costs are optimized.

With so many options available for both the software and hardware platforms, the task of codesign becomes almost intractable, unless the target architecture is explicitly specified. The target architecture may consist of one or more of the following components.

- One or more general-purpose processors along with individual program- and data-memory.

- An FPGA chip to realize tasks in hardware.
- An ASIC for the hardware part.

A communication mechanism between the components has to be fixed as well. Fig 6.1 shows a typical target architecture consisting of one ARM processor and an ASIC communicating over a *PCIe* bus.

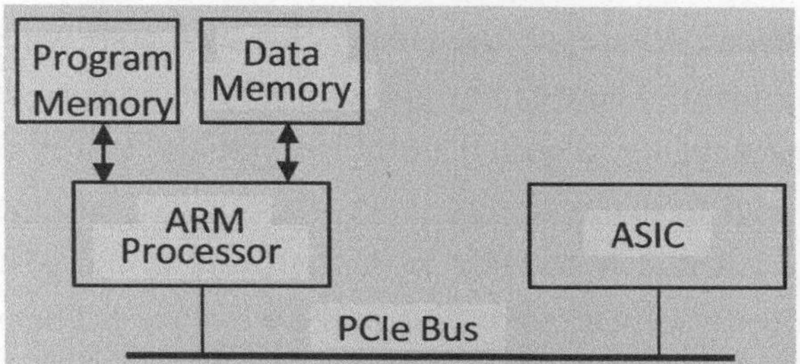

Fig 6.1: Typical target architecture

The codesign problem is to decide the implementation platform (hardware or software) for each individual task of the application. If there is a data-dependency between two tasks of the application, communication takes place over the bus, incurring delay and power. While checking for performance of the resultant system, this communication delay needs to be factored in. To ensure the correctness of the combined system with both hardware and software components, it is essential to perform a simulation of the system. As this simulation has two different types of platforms to be simulated, it is known as *cosimulation*. Thus, the codesign problem consists of two important subproblems – *cosimulation* and *hardware-software partitioning*. In the following, we shall be discussing on these two topics in detail.

6.2 Cosimulation

Simulation happens to be one of the most powerful tools for checking system correctness. A complex embedded system consists of both software and hardware modules that exchange information between them to carry out the designated system functionality. On the other hand, traditional simulation techniques are applicable to either the hardware systems or the software systems. Fundamentally, the software systems are inherently sequential in nature while the hardware is inherently parallel. This characteristic difference precludes the usage of software simulator to simulate hardware modules and vice versa. Simulators used for simulating the software modules developed using parallel programming languages also cannot capture the delays involved in carrying a signal value from one place to another in the hardware.

Hence, designing a single simulator to cater to both the hardware and software modules of an embedded system is difficult, if not impossible. At the same time, a joint simulation of the hardware and the software modules is essential to prove the correctness of the designed system that spans over both hardware and software platforms. The major difficulty in the process is the non-existence of the actual hardware in the initial phase of the design process. Thus, joint simulation cannot be taken up till a basic hardware module is ready to interact with the software simulator. Previously, software developers used to develop their code with perceived assumptions about behaviour of the hardware. There can be gross mismatch between this presumption and the actual hardware behaviour, leading to quite painful integration steps at some later stage. Minor miscommunication may lead to major design flaws. As the software modification is relatively simple, the behavioural mismatch is patched in the software at the cost of performance, even leading to expensive hardware/software redesign, in the worst case. The problem can be reduced significantly through the usage of proper cosimulation at an early stage. Fig 6.2 shows the integration of cosimulation with the hardware-software codesign process. Cosimulation is primarily used for the purposes of verification and estimation at different stages of the codesign process, as noted next.

- After the system specification has gone through refinement step, the resulting system description needs to be verified to ensure that the desirable features are properly captured in the resulting document.
- At hardware-software partitioning stage, the embedded system designer needs to take prudent decision about the modules to be put into the two partitions. Cosimulation is necessary to ensure that the resulting system will meet the performance requirements.
- After the system has been implemented, verification of the whole system is carried out via cosimulation.

In a broader sense, cosimulation refers to simultaneous simulation of two or more parts of a system at different abstraction levels. For example, in the hardware domain, if the circuit contains both analog and digital components, the full circuit simulation needs both the analog- and the digital- simulators to work in conjunction. A major problem with cosimulation is to create a bridge between the component simulators and also to ensure synchronization between the component simulators.

6.2.1 Major Issues

In cosimulation, different components of the system are simulated together. These individual component level simulators may not be able to capture the speed mismatch among the components. Further, the simulators need to interact with each other and exchange signal values. However, the major problem occurs due to speed mismatch between the real components, which may not be captured in the individual component level simulators. The component level simulators need to interact with each other to exchange signal values. As a result, a number of issues arise that are to be resolved in any successful cosimulation implementation. The major issues involved are as follows.

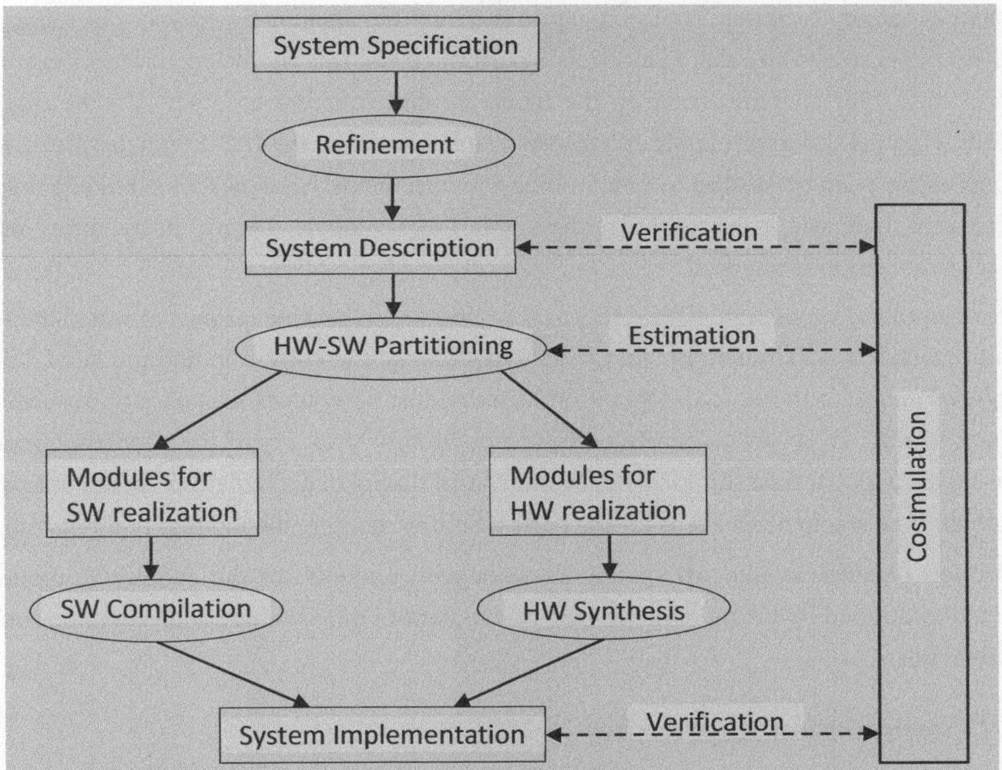

Fig 6.2: Cosimulation in Codesign process

1. *Communication between simulators*. Cosimulation for an embedded system needs communication between the hardware and the software simulators. Efficiency of cosimultaion (accuracy, speed of simulation etc.) is highly dependent upon the communication mechanism adopted. Typically, modern operating systems provide facilities for *interprocess communication* (IPC) using *pipes*, *message queues* etc. IPCs can be used for exchanging signal values between the two simulators. Further, the programming languages like C/C++ support facilities to call procedures written in another language. The facility can be used to call

procedures written in VHDL/Verilog. Languages like VHDL and Verilog can link to C code via *foreign language kernel* (VHDL) or *programming language interface* (Verilog).

2. *Synchronization of simulators*. As the hardware- and software- simulators are used to simulate the behaviour of one full system, it is often necessary to synchronize between the modules. Such communication and synchronization take place via the usage of shared memory. Typically, a *read-modify-write* cycle is followed by the two simulators while accessing any shared memory location. Synchronization is ensured by locking the memory locations so that, the write access to any shared location is performed exclusively by any of the simulators. This creates a tight coupling between the hardware and software modules. On the other hand, following the design principle of loosely-coupled systems, the IPC channels (pipes, message queues etc.) can be utilized to synchronize between the two modules. One module may send a message and wait for response from the other module before proceeding, whenever synchronization is required.
3. *Scheduling of simulators*. This refers to the issue about the time instants at which the software and the hardware simulators will activate to simulate the corresponding modules. For this, a *global timing* is introduced. Operation of individual simulators happen with respect to their *local timing*. Every event generated by the environment or any of the simulation modules is assigned a global time stamp. Whenever the local timing of a simulator matches with any such global time stamp of an event for the corresponding module, the module is simulated.
4. *Models of computation*. All simulators work with a model for the underlying module. The details captured by the model play vital role to control the accuracy and execution time of the simulator.

6.2.2 Cosimulation Approaches

There are two major approaches towards the cosimulation process – *homogeneous cosimulation* and *heterogeneous cosimulation* as noted next.

1. *Homogeneous cosimulation*. In this approach a single simulator is used to simulate both the hardware and the software modules. For this, a *hardware description language* (HDL) model is used corresponding to the microprocessor/microcontroller targeted to execute the software module. For the hardware module, the corresponding HDL description is used. Now that both the software and the hardware parts are available at HDL level, a simulator for the hardware description language can be utilized to simulate the overall behaviour of the system. The approach is simple, however, the accuracy and correctness of the simulation results depend significantly on the model created for the processor hosting the software module.

2. *Heterogeneous cosimulation*. In contrast to the homogeneous cosimulation, heterogeneous cosimultaion of an embedded design works with two different simulators – an *instruction-set simulator* for the microprocessor/microcontroller executing the software part of the system and an HDL simulator for the hardware part. It may be noted that the instruction-set simulator of a target processor is a software module that runs on a host processor (with possibly a different instruction set from the target) and can simulate all instructions of the target processor. Thus, the software part of the embedded system can be executed on this instruction-set simulator. Apart from the hardware and software simulators, it is also necessary to create communication channels between the two simulator modules for the data items to be exchanged between the software and hardware parts of the system.

Apart from the two cosimulation approaches discussed above, another policy, known as *emulation* is often used to check the correctness of the system design process. A basic problem with hardware simulation is the speed mismatch between the actual hardware and its simulated version. The simulated version works at a much slower rate, and thus no timing verification can be carried out to determine the system correctness. Emulation uses some simplified hardware implementation for the modules dedicated to be realized in hardware. FPGAs are typically used for this purpose. It provides a number of advantages as noted next.

- The FPGA implementation runs the full hardware module, while the hardware simulators may be concentrating on only a few of the submodules limited by the speed of simulation.
- FPGA implementation may run within 10% of the speed achievable by the target hardware. The speed is much closer to the actual hardware operation compared to the speed of a hardware simulator.
- Full hardware being simulated together may help the designer to detect problems which are otherwise not possible with partial hardware simulations.
- Another big advantage is the possibility of attaching actual devices (sensors, actuators etc.) with the FPGA based hardware emulators. This facilitates viewing the entire system and check for functional correctness.

6.2.3 Cosimulation Environment

A heterogeneous cosimulation environment consists of two or more software processes. Typically, there can be three such processes – one each for the software and hardware simulators and one for the interprocess communication. An optional FPGA based custom board may be used to emulate the hardware part, increasing the overall speed of cosimulation. The situation has been shown in

Fig 6.3. Depending upon the time at which it is carried out, there can be two types of cosimulation – *abstract-level* and *detailed-level*. The abstract-level cosimulation is useful when the target processor/platform has not been selected. Due to the absence of detailed information about the processor and hardware, the abstract-level simulation is not very accurate, as compared to the detailed-level cosimulation.

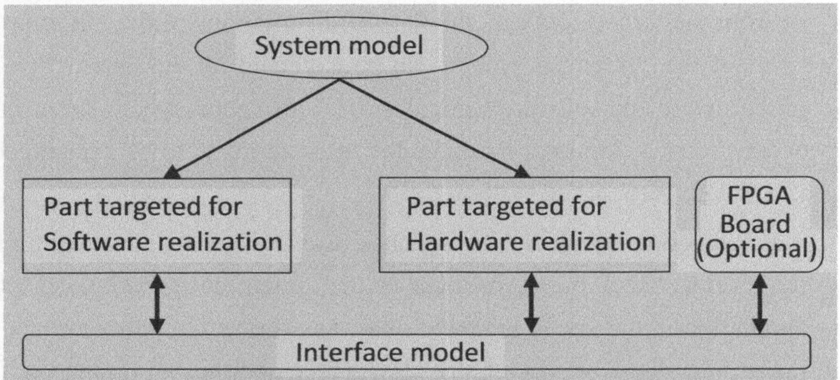

Fig 6.3: Cosimulation environment

1. *Abstract-level Cosimulation*. Programming languages like C/C++ and also the hardware description language like VHDL support socket calls that can be inserted into the descriptions for the purpose of communication. The interprocess communication primitives (IPCs) of the underlying operating system act as the communication channel. No concrete software and hardware module implementations are available at this stage. The IPC routine calls in the hardware component is grouped into an IPC handler process. In languages like VHDL, such handler process can be realized in terms of *foreign* routines. Fig 6.4 explains the abstract-level cosimulation.

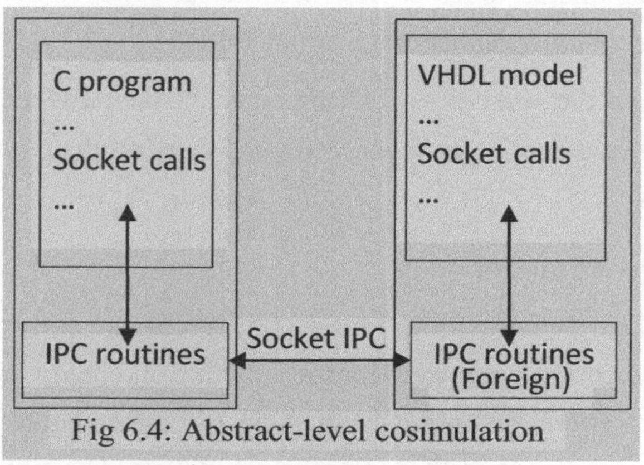

Fig 6.4: Abstract-level cosimulation

2. *Detailed-level Cosimulation.* This is used after the designer has finalized the target architectures for both the hardware and the software modules, the interface protocol has been decided upon. For the hardware side, the interface module is synthesized by automatic generation of *decoder/signal register* and the *channel unit* model available in the library. The channel unit consists of abstract model of a physical channel device (for example, DMA controller). Signal registers are additional registers introduced in the hardware unit to interface with the communication channel. The core hardware corresponding to the embedded hardware module may have ports of width different from the width of the interface channel. Thus, the data transferred through the channel need to be reformatted to match with the width of the core hardware ports. For example, the core hardware may have four 32-bit ports while the channel may be of 16-bit width. Hence, eight number of 16-bit signal registers may be introduced in the hardware part. Two such registers may feed one port of the core hardware. Fig 6.5 shows the detailed cosimulation scheme.

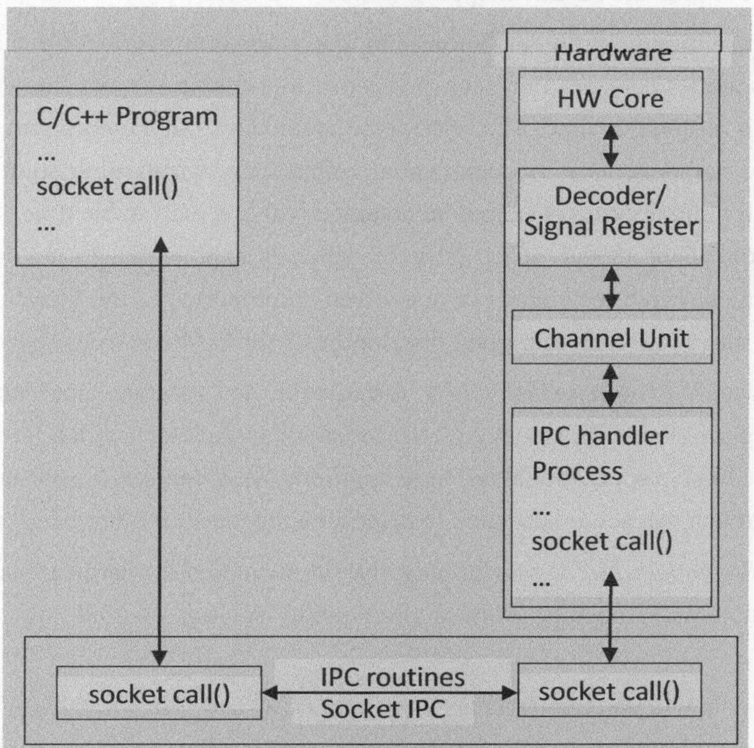

Fig 6.5: Detailed-level cosimulation

6.3 Hardware-Software Partitioning

The problem of hardware-software partitioning is to decide the target component for each task of the application. As discussed earlier, codesign works on mapping the tasks on a given target platform. Assuming that there are n tasks in the application and that the target architecture contains only a general-purpose processor and an ASIC (both of which can realize any of the tasks), there are 2^n ways in which the tasks can be assigned to either of the target architecture components. Each such mapping has got associated performance metrics, in terms of memory, hardware area, power consumption and delay. The best mapping solution is the one with the minimum cost (as defined by the optimization goal). The optimization process, apart from task graph and target architecture, needs cost estimates for each task of the application on each of the target architecture components. Also, the communication cost has to be estimated for each pair of tasks mapped on different architecture components. With all these estimates available, the partitioning tool can compute the cost estimate for any mapping solution explored by it.

The partitioning problem belongs to the *computationally hard* class of problems in theoretical computer science. For such problems, algorithms are not known to obtain optimal solution within reasonable time. The brute force method to find the optimum distribution of tasks to architecture components is of exponential complexity. Partitioning solution for applications beyond a small number of tasks cannot be obtained within a reasonable time. The process requires fast exploration of the design space (size of which is exponential in nature). For this, several heuristic and metasearch techniques have evolved and reported in the literature. In the following, we shall look into some such important developments for hardware-software partitioning.

1. *Integer Linear Programming* (*ILP*) formulation to generate optimum solution for the partitioning problem. The strategy works for small applications with a limited number of tasks only, due to huge computational resource requirements. However, the optimum results produced by the approach can act as yardstick to determine the merit of other heuristic techniques.
2. *Extended Kernighan-Lin Bi-partitioning* algorithm applied for hardware-software partitioning, is an alternative approach to produce good quality solutions within a reasonable computation time.
3. *Metasearch* techniques like *Genetic Algorithm* (*GA*) and *Particle Swarm Optimization* (*PSO*) have been reported to work well for the partitioning problem.
4. Producing partitioning solutions that can take area, delay and power into consideration have been addressed in some of the heuristic approaches.

5. Starting at the specification level, *functional partitioning* methods restructure the application task graph and then apply partitioning heuristics on it to obtain good quality mapping solutions.

6.3.1 Partitioning with Integer Programming

Integer programming is a mathematical tool to obtain exact solution of constrained optimization problems. Several mathematical packages are available that can be used to solve any instance of an integer programming problem. Hardware-software partitioning problem is also an optimization problem aiming to distribute the application tasks to either the hardware or the software partition with an objective of minimizing area requirement and power consumption subject to satisfying the deadlines of individual tasks. To use the integer programming tool, the designer needs to formulate the instance of partitioning problem as an instance of integer programming problem. Once the formulation has been done, the task of solving the resultant problem could be left to the tool. Many researchers have followed this avenue to solve the hardware-software partitioning problem instances. It may be noted that the solvers can come up with solutions for problem instances of small to moderate sizes only (in terms of number of variables, relations etc.). However, as the method can provide the optimum solutions, it can be used to judge the quality of solutions provided by heuristic methods of lesser complexity. As the formulation of partitioning problem is quite involved, to understand the basic philosophy of integer programming, in the following, a formulation has been shown for a constrained optimization example.

Consider the problem of minimizing the value of the expression $C = 7x_1 + 3x_2 - 4x_3 - 2x_4$, subject to the constraints that each x_i can pick up a value of 0 or 1 and at least three of the variables must assume the value 1. The integer programming formulation for this instance has been given in the following.

$$Minimize\ C = 7x_1 + 3x_2 - 4x_3 - 2x_4$$

such that,

$$x_1 + x_2 + x_3 + x_4 \geq 3,$$

$$0 \leq x_1 \leq 1, \quad 0 \leq x_2 \leq 1,$$

$$0 \leq x_3 \leq 1, \quad 0 \leq x_4 \leq 1.$$

Once this problem instance has been posed to the solver, it will come up with the answer $C = -3$ with the assignment to the variables $x_1 = 0$, $x_2 = 1$, $x_3 = 1$, $x_4 = 1$. In the following, we present an integer programming formulation of the hardware-software partitioning problem. To start with, a few definitions have been introduced.

1. *Target Architecture.* Any codesign problem works for a *target architecture* on which the application will run. The target architecture consists of both processor(s) to run the software part and ASIC/FPGA to run the hardware part. More formally, if the embedded system implementation platform consists of ASIC h and a set of processors $P = \{p_1, p_2 \dots p_n\}$ along with external memory and buses for communication, the set of target architecture components for the system can be represented as,

$$TA = \{h\} \cup P.$$

For the sake of uniformity, the ASIC can be considered as the first component in the set TA and denoted as ta_0, while the processors may be marked as ta_1 through ta_n.

2. *System.* It represents the application to be realized. An application is represented by a task graph with nodes corresponding to the individual tasks. Each task is of certain entity type. For example, there may be two filtering operations in the application, each of them representing a task while both of them are of the same entity type *filter*. Edges between the nodes of the task graph represent the interconnection requirements between the corresponding pair of tasks. Formally, a system is defined by the tuple $S = < EN, V, E, I >$, where,

$EN = \{en_1, \dots, en_{n_{EN}}\}$ is the set of entity types,

$V = \{v_1, \dots v_{n_V}\}$ is the set of nodes which are instances of entity types.

$E \subset V \times V$ is the set of edges corresponding to the interconnections.

$I: V \rightarrow EN$, with $I(v_j) = en_l$, defining the type of node v_j to be en_l.

3. *Cost Metrics.* For entity type en_l, the associated cost metrics are as follows.

- $c^a(en_l)$ – Hardware area.
- $c^{th}(en_l)$ – Hardware execution time.
- $c^{dm}(en_l)$ – Software data memory requirement.
- $c^{pm}(en_l)$ – Software program memory requirement.
- $c^{ts}(en_l)$ – Software execution time.

The interface cost for an edge $e = (v_1, v_2)$ consists of the following.

- $ci^a(e)$ – Additional hardware area.
- $ci^t(e)$ – Communication time.

4. *Design Quality.* It is identified by the following design metrics.

- $C^a(S)$ – Hardware area for the system.

- $C^{pm}(S)$ – Software program memory used by the system.
- $C^{dm}(S)$ – Software data memory used by the system.
- $C^{t}(S)$ – Total execution time for the system.

Hardware-Software Partitioning Problem Statement: *Find a mapping, map: $V \rightarrow TA$, such that all performance and resource constraints are satisfied and the design costs are minimized.*

In order to formulate the constraints for the integer programming problem, some additional notations are required, as noted next.

- $J = \{1, \ldots, n_V\}$ is the set of indices of $v_j \in V$.
- $K = \{1, \ldots, n_P\}$ is the set of indices of $ta_k \in TA$.
- $L = \{1, \ldots, n_{EN}\}$ is the set of indices in $en_l \in EN$.
- $c_{l,k}^{x}$ is the cost metric $c^{x}(en_l)$ on target architecture component ta_k, $x \in \{a, pm, dm, t\}$.
- $c_{j,k}^{x}$ is the cost metric $c^{x}(v_j)$ on target architecture component ta_k, $x \in \{a, pm, dm, t\}$.
- C_k^{x} is the design quality metric $C^{x}(S)$ of S on target architecture component ta_k, $x \in \{a, pm, dm, t\}$.
- MAX_k^{x} is the design constraint $MAX^{x}(S)$ on ta_k of S, $x \in \{a, pm, dm, t\}$.
- T_j^{S} is the execution start time of node v_j.
- T_j^{D} is the execution time duration of node v_j.
- T_j^{E} is the execution ending time of node v_j.

Apart from these, a few 0/1 variables are needed in the formulation process. The solver will assign values to these variables and T_j^{S} for all nodes v_j. It may be noted that a task graph node may be executed either in shared mode or in unshared mode in the hardware. For example, if there are two filter operation tasks, they may share the same filtering hardware or may have separate filtering modules in the hardware. On the other hand, the tasks mapped onto software on the same processor share the processor.

- $x_{j,0} = 1$, if v_j is executed unshared on ta_0, 0 otherwise.
- $y_{j,k} = 1$, if v_j is executed shared in ta_0 or ta_k $(k \geq 1)$, 0 otherwise.
- $sh_{l,k} = 1$, if en_l is executed shared in ta_0 or ta_k $(k \geq 1)$, 0 otherwise.
- $i_{j_1,j_2} = 1$, if an interface needed between v_{j_1} and v_{j_2}, 0 otherwise.

- $b_{j_1,j_2,k} = 1$, if v_{j_1} and v_{j_2} are mapped to different components or

  v_{j_1} finishes before v_{j_2} starts on ta_k, 0 otherwise.

Next, we shall look into the formulation of constraints to be satisfied by the solver to obtain the *map* function of hardware-software partitioning.

1. *General Constraints*. Each node v_j of the task graph must be mapped to exactly one target architecture component ta_k.

$$\forall j \in J: x_{j,0} + \textstyle\sum_{k \in K} y_{j,k} = 1.$$

For the node v_j, either $x_{j,0}$ or one of the $y_{j,k}$'s can be 1, identifying the target to which v_j has been mapped.

2. *Resource Constraints*. For the software side, the program and data memory constitute the resources. In hardware implementation, area is the resource. Considering data memory requirement, for each processor, the total data memory used should not exceed the maximum available data memory in it. Similar constraint holds for the program memory requirement. For the hardware side, area requirement is given by the area used by mapped tasks in unshared mode and in shared mode along with the area needed to realize the interface. The total hardware area requirement should not exceed the maximum available area. The corresponding conditions can be captured by the following expressions.

$$\forall k \in K - \{0\}: C_k^{dm} = \textstyle\sum_{l \in L} sh_{l,k} \times c_{l,k}^{dm} \le MAX_k^{dm}.$$

$$\forall k \in K - \{0\}: C_k^{pm} = \textstyle\sum_{l \in L} sh_{l,k} \times c_{l,k}^{pm} \le MAX_k^{pm}.$$

$$C_0^a = \textstyle\sum_{j \in J} x_{j,0} \times c_{j,0}^a + \textstyle\sum_{l \in L} sh_{l,0} \times c_{l,0}^a + CI_0^a \le MAX_0^a.$$

3. *Timing Constraints*. To formulate the timing constraints, first a scheduling has to be done for the task graph nodes. The schedule is obtained once by following the *As Soon As Possible* (*ASAP*) policy and then with *As Late As Possible* (*ALAP*) policy. The start time allotted to a node v_j, T_j^S must be between the ASAP and ALAP times for the node. Execution time of the node, T_j^D must be equal to either its software execution time or the hardware execution time, depending upon the target architecture component to which the node has been mapped. The finish time for the node, T_j^E is equal to the sum of T_j^S and T_j^D. In the following, the constraints have been formulated.

$$\forall j \in J: T_j^D = x_{j,0} \times c_{j,0}^{th} + y_{j,0} \times c_{j,0}^{th} + \textstyle\sum_{k \in K-\{0\}} y_{j,k} \times c_{j,k}^{ts}.$$

$$\forall j \in J: T_j^E = T_j^S + T_j^D.$$

$$\forall j \in J: ASAP(v_j) \leq T_j^S \leq ALAP(v_j).$$

$$\forall e = (v_{j_1}, v_{j_2}) \in E: T_{j_2}^S \geq T_{j_1}^E + T_{j_1,j_2}^I.$$

$$\forall j \in J: T_j^E \leq C^t \leq MAX^t.$$

Here, T_{j_1,j_2}^I is the time needed to pass information through the interface from node v_{j_1} to node v_{j_2}. An interface corresponding to an edge $e = (v_{j_1}, v_{j_2})$ is necessary only if the nodes are mapped onto different architecture components. The requirement of the interface along with the cost computations can be done by the following set of equations and inequalities.

$\forall e = (v_{j_1}, v_{j_2}) \in E$:

$$i_{j_1,j_2} \geq x_{j_1,0} + y_{j_1,0} + \sum_{k \in K-\{0\}} y_{j_2,k} - 1.$$

$$i_{j_1,j_2} \geq x_{j_2,0} + y_{j_2,0} + \sum_{k \in K-\{0\}} y_{j_1,k} - 1.$$

$$i_{j_1,j_2} \geq \sum_{k_1 \in K-\{0\}} \sum_{k_2 \in K-\{0\}, k_2 \neq k_1} y_{j_1,k_1} + y_{j_2,k_2} - 1.$$

$$T_{j_1,j_2}^I = i_{j_1,j_2} \times ci_{j_1,j_2}^t.$$

$$A_{j_1,j_2}^I = i_{j_1,j_2} \times ci_{j_1,j_2}^a.$$

$$CI_0^a = \sum_{e=(v_{j_1},v_{j_2}) \in E} A_{j_1,j_2}^I.$$

4. *Node Sharing*. Regarding the sharing of computational resources, the tasks mapped onto one processor (that is, target architecture component ta_1 through ta_n) are considered to be sharing it. On the other hand, for ta_0, the ASIC part, an entity en_l is shared only if at least two nodes v_{j_1} and v_{j_2} that are instances of en_l, are mapped in shared mode onto it.

$$\forall l \in L: \forall j_1, j_2 \in J: I(v_{j_1}) = I(v_{j_2}) = en_l: sh_{l,0} \geq y_{j_1,0} + y_{j_2,0} - 1.$$

$$\forall k \in K - \{0\}: \forall l \in L: \forall j \in J: I(v_j) = en_l: sh_{l,k} \geq y_{j,k}.$$

The $sh_{l,k}$ values so computed are used to satisfy the inequalities noted earlier under *Resource Constraints*.

5. *Shared Node Scheduling*. Sharing of nodes on to the same resource also leads to the requirement of scheduling of nodes for execution. This is expressed by a set of constraints involving the 0/1 variables $b_{j_1,j_2,k}$ and $b_{j_2,j_1,k}$ for a pair of nodes v_{j_1} and v_{j_2} mapped onto the same architecture component ta_k. The first five inequalities ensure that the two variables cannot be assigned the value 1 simultaneously, as $y_{j_1,k}$ and $y_{j_2,k}$ are both already 1's (due to sharing on ta_k).

$$b_{j_1,j_2,k} + y_{j_1,k} \leq 1.$$

$$b_{j_1,j_2,k} + y_{j_2,k} \leq 1.$$

$$b_{j_2,j_1,k} + y_{j_1,k} \leq 1.$$

$$b_{j_2,j_1,k} + y_{j_2,k} \leq 1.$$

$$b_{j_1,j_2,k} + b_{j_2,j_1,k} + y_{j_1,k} + y_{j_2,k} \leq 3.$$

Assuming that BIGNUM is a very large positive number, the next two inequalities will control the assignment of start and end times of the two nodes shared on ta_k. The conditions also make it impossible to assign the value 0 to both the variables $b_{j_1,j_2,k}$ and $b_{j_2,j_1,k}$, simultaneously (as that will create a contradiction between the time schedules of the two nodes). Hence, finally only one of the two variables is assigned the value 1 while the other gets the value 0. If the variable $b_{j_1,j_2,k}$ gets the value 0, the solver will schedule the node v_{j_1} to start execution after v_{j_2} has finished. If $b_{j_2,j_1,k}$ gets the value 0, the node v_{j_1} finishes earlier than the start of execution of v_{j_2}.

$$\forall k \in K: T^S_{j_1} \geq T^E_{j_2} - BIGNUM \times b_{j_1,j_2,k}.$$

$$T^S_{j_2} \geq T^E_{j_1} - BIGNUM \times b_{j_2,j_1,k}.$$

Once all these constraints have been formulated, any standard IP-solver can be used to optimize one or more of the design quality metrics – $C^a(S)$, $C^{pm}(S)$, $C^{dm}(S)$ and $C^t(S)$. However, the solver needs considerable amount of time even for moderately sized problems, though the result produced is optimal. In the following we shall look into some heuristic and metasearch techniques that are quite fast and have the potential to produce reasonably good partitioning solutions.

6.3.2 Kernighan-Lin Heuristic Based Partitioning

Kernighan-Lin algorithm is a fast heuristic that can be used to bi-partition an edge-weighted graph/hypergraph, with each partition containing the same number of nodes. Each edge has an associated weight. The partition introduces a cut into the graph with the cut-cost being equal to the sum of the costs of the edges crossing the cut. The algorithm attempts to minimize the cut-cost by suitable grouping of nodes into two partitions. The algorithm starts with any arbitrary bi-partition. It attempts to improve the cut-cost in an iterative fashion by exchanging nodes across the partitions, keeping the partition sizes unaltered. The algorithm was originally developed for partitioning VLSI physical designs. A VLSI chip in its design stage consists of number of library modules with interconnections between them. Unfortunately, the optimization tools in physical design work well for small problem sizes with less number of modules. Thus, before running the place-and-route tools, it becomes imperative to group the highly communicating modules into same partition so that they are placed close to each other in the silicon floor. The algorithm has been extended for usage in many other domains. The algorithm has extremely low runtime (of the order of few seconds for moderately sized graph) and produces excellent results. While applying to other domains, many augmentations have been made to the basic algorithm. Some such augmentations include supporting imbalanced partitioning with unequal number of nodes in the two partitions, using efficient data structures to make the implementation more strategic etc.

Table 6.1: Attributes of task graph in Fig 6.6(a)

Attributes of tasks						*Attributes of communication*		
	ict (μS)		*size (gates)*				*freq.*	*bits*
	Software	*Hardware*	*Software*	*Hardware*		e_1	4	16
v_1	10	5	10	200		e_2	2	32
v_2	25	10	150	1500		e_3	15	8
v_3	5	5	10	70		e_4	2	16
v_4	100	20	50	750		e_5	3	16
v_5	200	10	100	350		e_6	5	32

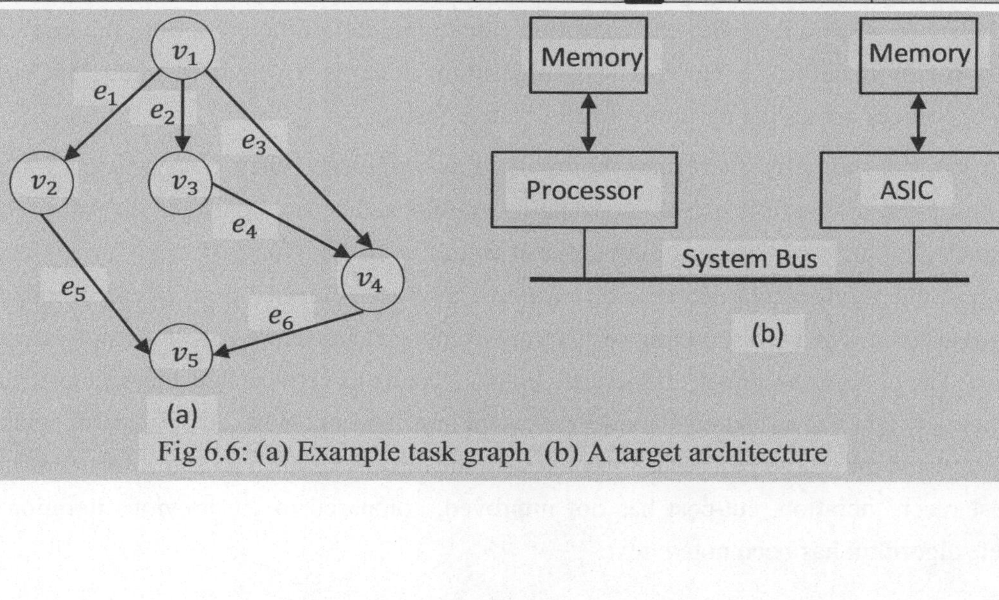

Fig 6.6: (a) Example task graph (b) A target architecture

The codesign problem can be viewed as an instance of graph-partitioning problem. The application is represented as a task graph – individual tasks constituting the nodes of the graph while the edges representing communication requirements. Fig 6.6(a) shows an example application task graph having five nodes and six edges between them. The target architecture consists of a standard processor that can execute the tasks realized in software and a custom processor (ASIC/hardware) for the tasks that require hardware realizations. The architecture has been shown in Fig 6.6(b). It is assumed that each of the tasks can be realized in both software and hardware. Thus, each node possesses *internal computation time* (*ict*) corresponding to its software and hardware implementations. An edge in the task graph is directed from a source task to a destination task. The source task calls the destination task to get some computation carried out. Each such invocation involves data transfer. Thus, each edge has got two attributes associated with it – number of times the destination task is called by the source task (*frequency*) and number of bits transmitted in each such call (*bits*). This can provide an estimation of the time needed to communicate over the system bus if the source and the destination tasks are mapped onto different components of the target platform. Table 6.1 lists some such attribute values for the task graph shown in Fig 6.6(a).

Kernighan-Lin Heuristic

In the following, we shall look into the basic Kernighan-Lin bi-partitioning heuristic for graphs and hypergraphs. A bi-partitioning corresponds to a cut of the vertices of the graph. The cost of the cut is equal to the sum of the edge-costs of all edges crossing the cut. The algorithm starts with a balanced partitioning with each partition containing half of the vertices of the graph. This initial bi-partition defines a cut-cost. The algorithm attempts to improve upon this cost by swapping vertices across the partitions in an iterative fashion.

At each iteration, initially all vertices are marked as *unlocked* – they can participate in swap operations. Next, all possible pair-wise swapping of unlocked vertices between the two partitions are evaluated in terms of their resulting cut-cost values. Among all such possible swaps, the one resulting in the greatest cost decrease or least cost increase (in case no swap can produce cost decrease) is taken. The corresponding vertices are exchanged across the partitions and are marked as *locked*. The process continues till there are unlocked pairs of vertices in the partitions. Once all the vertices are labelled as locked, it marks the end of one iteration. Now, all vertices are relabelled as unlocked and the whole process is repeated with the next iteration. The algorithm stops if after the most recent iteration, cut-cost has not improved, compared to the previous iteration. The complete algorithm has been noted next.

Algorithm Kernighan-Lin

Input: Vertex set $V = \{v_1, v_2, \dots\ v_m\}$ partitioned into two equal-sized partitions p_1 and p_2, such that, $p_1 \cup p_2 = V$ and $p_1 \cap p_2 = \emptyset$.

Output: A refined partition with reduced cut-cost.

```
Begin
    do
        current-partition = best-partition = (p1, p2);
        Unlock all vertices;
        while unlocked-vertices-exist(current-partition) do
            swap = select-next-move(current-partition);
            current-partition = move-and-lock-vertices(current-partition, swap);
            best-partition = get-better-partition(best-partition, current-partition);
        end while;
        if not(cut-cost(best-partition) < cut-cost(p1, p2)) then return (p1, p2);
        else // Start next iteration
            (p1, p2) = best-partition;
            Unlock all vertices;
        end if;
    end do;
End.
```

```
Procedure select-next-move(P)
begin
    Let P have partitions r1 and r2;
    for each unlocked((vi ∈ r1, vj ∈ r2) do append(costlog, cut-cost(Swap(P, vi, vj)));
    return (vi, vj) swap in costlog with minimum cost;
end;
```

To illustrate the operation of the algorithm, consider the graph shown in Fig 6.7. It has to be bi-partitioned with minimum cut-cost. The graph has eight vertices and ten edges with cost of each edge equal to 1. Let us assume that the algorithm starts with initial partition having $p_1 = \{1, 2, 3, 4\}$ and $p_2 = \{5, 6, 7, 8\}$. The initial cut-cost is equal to 6. The first iteration of the partitioning process has been shown in Table 6.2. At the end of this iteration, the *best-partition* is {{1, 2, 5, 6}, {3, 4, 7, 8}} with *cut-cost* 2. Now, all nodes will get unlocked and the next iteration of the partitioning process will start. It may be shown that the second iteration cannot improve the *cut-cost*, as it has already reached the minimum value for this example. Thus, the algorithm terminates at the end of the second iteration.

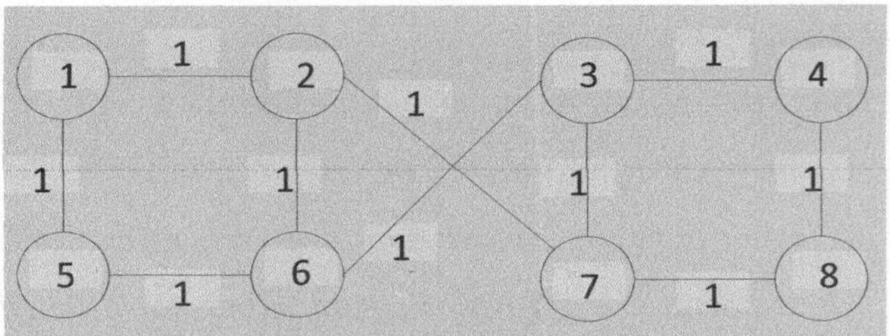

Fig 6.7: Example graph

Table 6.2: First iteration of partitioning

Swaps	(1,5)	(1,6)	(1,7)	(1,8)	(2,5)	(2,6)	(2,7)	(2,8)	(3,5)	(3,6)	(3,7)	(3,8)	(4,5)	(4,6)	(4,7)	(4,8)
cut-cost	8	5	5	6	5	6	6	5	5	6	6	5	6	5	5	8
current-partition = {{1,2,4,5}, {3,6,7,8}}, *locked* = {3, 5}, *cut-cost* = 5																
Swaps	(1,6)	(1,7)	(1,8)	(2,6)	(2,7)	(2,8)	(4,6)	(4,7)	(4,8)							
cut-cost	6	8	7	5	7	4	2	4	5							
current-partition = {{1,2,5,6}, {3,4,7,8}}, *locked* = {3,4,5,6}, *cut-cost* = 2*																
Swaps	(1,7)	(1,8)	(2,7)	(2,8)												
cut-cost	5	6	6	5												
current-partition = {{2,5,6,7}, {1,3,4,8}}, *locked* = {1,3,4,5,6,7}, *cut-cost* = 5																
Swaps	(2,8)															
cut-cost	6															

current-partition = {{5,6,7,8}, {1,2,3,4}}, *locked* = {1,2,3,4,5,6,7,8}, *cut-cost* = 6
best-partition = {{1,2,5,6}, {3,4,7,8}}, *cut-cost* = 2

Extension for Hardware-Software Partitioning

While adapting the Kernighan-Lin partitioning heuristic in the hardware-software codesign problem, the following differences from the graph-partitioning problem can be noted.

1. *Change in objective.* The codesign problem partitions the task graph modules into hardware and software parts with an aim to achieve better performance. Thus, the cost function *cut-cost* of the graph-partitioning problem should be replaced by more relevant execution-time metric. Execution-time of task graph node v, represented as $v.et$ is given by,

$$v.et = v.ict + v.ct$$

where, $v.ict$ is the internal computation time of the task (determined by its mapping on hardware or software) and $v.ct$ includes the computation times of all other tasks called by task v. The quantity $v.ct$ is given by,

$$v.ct = \sum_{e_k \in v.outedges} e_k.freq \times (e_k.tt + (e_k.dst).et)$$

Here, $e_k.tt$ is the time to transfer the bits corresponding to edge e_k over the bus. If the bus has a width of W bits and one W-bit transfer over the bus takes B time, $e_k.tt$ can be expressed as,

$$e_k.tt = \left\lceil B \times \frac{e_k.bits}{W} \right\rceil$$

For the task graph shown in Fig 6.6(a), the execution times of individual tasks can be formulated as follows.

$$v_5.et = v_5.ict$$

$$\begin{aligned} v_4.et &= v_4.ict + e_6.freq \times (e_6.tt + v_5.et) \\ &= v_4.ict + e_6.freq \times (e_6.tt + v_5.ict) \end{aligned}$$

$$\begin{aligned} v_3.et &= v_3.ict + e_4.freq \times (e_4.tt + v_4.et) \\ &= v_3.ict + e_4.freq \times (e_4.tt + v_4.ict + e_6.freq \times (e_6.tt + v_5.ict)) \end{aligned}$$

$$\begin{aligned} v_2.et &= v_2.ict + e_5.freq \times (e_5.tt + v_5.et) \\ &= v_2.ict + e_5.freq \times (e_5.tt + v_5.ict) \end{aligned}$$

$$\begin{aligned} v_1.et = {} & v_1.ict + e_1.freq \times (e_1.tt + v_2.et) + e_2.freq \times (e_2.tt + v_3.et) + \\ & e_3.freq \times (e_3.tt + v_4.et) \\ = {} & v_1.ict + e_1.freq \times (e_1.tt + v_2.ict + e_5.freq \times (e_5.tt + v_5.ict)) + \\ & e_2.freq \times (e_2.tt + v_3.ict + e_4.freq \times (e_4.tt + v_4.ict + \\ & e_6.freq \times (e_6.tt + v_5.ict))) + e_3.freq \times (e_3.tt + v_4.ict + \\ & e_6.freq \times (e_6.tt + v_5.ict)) \end{aligned}$$

As $v_1$is the root node of the application task graph, minimization of $v_1.et$ ensures optimizing the overall execution time requirement. In the real hardware, computation and communication go in parallel, however, this formulation has ignored that phenomena. Loading of the bus may also affect the data transfer time through it. This factor has also been ignored, leading to some inaccuracies in the overall model.

2. *Single Object Move.* The basic Kernighan-Lin heuristic works with two balanced partitions, each having the same number of vertices in it. This requirement is justified in VLSI physical design as the two partitions represent two segments of the chip area, which are required to be mostly balanced. However, in hardware-software partitioning, this requirement is not much meaningful. For the software modules the memory required to store the instructions is meaningful, whereas for the hardware part, number of gates is important. Balancing the partitions in terms of number of modules mapped is not of much significance. Hence, instead of swapping the vertices across the partitions, it is better to explore the design space by first assuming that all vertices belong to one of the partitions – each iteration then moves vertices from this partition to the other. Thus, instead of "swap", a "move" operation is followed.

3. *Change Equations.* When a task vertex is moved from its currently assigned partition to the other one, it may result in the change in execution times of many of the tasks. The changes come in the internal execution time of the vertex and the transfer times for all edges associated with the vertex. This change in transfer time will affect the execution times of many other task vertices. This requires recomputation of many of the equations corresponding to $v_i.et$. However, all equations may not be affected by such a move. For example, in the given task graph of Fig 6.6(a), if the vertex v_1 changes its partition, the quantities affected are $v_1.ict$, $e_1.tt$, $e_2.tt$ and $e_3.tt$. If these quantities change by the amounts $Dv_1.ict$, $De_1.tt$, $De_2.tt$ and $De_3.tt$, the change in the execution time of the vertex can be expressed by the following equation of $Dv_1.et$.

$$Dv_1.et = Dv_1.ict + De_1.tt \times e_1.freq + De_2.tt \times e_2.freq + De_3.tt \times e_3.freq$$

Similar change equations can also be derived for the change in the quantity $Dv_1.et$ for the movement of other vertices as well. Table 6.3 notes all such change equations. By computing these equations, at any iteration, the algorithm can identify the vertex to be moved to minimize the execution time $v_1.et$. The vertex may be moved and locked for the remaining part of the iteration.

Table 6.3: Change equations for the example task graph

Vertex moved	*Change Equation*
v_1	$Dv_1.ict + De_1.tt \times e_1.freq + De_2.tt \times e_2.freq + De_3.tt \times e_3.freq$
v_2	$e_1.freq \times (De_1.tt + Dv_2.ict + e_5.freq \times De_5.tt)$
v_3	$e_2.freq \times (De_2.tt + Dv_3.ict + e_4.freq \times De_4.tt)$
v_4	$e_2.freq \times e_4.freq \times (De_4.tt + Dv_4.ict + e_6.freq \times De_6.tt) + e_3.freq \times (De_3.tt + Dv_4.ict + e_6.freq \times De_6.tt)$
v_5	$e_1.freq \times e_5.freq \times (De_5.tt + Dv_5.ict) + e_2.freq \times e_4.freq \times e_6.freq \times (De_6.tt + Dv_5.ict) + e_3.freq \times e_6.freq \times (De_6.tt + Dv_5.ict)$

Table 6.4: Edge transfer times

Edge	*Transfer time (μs)*
e_1	$2 \times (16 \div 8) = 4$
e_2	$2 \times (32 \div 8) = 8$
e_3	$2 \times (8 \div 8) = 2$
e_4	$2 \times (16 \div 8) = 4$
e_5	$2 \times (16 \div 8) = 4$
e_6	$2 \times (32 \div 8) = 8$

Next we shall consider the partitioning of the application task graph of Fig 6.6(a) onto the platform in Fig 6.6(b). Assuming that all the tasks are initially mapped onto software, the execution time of the application, given by the execution time of vertex v_1 is,

$$v_1.et = 10 + 4 \times (25 + 2 \times 200) + 2 \times \big(5 + 3 \times (100 + 5 \times 200)\big) + 15 \times (100 + 5 \times 200)$$

$$= 24820\ \mu s.$$

Let the bus width W be 8-bit and the time taken for one transfer over the bus, B be 2 µs. If for all edges, the source and destination tasks are mapped onto different components of the target architecture, the transfer times over the bus will be as shown in Table 6.4. It may be noted that if the source and destination tasks of an edge are both realized either in software or in hardware alone, the data transfer time for the edge can be neglected. This is because for software realizations, the source task writes at some memory location to be read by the destination task and for hardware realizations, data is transferred over internal electrical signal lines – no bus activities are involved.

Table 6.5: First iteration of hardware-software partitioning					
Moves	v_1	v_2	v_3	v_4	$\boldsymbol{v_5}$
$Dv_1.et$	57	-12	40	-456	**-20598**
hardware = $\{v_5\}$, *software* = $\{v_1, v_2, v_3, v_4\}$, *locked* = $\{v_5\}$, $v_1.et$ = 4222					
Moves	v_1	v_2	v_3	$\boldsymbol{v_4}$	
$Dv_1.et$	57	-76	40	**-2466**	
hardware = $\{v_4, v_5\}$, *software* = $\{v_1, v_2, v_3\}$, *locked* = $\{v_4, v_5\}$, $v_1.et$ = 1756					
Moves	v_1	$\boldsymbol{v_2}$	v_3		
$Dv_1.et$	-3	**-76**	-8		
hardware = $\{v_2, v_4, v_5\}$, *software* = $\{v_1, v_3\}$, *locked* = $\{v_2, v_4, v_5\}$, $v_1.et$ = 1680					
Moves	$\boldsymbol{v_1}$	v_3			
$Dv_1.et$	**-35**	-8			
hardware = $\{v_1, v_2, v_4, v_5\}$, *software* = $\{v_3\}$, *locked* = $\{v_1, v_2, v_4, v_5\}$, $v_1.et$ = 1645					
Moves	$\boldsymbol{v_3}$				
$Dv_1.et$	**-40**				
hardware = $\{v_1, v_2, v_3, v_4, v_5\}$, *software* = $\{\}$, *locked* = $\{v_1, v_2, v_3, v_4, v_5\}$, $v_1.et$ = 1605					

The first iteration of the partitioning process has been shown in Table 6.5. Initially, all the tasks are assumed to be mapped to software. Thus, the overall execution time is 24820 μs. At the end of the first iteration, all tasks have moved to hardware and all the task vertices are locked. The execution time becomes 1605 μs which is the case when all tasks are realized in hardware. Now, all the vertices will be unlocked and the next iteration of the partitioning process will start. It can be verified that this iteration does not improve the execution time further. Hence, the algorithm terminates with the solution that all tasks be mapped to hardware. It may be noted that instead of execution time, if some other metric (such as, area occupied or a weighed sum of area and execution time) is tried to be minimized, some different partitioning result may be obtained.

6.3.3 Genetic Algorithm Based Partitioning

The meta-search heuristic of Genetic Algorithm (GA) has been used to solve many of the optimization problems. Based upon the operations of natural genetics, these search algorithms mimic the evolution process of a population. The problem should be such that producing a large number of candidate solutions is easy, however, getting the optimal solution is difficult and require exploring a huge search space. The algorithm works with a population of solutions, each of them called a *chromosome*. A chromosome has its *fitness value* determining its quality. Chromosomes participate in operations equivalent to *crossover* and *mutation* in natural genetics. For a pair of parent chromosomes in a generation, a crossover of them exchanges their parts, creating offspring chromosomes. The mutation operation creates an offspring by introducing some random modifications into the parent chromosome. The offspring chromosomes create the new generation of the population. It is expected that through these genetic operators, newer promising regions of the search space will get explored and better solutions will get discovered. However, compared to natural genetics, the population size in genetic algorithms is limited, thus limiting the varieties in the population.

For hardware-software partitioning problem, generating a large number of solutions is not difficult – any random distribution of tasks to the hardware and software platforms constitutes a solution. The distribution results in execution time, area requirement of the application. Thus, a random distribution can be considered as a chromosome. For computer representation, a chromosome can be a bit-stream. If there are n tasks in the application task graph, the chromosome can be taken to be a n-bit stream, the ith bit being 0 may mean the task i to be realized in hardware, whereas the bit being 1 may indicate software realization, or vice versa. To start with, a fixed number of chromosomes may be created to represent the initial population. The overall execution time corresponding to the partition indicated by a chromosome may be computed to represent the fitness of the chromosome. The lower the numeric value of the fitness measure, more fit is the chromosome.

To evolve the next generation from the current population, first the chromosomes are sorted in the ascending order of their fitness. In order to ensure that good solutions are not lost in the evolution process, a small percentage of better fit chromosomes are directly copied to the next generation. The remaining population is created through the genetic operators – crossover and mutation. Crossover operator selects two random chromosomes from the current population (with a bias towards selecting better fit chromosomes). Parts of these parent chromosomes are exchanged to create the offsprings. The crossover may be single-point or multi-point. For example, consider two chromosomes, "1010001010" and "1111001101" for an application with ten tasks. If the single-point crossover is followed with the crossover-point after four bits from the left, the offsprings created are "1010001101" and "1111001010". The mutation operator randomly changes some bits of a parent chromosome to create an offspring. For example, in the chromosome "1100101011" if mutation is applied at bits 1, 3 and 5 from the left side, the resulting offspring will be "0110001011". The rate of mutation may control the rate of convergence of the search algorithm.

A major concern with the genetic algorithm is its slow rate of convergence. To converge to a solution, a large number of iterations are to be carried out. Since the optimal fitness value for a problem is not known, it is difficult to terminate the genetic algorithm. Typically, the termination criteria is set to be "no improvement over last fixed number of generations" or completion of a maximum number of generations for which the genetic algorithm has run. Once the terminating criteria is met, the evolution process stops. The best solution at that point is declared as the output of the optimization process. Increasing the mutation rate may ensure quicker convergence. However, it often converges to some local optima rather than the global optima.

6.3.4 Particle Swarm Optimization Based Partitioning

In the line of genetic algorithms, many more stochastic search techniques have been developed, inspired by natural phenomena. One such popular technique is known as *Particle Swarm Optimization* (*PSO*). The strategy is based upon the social behaviour of bird flocking and fish schooling. In both the cases, there is a leader who is followed by the others. The travel pattern is shaped like the English alphabet 'V' in which the leader is at the peak of V. However, there may be a change in the leadership as well. All on a sudden, one bird/fish may deviate from the group and all others start following this new leader. Based on this observation, the behaviour of a flock of birds flying in the sky can hypothesized as follows.

It is assumed that the birds are searching randomly for food items in an area. It is also assumed that there is only one piece of food and none of the birds know where exactly the food is located. However, each of them can estimate how far it is from the food, based on its own intelligence and through learning via inter-communications with fellow birds. Naturally, among all the birds, one will have the best estimation and assumes the leader role. Other birds decide on their flight based upon the information from the leader and also its own intelligence captured in the history (that is, different estimations about distance from food that it had over the past). All birds effectively attempt to decide their movements at each time instant to ultimately reach the location of the food.

The PSO formulation applies the concept of bird flocking to optimization problems in which proposing a large number of solutions and their cost estimation is easy, however, getting the optimum solution is difficult. Similar to GA, PSO also works with a population, each element of it called a *particle*. A particle constitute a solution to the partitioning problem. If the target architecture consists of a hardware and a software platform, a binary stream similar to the GA chromosome structure can be used to represent a particle. The particle may be thought of containing two parts – the bit stream (named as *position vector*) and the fitness value. The updating of a particle is guided by two *best* values. The first one is the best solution that the particle has achieved so far during the evolution process. The corresponding position is called its *pbest*. The second parameter is the global best position that the optimizer has obtained so far, known as current global best or *gbest*. Once these two positions have been identified, a particle updates its velocity and position using the following two equations.

$$v_{k+1}^{i} = w \times v_{k}^{i} + c_1 \times r_1 \times (pbest^{i} - x_{k}^{i}) + c_2 \times r_2 \times (gbest_k - x_{k}^{i})$$

$$x_{k+1}^{i} = x_{k}^{i} + v_{k+1}^{i}$$

Here,

v_{k+1}^{i} : Velocity of particle i at $(k+1)^{th}$ iteration

v_{k}^{i} : Velocity of particle i at k^{th} iteration

x_{k+1}^{i} : Position of particle i at $(k+1)^{th}$ iteration

x_{k}^{i} : Position of particle i at k^{th} iteration

r_1, r_2 : Two random numbers between 0 and 1

w : Inertia factor

c_1 : Self-confidence (Cognitive) factor

c_2 : Swarm-confidence (Social) factor

Velocity computation has three parts in it. The first term captures the inertia of the particle to maintain its current velocity. The second term captures the influence of particle memory in deciding the velocity. The third term is responsible to incorporate the influence of swarm-intelligence (position of the current best particle) into the velocity determination process. Velocity of a particle is clamped at V_{max} specified by the user. It has been found that in many optimization problems, PSO performs better than GA due to lesser number of tunable parameters and the linear complexity of the main loop.

For the hardware-software partitioning problem, every task in a particle may be initialized with a velocity in the range –1 to +1. A negative velocity may indicate the task is moving towards 0 (software platform) while a positive velocity takes the task towards the hardware platform. If the position goes beyond 0 and 1, it may be clamped to the nearest value. The particles may be allowed to evolve over the generations and the process may be terminated if the improvement in global best solution becomes less than a small predefined number.

6.3.5 Power-Aware Partitioning on Reconfigurable Hardware

The hardware-software partitioning formulations discussed so far, primarily targeted the execution time optimization. The architecture consisted of an ASIC (for the hardware part) and one or more general-purpose processors (for the software part), communicating over a bus. A different type of codesign problem emerges if the ASIC is replaced by reconfigurable hardware, like FPGAs. An FPGA can be programmed to realize any functionality. Moreover, the FPGA chip has to be used in its entirety. As a result, the hardware area possesses a maximum limit (dictated by the amount of logic that the chip can host) with little scope for optimization. The embedded application has upper bound limits on its deadline and the overall power consumption. Thus, assuming that the overall embedded architecture contains an FPGA and a general-purpose processor communicating over a bus, a power-aware partitioning problem can be stated as follows.

"Given an application A with deadline D consisting of a set of tasks, the total available hardware area Ah_{total} (total logic that can be accommodated in the FPGA chip) and the maximum power rating of the system P_{Max}, generate a partition of the tasks of the application so that the deadline, maximum power requirement and hardware area capacity are met."

It may be noted that from the power optimization angle, all tasks should be mapped onto the software partition for execution by the processor. However, the software being an order of magnitude slower than the FPGA, mapping all tasks to it has a high chance of leading to deadline miss for the application. Hence, certain selected tasks must move to hardware, which in turn increases the power consumption of the system. This may create occasional power limit violations. Thus, the tasks to be moved to FPGA are to be chosen carefully. Once a task is mapped onto hardware, if its predecessor and/or successor task(s) are mapped onto software, the bus communication time and the associated bus power consumption also need to be accounted for. These extra amounts may lead to deadline violations and/or power limit violations.

The partitioning process followed here uses iterative improvement to produce valid solutions. It assumes that initially all tasks are mapped onto software. This realization is expected to be satisfying the power-constraint, as hardware execution of tasks will need more power. Hardware mapping of tasks may not be satisfying the power constraint and lead to power spikes in the execution life-time of the application. The algorithm discussed here prioritizes between the software tasks that are candidates for moving to FPGA, based on a *mobility* index detailed next.

For the set of tasks mapped onto software, the processor can execute only one at a time. A software task can start executing only after all its predecessor tasks (in software and in FPGA) are over. Thus, for a task i, its *earliest possible start time*, E_i is given by,

$$E_i = MAX_{k \in pred(i)} \ \delta(k)$$

where, $pred(i)$ is the set of predecessors of task i and $\delta(k)$ is the finish time of task k. Similarly, the latest possible start time, L_i is defined as,

$$L_i = MIN_{k \in succ(i)} \ (\sigma(k) - t_i)$$

where, $succ(i)$ is the set of successor tasks of task i, $\sigma(k)$ is the start time of task k. The quantity t_i is equal to either the software execution time (ts_i) or the hardware execution time (th_i) of task i, depending upon whether the task has been mapped onto software or hardware, respectively. *Mobility*, denoted as $\mu(i)$ for task i, is a binary quantity defined as follows.

$$\mu(i) = 1 \text{ if } L_i > E_i, 0 \text{ otherwise}$$

The tasks with mobility value 1 are better suited for moving to hardware because of two reasons. First, there is time to take care of communication over the bus. Second, the movement will reduce the execution time of the task providing better parallelism opportunities.

Next we shall look into the computation of time needed to communicate N_{sample} number of bits over a bus of width N_{bus} bits. The number of communication cycles needed per transfer is CC. Then, the total number of cycles for the communications is $\frac{CC \times N_{sample}}{N_{bus}}$. If the arbitration decision takes additional AC cycles and the frequency of the channel is F, the communication time is given by,

$$t_{comm} = \frac{\frac{CC \times N_{sample}}{N_{bus}} + AC}{F}$$

The communication between tasks i and j is needed if task i has been mapped to software and task j to hardware. This communication must be scheduled during the execution of task j, that is between the earliest possible start time E_j and latest possible finish time F_j. Thus, if $\sigma(i)$ and $\sigma(j)$ be the start times of the two tasks with their execution times t_i and t_j, $\sigma(comm)$ the start time of the communication, the following inequalities must hold.

$$\sigma(i) + t_i \leq \sigma(comm) < F_j$$

$$E_j < \sigma(j) + t_j \leq F_j$$

The bus transfer activity also incurs power consumption. Assuming that the operating voltage of the bus is V, capacitance C_{bus}, number of words transmitted per second is m with the number of bits per word as n, the power consumption is given by the following equation.

$$P_{bus} = \frac{1}{2} \times C_{bus} \times V^2 \times m \times n$$

Algorithm Power-Aware-Partitioning

Begin

Map all tasks to software; // Schedule assumed to be power-valid

While schedule is not time-valid do

Begin

Call *Task-Selection-Routine*() to select task i to go to hardware;

Determine start time $\sigma(i)$ using mobility $\mu(i)$;

Update bus activity;

Reschedule task graph;

Update hardware requirement Ah;

If (execution time decreases) AND (schedule is power-valid) AND

($Ah < Ah_{total}$) then

Note new schedule; Continue next iteration of the loop;

Else if ($Ah < Ah_{total}$) then

Invalidate selection of task i for hardware mapping for all future iterations;

Continue the loop;

Else if (schedule is not power-valid) then

Invalidate selection of task i for hardware mapping for the next iteration;

Continue the loop;

Else if (no time improvement) then

Invalidate selection of task i for hardware mapping for the next iteration;

Continue the loop;

End While;

End.

Procedure *Task-Selection-Routine*()

Begin

Let N_S constitute the set of software tasks in decreasing order of execution time ts_i;

Compute mobility of all tasks in N_S;

If ($\mu(i) = 0$) for all $i \in N_S$

Select task i with the maximum execution time ts_i;

Else

Select task i with the maximum execution time ts_i and non-zero mobility;

End;

6.3.6 Functional Partitioning

The hardware-software partitioning strategies discussed so far attempts to distribute the tasks of an application across the components of the target architecture platform. For example, if the target architecture consists of a general-purpose processor and an ASIC, some of the critical tasks may get mapped onto the ASIC while others may be realized in software and executed on the general-purpose processor. However, the identification of tasks constituting the system is left largely to the person writing the specification of the system. At specification stage, the major emphasis is put on a clean description understandable by the system designers. Little effort is put on ensuring good implementability of the system. Thus, it is very much possible that the specification is not highly suitable for implementation. For example, functionality of an application may be specified in terms of some user-defined procedures. These modules represent user-level views of the system functionality. However, there may be commonalities between a number of procedures, a procedure may be too large or too small, etc. Taking these individual procedures as tasks in the task-graph to be partitioned may lead to poor system implementations.

Functional partitioning is the process of dividing a given functional specification into a set of sub-specifications. These individual sub-specifications correspond to the tasks in the task-graph. Individual tasks in the task-graph will get mapped onto hardware and software components of the target architecture. Thus, functional partitioning modifies a large functional specification into a number of smaller specifications. Functional partitioning provides a number of advantages, as noted next.

1. In ASIC/FPGA based hardware realizations, optimization tools (such as, logic synthesis tools) are used to synthesize the logic structure. These optimization problems being quite complex in nature, the tools can produce reasonably good circuits if the input problem size is not too large. The heuristic tools work well for small-to-medium sized inputs. Also, the runtimes of these tools increase at a rapid rate with increase in the input size.
2. For smaller designs synthesized in the hardware, the clock frequency can be made significantly high. This may offset the delay of data transfer over the bus for communicating with tasks mapped to software.
3. The FPGAs possess limited resources in terms of logic capacity and input-output pins. If the mapped task is large, it may necessitate multiple FPGA chips with inter-chip communication overheads.
4. Partitioning a large procedure may create scope for further parallelization.

Input to the functional partitioning process is a single behavioural process specification X, consisting of a set of user-defined procedures $F = \{f_1, f_2, \dots f_n\}$. Amongst them, one is the main procedure, which calls some other procedures, however this procedure cannot be called by others. All procedures excepting main may call other procedures. It may be noted that a variable access can also be treated as procedures –procedure *read* (to get the value of the variable) and procedure *write* (to assign value to the variable). The functional partitioning of F creates a set of parts $P = \{p_1, p_2, \dots p_m\}$, such that each procedure is put into one of these parts. That is, $p_1 \cup p_2 \cup \dots \cup p_m = F$ and $\forall i, j \in \{1, 2, \dots n\}, i \neq j: p_i \cap p_j = \emptyset$. The hardware-software partitioning techniques can work on these parts of P and put each of its components either in hardware or in software. In that way, each part is looked as tasks in the task-graph to be partitioned by the codesign process. The situation has been explained in Fig 6.8.

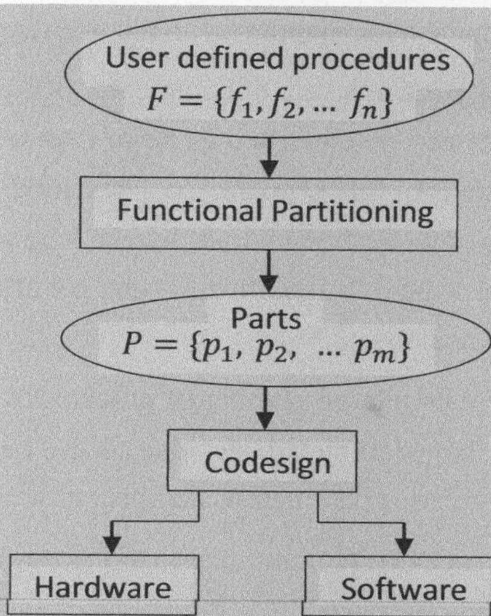

Fig 6.8: Role of functional partitioning

By analysing the behavioural process specification X, the *call graph* of the same can be constituted enumerating the procedures defined in the specification and their interrelations in terms of caller-callee relationships. Any standard program analysis tool can be utilized to obtain the call graph for X. For the sake of discussion in this section, let us assume that it contains nine procedures apart from the main procedure and the calling pattern of the procedures is as shown in the call graph in Fig 6.9.

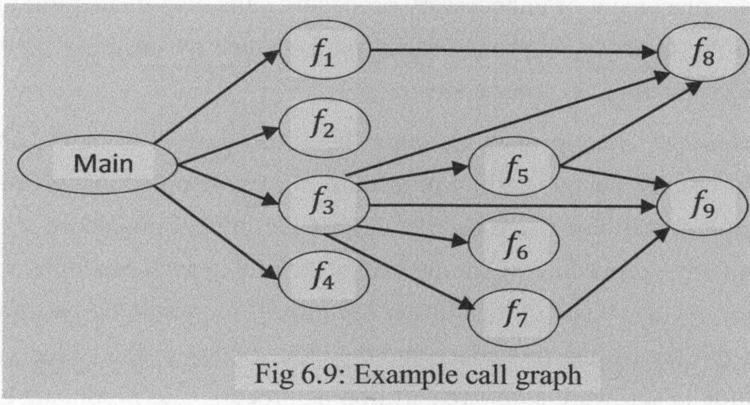

Fig 6.9: Example call graph

Methodology for Functional Partitioning

Functional partitioning is a three-step process consisting of *Granularity Selection*, *Preclustering* and *N-Way Assignment.* The steps have been elaborated in the following.

1. *Granularity Selection*. Granularity is a measure of complexity of a procedure. A big procedure with a large number of variables can be classified to be of *coarse granularity*. On the other hand, a low complexity procedure is of *fine granularity*. Thus, module level coarse granularity leads to fewer complex procedures while fine granularity can lead to a large number of simple small procedures. Partitioning process of a specification can get affected by the granularity of procedures due to the following reasons.

   - Too fine a granularity will create a large number of procedures for the specification. This may create difficulty in the partitioning process due to the enhanced complexity of the problem. Estimation of performance parameters also becomes an issue.
   - A coarse granularity will put lot of computations into a single task. It will exclude potential solutions that may be obtained otherwise.

   The process of ensuring a good granularity for the behavioural specification starts with the user defined procedures – they represent a grouping of related statements into procedures based upon human intelligence. The granularity can be improved by applying certain transformations to the specification, as noted next.

   (i) *Procedure inlining*. This transformation replaces a call to a procedure by the content of the called procedure. The parameters are suitably replaced in the body. As an outcome, the called procedure disappears, however all such procedures calling this one, become more complex. This replacement of unnecessary procedure calls help in keeping the executable codes close in the memory, improves cache performance by ensuring better locality of reference. The granularity becomes coarser.

   (ii) *Procedure cloning*. Cloning makes a copy of a procedure. The newly created cloned procedure is for use by a single calling procedure. It may be noted that procedure inlining may increase the overall code size significantly if the inlined procedure was called by a good number of other procedures. Cloning may be helpful in such situations. Cloning make a local copy for exclusive use of a calling procedure. If required, the partitioning process may decide to put the calling procedure and the cloned copy of the called procedure into the same partition in hardware-software partitioning process, thus producing good mapping solutions.

(iii) *Procedure exlining*. This is the reverse of inlining. A related portion of statements within a procedure is taken out to constitute a new procedure. The original procedure is made to contain a call to this new procedure, replacing the code fragment. The granularity becomes finer. The following are the types of exlining followed in functional partitioning.

- *Redundancy exlining*. A redundancy corresponds to the occurrence of two or more near identical code segments within a single procedure. The program is encoded as a string of characters. Approximate string matching algorithms are used to identify the matching code segments.

- *Distinct-computation exlining*. The technique attempts to determine tightly-coupled portions within a procedure. Each statement is considered as an atomic unit. The statements affect the values of variables. A dependency analysis is performed between the values computed by the statements. This reveals relationship between the statements. It has the potential to identify a group of highly related statements. Statements within a group are highly related, whereas those between the groups are rather uncorrelated.

To illustrate the granularity transformations, let us consider the situation that almost every system contains an initialization routine which is called on resetting the system. For the example call graph shown in Fig 6.9, the routine f_1 may be an initialization routine. As it is called only once, it may be inlined with the procedure Main. Procedure f_2 may be first computing some data and then packetize it and send through a transmission channel to a distant place – a typical situation of an embedded application employed in remote processing. Now, f_3 may be exlined into two parts – f_3 and f_{3a}, where f_3 is responsible for doing the computation and f_{3a} takes care of the communication task. The procedure f_3 calls f_5, f_8 and f_9, while f_{3a} calls f_6 and f_7. The situation has been shown in Fig 6.10.

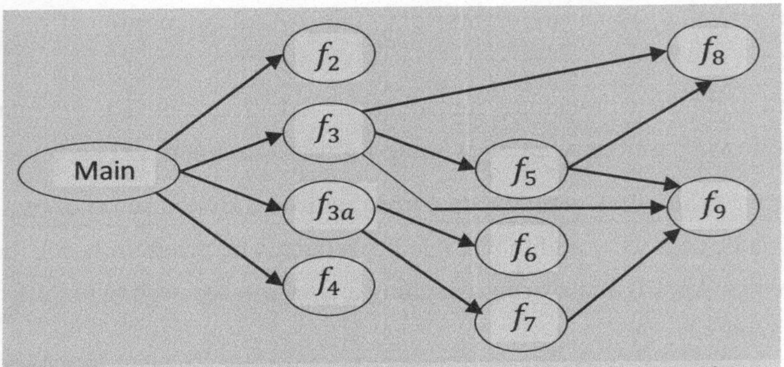

Fig 6.10: Call graph after granularity transformations

2. *Pre-Clustering*. This phase attempts to do a grouping of the procedures so that the job of next phase becomes simpler. It identifies the procedures such that, putting them on different architecture components will definitely degrade the solution quality. At the same time, these procedures cannot be inlined into a single one, may be due to the size of the resulting procedure. It may be noted that pre-clustering does not do any partitioning of the tasks, it just groups the procedures into clusters. All procedures belonging to a cluster should be put into the same architecture component by the actual partitioning tool, at the next phase. Grouping of procedures may be guided by a *closeness* measure. The closeness is defined as a weighted sum of metrics, such as, amount of parameter passing, number of calls etc. For example, in the call graph of Fig 6.10, procedures f_5 and f_8 may be very close and thus put into the same cluster. This has been shown in Fig 6.11.

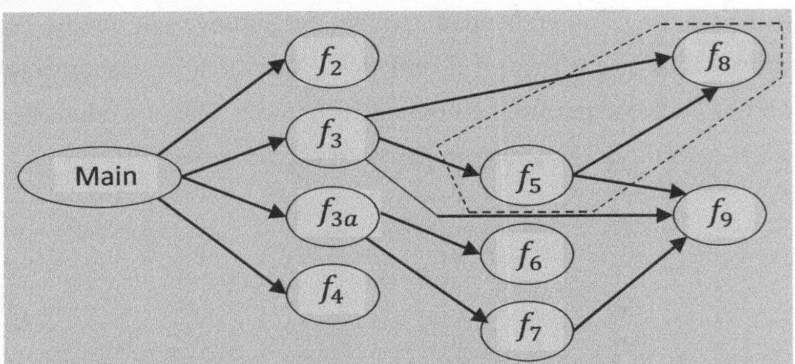

Fig 6.11: Call graph after pre-clustering

3. *N-Way Assignment*. This is the stage performing the actual hardware-software partitioning. Any of the partitioning techniques discussed in Section 6.3 can be employed to perform this stage. For example, assuming that the target architecture contains only two components – one

general-purpose processor and one hardware platform, a *2-Way Assignment* of procedures of call graph in Fig 6.11 has been shown in Fig 6.12.

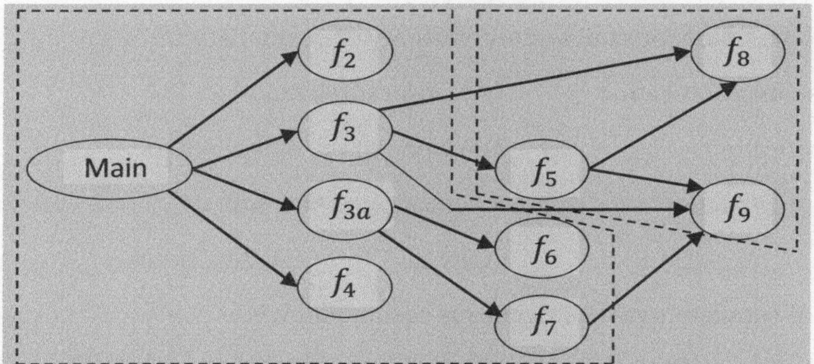

Fig 6.12: Call graph after 2-Way Partitioning

UNIT SUMMARY

An embedded system design may be highly constraint by its performance requirements, size and cost. From the performance perspective, the system should be implemented in hardware, while from the cost point of view software realization may be preferable. All functions in an embedded system are not equally critical. Thus, a partitioning of the tasks to target hardware or software realization becomes an optimization challenge. This leads to the field of Hardware-Software Co-design. Ensuring the functional correctness of such a system distributed over the hardware and the software platforms necessitate a new class of combined simulation, called cosimulation. Several software development techniques have been reported for the design of cosimulators. For the codesign problem, several optimization approaches are available. A fully mathematical approach based on integer programming, can produce optimal partitioning results. However it is computationally infeasible for moderate to large task graphs. An iterative improvement based approach, known as Kernighan-Lin bi-partitioning has been used for the optimization. The metasearch techniques like Genetic Algorithm and Particle Swarm Optimization have been used to achieve good partitioning solutions within reasonable CPU time. For the reconfigurable platforms like FPGA, power-aware partitioning has been carried out. To take care of large specification, a functional partitioning of the procedures have been developed to aid in the hardware-software partitioning process.

EXERCISES

Multiple Choice Questions

MQ1. Which of the following is not a responsibility of cosimulation?

(A) System specification (B) Cost estimation

(C) Verification (D) None of the other options

MQ2. Number of simulators used in homogeneous cosimulation is

(A) 0 (B) 1 (C) 2 (D) Any number

MQ3. Number of simulators in heterogeneous cosimulation is

(A) 0 (B) 1 (C) 2 (D) 2 or more

MQ4. After the target architecture has been fixed, the cosimulation is at

(A) Abstract level (B) Detailed level

(C) Medium level (D) None of the other options

MQ5. Solution produced via integer programming of a problem is

(A) Exact (B) Constant

(C) Sub-optimal (D) None of the other options

MQ6. Partitions in basic Kernighan-Lin technique are

(A) Balanaced (B) Empty

(C) Unbalanced (D) Full

MQ7. In Kernighan-Lin algorithm, when all vertices are locked, it marks the end of

(A) Algorithm (B) Iteration

(C) Selection (D) None of the other options

MQ8. Partitions in Extended Kernighan-Lin technique are

(A) Balanaced (B) Empty

(C) Unbalanced (D) Full

MQ9. Change equations help in reducing

(A) Computation (B) System cost

(C) Area (D) None of the other options

MQ10. Which of the following is not used in Genetic Algorithm?

(A) Crossover (B) Mutation

(C) Initialization (D) None of the other options

MQ11. In PSO, particle evolution is guided by

(A) Local best (B) Global best

(C) Particle inertia (D) All of the other options

MQ12. Mobility value of a task is

(A) Binary (B) Integer

(C) Real (D) Any of the other options

MQ13. Priority of task to be moved in task selection routine is guided by

(A) Mobility (B) Execution time

(C) Both mobility and execution time (D) None of the other options

MQ14. Power-aware partitioning initially puts all tasks in

(A) Software (B) Hardware

(C) Either software or hardware (D) None of the other options

MQ15. Functional partitioning restructures

(A) Task graph (B) Target architecture

(C) Partitioning algorithm (D) None of the other options

MQ16. Procedure size will be more for

(A) Coarse granularity (B) Fine granularity

(C) Mean granualaity (D) None of the other options

MQ17. In procedure inlining, the inlined procedure gets

(A) Emphasized (B) Removed

(C) Lesser calls (D) None of the other options

MQ18. Procedure inlining makes granularity

(A) Coarser (B) Finer

(C) Zero (D) One

MQ19. Cloning is useful for procedure with

(A) Multiple calls from another (B) Large number of calls

(C) No calls (D) None of the other options

MQ20. New procedure is created in

(A) Inlining (B) Exlining

(C) Both inlining and exlining (D) None of the other options

MQ21. String-matching algorithms are used in

(A) Redundancy exlining (B) Distinct computation exlining

(C) Inlining (D) None of the other options

MQ22. Dependency analysis is useful for

(A) Redundancy exlining (B) Distinct computation exlining

(C) Inlining (D) None of the other options

MQ23. Pre-clustering is close to

(A) Inlining (B) Exlining

(C) Cloning (D) None of the other options

MQ24. Preclustered procedures are put into

(A) Same partition (B) Different partitions

(C) Software partition (D) Hardware partition

MQ25. In functional partitioning, actual partitioning algorithm is used in

(A) Granularity selection (B) Pre-clustering

(C) N-way partitioning (D) None of the other options

Answers of Multiple Choice Questions

1:A, 2:B, 3:D, 4:B, 5:A, 6:A, 7:B, 8:C, 9:A, 10:D, 11:D, 12:A, 13:C, 14:A, 15:A, 16:A, 17:B, 18:A, 19:A, 20:B, 21:A, 22:B, 23: A, 24: A, 25: C

Short Answer Type Questions

SQ1. How does cosimultaion differ from simulation of hardware and software systems?

SQ2. Differentiate between homogeneous and heterogeneous cosimulation.

SQ3. How does emulation differ from simulation?

SQ4. Differentiate between abstract and detailed cosimulation.

SQ5. State the main advantages and disadvantages of ILP-based partitioning.

SQ6. Why Kernighan-Lin partitioning should be considered as a hill-climbing technique?

SQ7. How does Kernighan-Lin algorithm attempt to overcome local minima?

SQ8. Why is functional partitioning important in hardware-software codesign?

SQ9. Distinguish between procedure inlining and exlining.

SQ10. How does procedure inlining differ from clustering?

Long Answer Type Questions

LQ1. State and explain the requirement of cosimulation in the codesign process.

LQ2. How does a typical cosimulation environment look like?

LQ3. Explain the meaning of individual resource constraints and timing constraints in the ILP-based partitioning formulation.

LQ4. For the task-graph shown in Fig 6.6(a) perform extended Kernighan-Lin partitioning targeting area minimization.

LQ5. Write the change equations for vertex v_3 in Fig 6.6(a) for movement of all vertices from software to hardware.

LQ6. How can Genetic Algorithm be used in hardware-software partitioning?

LQ7. Explain how PSO can be used for hardware-software partitioning.

LQ8. Define task mobility in the context of hardware-software partitioning. If all nodes are of 0 mobility, why should the task with highest software-execution time be moved to hardware?

LQ9. Explain procedure inlining, exlining and cloning with suitable examples.

LQ10. Explain how pre-clustering aid in N-way partitioning process.

KNOW MORE

SystemC is a language for system-level design that can be used for specification, modelling and verification for systems spanning hardware and software. It is based upon standard C++, extended using class libraries. The language is suitable for modelling system partitioning, evluate and verify assignment of blocks to either hardware or software implementations. Leading EDA and IP vendors use this language for architectural exploration and platforms for hardware-software codesign. It has the capability to have several abstraction levels – functional level (in which algorithms are defined and system partitioned into communicating tasks), architecture level (tasks are assigned to execution units, communication mechanism is defined and implementation metrics, such as, performance are modelled), implementation level (precise method of implementation of the execution units).

REFERENCES AND SUGGESTED READINGS

[1] S. Chattopadhyay, "Embedded System Design", PHI Learning, 2023.

[2] P. Marwedel, "Embedded System Design", Springer, 2021.

[3] G.D. Micheli, R. Ernst, W.Wolf, "Readings in Hardware/Software Co-Design", Elsevier, 2002.

[4] R. Gupta, "Special Issue: Partitioning Methods for Embedded Systems", Journal of Design Automation of Embedded Systems 2, 1997.

[5] B. Kernighan, S. Lin, "An Efficient Heuristic Procedure for Partitioning Graphs", Bell System Technical Journal, 1970.

[6] J. Staunstrup, W. Wolf, "Hardware/Software Co-Design Principles and Practice", Springer, 1997.

[7] F. Vahid, T. Le, "Extending the Kernighan-Lin Heuristic for Hardware and Software Functional Partitioning", Journal of Design Automation of Embedded Systems 2, 1997.

Dynamic QR Code for Further Reading

1. S. Chattopadhyay, "Embedded System Design", PHI Learning, 2023.

2. P. Marwedel, "Embedded System Design", Springer, 2021.

CO AND PO ATTAINMENT TABLE

Course outcomes (Cos) for this course can be mapped with the programme outcomes (POs) after the completion of the course and a correlation can be made for the attainment of POs to analyse the gap. After proper analysis of the gap in the attainment of POs, necessary measures can be taken to overcome the gaps.

Course Outcomes	**Expected Mapping with Programme Outcomes** ***(1-Weak Correlation; 2- Medium Correlation; 3- Strong Correlation)***											
	PO-1	PO-2	PO-3	PO-4	PO-5	PO-6	PO-7	PO-8	PO-9	PO-10	PO-11	PO-12
CO-1												
CO-2												
CO-3												
CO-4												

The data filled in the above table can be used for gap analysis.

EC 21 Embedded System Laboratory

Experiments for the *Embedded System* laboratory can be carried out by using the embedded system trainer boards developed around 8051 and/or ARM processor. The trainer board is to be interfaced with the host PC in which the software part can be developed, simulated and compiled for the target system. Once satisfied with the simulation, the machine code can be downloaded onto the trainer board via USB/JTAG port. The trainer boards, in general, contain the basic input-output facilities in terms of DIP switches, onboard LEDs, ADC (with variable resistance to feed analog voltage) and DAC. Additional circuitry can be developed on breadboards and connected to the system to prototype the complete system. The trainer boards often support the interfaces like SPI, I2C, CAN, USB, Bluetooth etc. The boards also contain rudimentary monitor routine to support some simple RTOS (such as, FreeRTOS). The following is a tentative list of experiments that can be carried out on such trainer boards.

Experiment 1: Familiarization with trainer board.

1.1 Familiarize with the trainer board operations and its development environment on desktop.

1.2 Use on-board LEDS and write an embedded C program to display some specific patterns.

Experiment 2: Digital I/O interface.

2.1 Use onboard LEDs and DIP switch. Set a pattern in the DIP switch and display the corresponding pattern onto the LEDs via an embedded C program.

2.2 Set switches on a breadboard. Make external LED connections on breadboard. Execute the program, so that both onboard and external LEDs display the pattern set by the external switches.

2.3 Modify the program to read a four bit number and display its 2's complement.

Experiment 3: RS-232 interfacing with PC.

3.1 Develop an embedded C program to access the RS-232 port of the trainer board.

3.2 Develop a program on PC to access its COM port.

3.3 Use the programs to send a byte from PC to the trainer board. The program in the board should compute the square of the byte and return to the PC. Assume the result to be confined within 8-bits.

Experiment 4: Traffic Light Controller.

4.1 Design the hardware and software for a traffic light controller system that has four LEDs – RED, YELLOW, GREEN, ADVANCE GREEN. The sequence in which the LEDs are turned on is as follows: RED for 1 min, YELLOW for 15 seconds, GREEN for 1 min, ADVANCE GREEN for the last 10 seconds of GREEN.

4.2 Interface a light-dependent resistor (LDR) with it. Whenever the LDR is covered, the controller goes to manual mode and all lights start blinking. The system returns to its normal condition as soon as the LDR is uncovered.

4.3 The master control lies with a program running in the PC. This program will be able to control all these timing and also the manual setting. That is, the program in PC should be able to transmit commands like “R <time>” to set the RED on-time, “M” to switch over to manual mode, “A” to come back to automatic mode.

Experiment 5: ADC interfacing.

Design the hardware and software for a temperature monitoring and control system. It uses a temperature sensor whose output is fed to the ADC. The ADC sends the digital output to the processor. There are two cutoff temperatures – *high* and *low*. A heating coil and a fan are interfaced with the processor. The heating coil is turned on. If the temperature is more than the *high* cutoff, a relay is triggered to turn on a fan working at 12V, the coil is turned off. Again when the temperature comes down to the *low* preset value, the fan is turned off and the coil is turned on. A program running in PC should communicate with the trainer board to set the cutoff temperatures *high* and *low*.

Experiment 6: FreeRTOS environment.

Repeat the LED and switch interfacing exercise in Experiments 1 and 2, using programming in FreeRTOS environment to create tasks. For each switch-LED pair there is a task monitoring and controlling the I/O operation.

Experiment 7: FPGA implementation.

For the Traffic Light Controller in Experiment 4, implement the task dedicated to the trainer board by an FPGA board. The embedded C program needs to be rewritten using Verilog/VHDL code and the FPGA should communicate with the PC using serial communication.

Experiment 8: SPI, I2C, CAN interfacings.

Take two trainer boards. Connect between them using three different interfaces – (a) SPI, (b) I2C, (c) CAN. For each case, one board will send a byte to the other one which will be doubled by the destination board and returned to the source board.

Experiment 9: Extended Kernighan-Lin partitioning.

Develop a C/C++ program to implement extended Kernighan-Lin partitioning strategy for hardware-software partitioning.

Experiment 10: GA/PSO based partitioning.

Develop a C/C++ program for Genetic Algorithm and/or Particle Swarm Optimization based strategy for hardware-software partitioning.

Index